The Mormon Doctrine Of Deity
The Roberts-Van Der Donckt Discussion

By

B. H. Roberts

The Mormon Doctrine Of Deity
The Roberts-Van Der Donckt Discussion
by B. H. Roberts

Copyright © 2023

All Rights reserved.

No part of this publication may be reproduced, stored in a retrieval system, or transmitted in any form or by any means, electronic, mechanical, photocopying or Otherwise, without the written permission of the publisher.
The author/editor asserts the moral right to be identified as the author/editor of this work.

ISBN: 978-93-59957-54-8

Published by

DOUBLE 9 BOOKS

2/13-B, Ansari Road
Daryaganj, New Delhi – 110002
info@double9books.com
www.double9books.com
Tel. 011-40042856

This book is under public domain

ABOUT THE AUTHOR

Brigham Henry Roberts (March 13, 1857 – September 27, 1933) was a Church of Jesus Christ of Latter-day Saints (LDS Church) historian, politician, and leader. He independently wrote the six-volume Comprehensive History of the Church of Jesus Christ of Latter-day Saints and edited the seven-volume History of the Church of Jesus Christ of Latter-day Saints. Roberts also wrote Studies of the Book of Mormon, which was released posthumously and explored the Book of Mormon's authenticity as an ancient record. Because of his polygamy, Roberts was denied a seat in the United States Congress. Roberts was born in Warrington, Lancashire, England, the son of alcoholic blacksmith and ship plater Benjamin Roberts and seamstress Ann Everington. Both of his parents converted to the LDS Church the year he was born. Then Benjamin Roberts abandoned his family. "My childhood was a nightmare; my boyhood was a tragedy," Roberts later wrote. B. H. Roberts and a sister departed England in April 1866, aided by the Perpetual Emigrating Fund. They boarded a wagon train in Nebraska and walked—barefoot for much of the way—to Salt Lake City, where they were met by their mother, who had preceded them.

CONTENTS

PREFACE 7

CHAPTER I 11

CHAPTER II 36

CHAPTER III 53

CHAPTER IV 128

CHAPTER V 155

CHAPTER VI 183

CHAPTER VII 195

CHAPTER VIII 214

PREFACE

In nothing have men so far departed from revealed truth as in their conceptions of God. Therefore, when it pleased the Lord in these last days to open again direct communication with men, by a new dispensation of the gospel, it is not surprising that the very first revelation given was one that revealed himself and his Son Jesus Christ. A revelation which not only made known the *being* of God, but the *kind* of a being he is. The Prophet Joseph Smith, in his account of his first great revelation, declares that he saw "two personages," resembling each other in form and features, but whose brightness and glory defied all description. One of these personages addressed the prophet and said, as he pointed to the other—

"*This is my beloved Son, hear him.*"

This was the revelation with which the work of God in the last days began. The revelation of God, the Father; and of God, the Son. They were seen to be two distinct personages. They were like men in form; but infinitely more glorious in appearance, because perfect and divine. The Old Testament truth was reaffirmed by this revelation—"God created man in his own image, in the image of God created he him." Also the truth of the New Testament was reaffirmed—Jesus Christ was shown to be the express image of the Father's person, hence God, the Father, was in form like the Man, Christ Jesus, who is also called "the Son of Man."

Again the Old Testament truth was revealed—"The *Gods* said let *us* make man in *our* image, and in *our* likeness." That is, more than *one* God was engaged in the work of creation. Also the truth of the New Testament was again reaffirmed—the Father and the Son are seen to be two separate and distinct persons or individuals; hence the Godhead is plural, a council, consisting of three distinct persons, as shown at the baptism of Jesus, and throughout the conversations and discourses of Jesus and his inspired apostles.

All this, coming so sharply in conflict with the ideas of an apostate Christendom which had rejected the plain anthropomorphism of the Old and New Testament revelations of God; also the scriptural doctrine of a plurality of Gods, for a false philosophy-created God, immaterial and passionless—all this, I say, could not fail to provoke controversy; for the revelation given to Joseph Smith challenged the truth of the conception of God held by the modern world-pagan, Jew, Mohammedan and Christian alike.

It was not to be expected, then, that controversy could be avoided, though it has been the policy of the Elders of the Church to avoid debate as far as possible—debate which so often means contention, a mere bandying of words—and have trusted in the reaffirmation of the old truths of revelation, accompanied by a humble testimony of their divinity, to spread abroad a knowledge of the true God. Still, controversy, I repeat could not always be avoided. From the beginning, "Mormon" views of Deity have been assailed. They have been denounced as "awful blasphemy;" "soul destroying;" "the lowest kind of materialism;" "destructive of all truly religious sentiment;" "the worst form of pantheism;" "the crudest possible conception of God;" "absolutely incompatible with spirituality;" "worse than the basest forms of idolatry." These are a few of the phrases in which "Mormon" views of Deity have been described. Defense against these attacks has been rendered necessary from time to time; and whenever Elders of the Church of Jesus Christ of Latter-day Saints have entered into discussions on the subject of Deity, they have not failed to make it clear that the scriptures sustained their doctrine, although they may not always have been successful in stopping the denunciations, sarcasm, and ridicule of their opponents. This, however, is matter of small moment, since making clear the truth is the object of discussion, not superior strength in denunciation, bitterness in invective, keenness in sarcasm, or subtilty in ridicule.

In the winter and summer of 1901, unusual interest was awakened in "Mormon" views of Deity, in consequence of a series of lectures on the subject delivered by a prominent sectarian minister of Salt Lake City, and other discourses delivered before sectarian conventions of one kind or another held during the summer months of the year named. Now it so happened that for that same year the General Board of the Young Men's Improvement Associations of the Church of Jesus Christ of Latter-day Saints had planned a course of theological study involving consideration of this same subject—the being and nature of God; therefore, when the Mutual Improvement Associations of the Salt Lake Stake of Zion met in conference on the 18th of August of that year, and the writer was invited to deliver an address at one of the sessions of the conference, the time to him seemed opportune to set forth as clearly as might be the doctrine of the Church of Christ as to God. Accordingly the discourse, which makes chapter one in this book, was delivered. The discourse attracted some considerable attention, being published both in the *Deseret News* and *Improvement Era*: in the latter publication, in revised form. Through a copy of this magazine the discourse fell into the hands of the Reverend C. Van Der Donckt, of Pocatello, Idaho, a priest of the Roman Catholic Church; and he wrote a Reply to it, which by the courtesy of the editors of the *Improvement Era* was published in that magazine, and now appears as chapter two in this work.

It was very generally conceded that Rev. Van Der Donckt's Reply was an able paper—a view in which I most heartily concur; and it had the additional merit of being free from offensive personalities or any indulgence in ridicule or sarcasms of those principles which the gentleman sought to controvert. Some were of opinion that the Rev. gentleman's argument could not be successfully answered. This was a view in which I did not concur; for however unequal my skill in debate might be as compared with that of the Rev. gentleman of the Catholic Church, I had, and have now, supreme confidence in the truth of the doctrines I believe and advocate; and I was sure this advantage of having the truth would more than outweigh any want of skill in controversy on my part. In this confidence the Rejoinder was written and published in the *Improvement Era*, and now appears as chapter three in this work. How successfully the Rejoinder meets the criticism upon our doctrines by the Rev. gentleman who wrote the Reply, will, of course, be determined by the individual reader.

The discourse with which this controversy begins appears in chapter one as it did in the *Era*; unchanged except by the enlargement of a quotation or two from Dr. Draper's works, and Sir Robert Ball's writings, and the addition of one or two notes, with here and there a mere verbal change which in no way affects the thought or argument of the discourse, as I recognize the fact that any alteration which would change the argument or introduce new matter in the discourse, would be unfair to Mr. Van Der Donckt. The Rev. gentleman's Reply is, of course, exactly as it appeared in the *Improvement Era* for August and September, 1902. In the Rejoinder I have felt more at liberty, and therefore have made some few changes in the arrangement of paragraphs, and have here and there strengthened the argument, though even in this division of the discussion the changes in the *Era* copy are but slight.

In chapter four I publish another discourse—*Jesus Christ: the Revelation of God*, which I trust will emphasize and render even more clear than my first discourse the belief of the Church that Jesus Christ is the complete and perfect revelation of God;—that such as Jesus Christ is, God is.

In chapters five, six, seven and eight is a collection of utterances from our sacred scriptures, and from some of the prophets in the Church, on the doctrine of Deity, which I may say without reserve will be found extremely valuable to the student of this great subject; and these passages are so arranged as to make clear the fact that our doctrines on the subject of Deity are today what they have been from the commencement; and while there may have been an unfolding of the doctrines, an enlargement of our understanding of them, there is nothing in our doctrines on Deity today but what was germinally present in that first great revelation received by the Prophet Joseph Smith, in which God made himself known once more to a prophet, who knew him, as Moses did, face to face—as a man knows his friend.

B. H. Roberts.

Salt Lake City,

December, 1903.

CHAPTER I

I.
FORM OF GOD.

MY brethren and sisters, there are two things which conjoin to make this conference of the Young Men's and Young Women's Improvement Associations of Salt Lake Stake of Zion an interesting occasion. One is the approaching working season of the Young Men's Associations. They will this winter take up a course of study in "Mormon" doctrine—the first principles of the Gospel, or at least, some of those principles; and a large division of the Manual which has been prepared for their use will deal with the subject of the Godhead. For this reason I thought the time opportune to call attention to some of the doctrinal features pertaining to this subject. The Prophet Joseph Smith made this important statement: "It is the first principle of the Gospel to know for a certainty the character of God;" then he added something which to some ears is a little offensive—"and to know that we may converse with him, as one man converses with another." On the same occasion, he also said: "God himself was once as we are now, and is an exalted man, and sits enthroned in yonder heavens.[A]" Since, then, to know the character of God is one of the first principles of the Gospel, the subject of the Godhead is given a prominent place in the Manual for our Young Men's Associations during the coming season. This is one thing which makes this conference an interesting occasion.

[Footnote A: History of Joseph Smith: *Millennial Star*, Vol. xxiii, p. 246.]

Another thing which contributes to the interest of this conference, and also to this subject of the Godhead, is the attention which of late has been given to what is called the "Mormon view of God" by sectarian ministers among us. The interest found expression in a course of lectures during the past few months by one of the prominent ministers of Salt Lake City,[A] and also in a discourse delivered by another minister before the Teachers' association of the Utah Presbytery,[B] in which certain strictures were offered concerning our doctrine of God. It will perhaps be well to read the report of what in substance was said on that occasion by the reverend gentleman who thought proper to take up this subject before that association. I read from the synopsis of his discourse published in one of the morning papers:

[Footnote A: This was Rev. Alfred H. Henry, Pastor First M. B. Church.]

[Footnote B: This was Dr. Paden of the Presbyterian church, August 16, 1901.]

> At this point Dr. Paden made his address, first taking up some of the standard writings on "Mormon" doctrine and reading from them the ideas of God as incorporated in the "Mormon" faith. He read from the Catechism in relation to the Godhead, wherein it is stated that there are not only more Gods than one, but that God is a being of parts, with a body like that of a man. He then read from the Doctrine and Covenants, where it is stated that the words of the priesthood are the words of God. After calling attention to the material view of God as set forth in these teachings, the speaker said that he thought he could see a tendency towards a more spiritual idea of God among the younger and more enlightened members of the dominant church, and noticed this in the writings of Dr. Talmage especially. Referring to the Adam-God idea, the speaker said that he had not investigated it much, but thought that the "Mormon" Church was ashamed of such an idea. He placed special stress on the idea that when men attempted to give God a human form they fashioned him after their own weaknesses and frailties. A carnal man, he said, had a carnal God, and a spiritual man a spiritual God. The teaching of a material God, said he, and of a plurality of Gods, I think is heathenish. The material conception of God is the crudest possible conception.

I take it that we may classify under three heads the complaints here made against us with reference to the doctrine of Deity.

First, we believe that God is a being with a body in form like man's; that he possesses body, parts and passions; that in a word, God is an exalted, perfected man.

Second, we believe in a plurality of Gods.

Third, we believe that somewhere and some time in the ages to come, through development, through enlargement, through purification until perfection is attained, man at last, may become like God—a God.

I think these three complaints may be said to cover the whole ground of what our reverend critics regard as our error in doctrine on the subject of Deity.

The task before me, on this occasion, is to take this subject and present to you what in reality the Church of Jesus Christ of Latter day Saints teaches with reference to the Godhead.

Very naturally, one stands in awe of the subject, so large it is, and so sacred it is. One can only approach it with feelings of reverential awe, and with a deep sense of his own inability to grasp the truth and make it plain to the understandings of men. In the presence of such a task, one feels like invoking the powers divine to aid him in his undertaking; and paraphrasing Milton a little, one could well cry aloud, what in me is dark, illumine; what low, raise and support, that to the height of this great argument I may justify to men the faith we hold of God.

Here let me say that we are dependent upon that which God has been pleased to reveal concerning himself for what we know of him. Today, as in olden times, man cannot by searching find out God.[A] While it is true that in a certain sense the heavens declare his glory, and the firmament showeth his handiwork, and proclaim to some extent his eternal power and Godhead, yet nothing absolutely definite with respect of God may be learned from those works of nature. I will narrow the field still more, and say that such conceptions of God as we entertain must be in harmony with the doctrines of the New Testament on this subject; for accepting as we do, the New Testament as the word of God—at least, as part of it—any modern revelation which we may claim to possess must be in harmony with that revelation. Consequently, on this occasion, all we have to do is to consider the New Testament doctrine with reference to the Godhead. This, I believe, will simplify our task.

[Footnote A: Job ii:7.]

Start we then with the teachings of the Lord Jesus Christ. It is to be observed in passing that Jesus himself came with no abstract definition of God. Nowhere in his teachings can you find any argument about the existence of God. That he takes for granted; assumes as true; and from that basis proceeds as a teacher of men. Nay more; he claims God as his Father. It is not necessary to quote texts in proof of this statement; the New Testament is replete with declarations of that character. What may be of more importance for us at the present moment is to call attention to the fact that God himself also acknowledged the relationship which Jesus claimed. Most emphatically did he do so on the memorable occasion of the baptism of Jesus in the river Jordan. You remember how the scriptures, according to Matthew, tell us that as Jesus came up out of the water from his baptism, the heavens were opened, and the Spirit of God descended like a dove upon him; and at the same moment, out of the stillness came the voice of God, saying, "This is my beloved Son, in whom I am well pleased." On another occasion the Father acknowledges the relationship—at the transfiguration of Jesus in the mount, in the presence of three of his apostles, Peter and James and John, and the angels Moses and Elias. The company was overshadowed by a glorious light, and the voice of God was heard to say of Jesus, "This is my beloved Son; hear him." Of this the apostles in subsequent years testified, and we have on record their testimony. So that the existence of God the Father, and the relationship of Jesus to him, is most clearly shown in these scriptures. But Jesus himself claimed to be the Son of God, and in this connection there is clearly claimed for him divinity, that is to say, Godship. Let me read to you a direct passage upon that subject; it is to be found in the gospel according to St. John, and reads as follows:

> In the beginning was the Word, and the Word was with God, and the Word was God. * * * And the Word was made flesh, and dwelt among us, (and we beheld his glory, the glory as of the inly begotten of the Father) full of grace and truth.[A]

[Footnote A: John 1.]

The identity between Jesus of Nazareth—"the Word made flesh"—and the "Word" that was "with God from the beginning," and that "was God," is so clear that it cannot possibly be doubted. So the Son is God, as well as the Father is God. Other evidences go to establish the fact that Jesus had the Godlike power of creation. In the very passage I have just read, it is said:

> All things were made by him [that is, by the Word, who is Jesus]; and without him was not anything made that was made. In him was life; and the life was the light of men.[A]

[Footnote A: Verses 3, 4.]

One other scripture of like import, but perhaps even more emphatic than the foregoing, is that saying of Paul's in the epistle to the Hebrews:

> God, who at sundry times and in divers manners spake in time past unto the fathers by the prophets, hath in these last days spoken unto us by his Son, whom he hath appointed heir of all things, by whom also he made the worlds.[A]

[Footnote A: Heb. 1:1-3.]

Not only one world, but many "worlds," for the word is used in the plural So that we find that the Son of God was God the Father's agent in the work of creation, and that under the Father's direction he created many worlds. There can be no question then as to the divinity, the Godship, of Jesus of Nazareth, since he is not only God the Son, but God the Creator also—of course under the direction of the Father.

Again, the Holy Ghost is spoken of in the scriptures as God. I think, perchance, the clearest verification of that statement is to be found in connection with the circumstance of Ananias and his wife attempting to deceive the apostles with reference to the price for which they had sold a certain parcel of land they owned, which price they proposed putting into the common fund of the Church; but selfishness asserted itself, and they concluded to lie as to the price of the land, and only consecrate a part to the common fund It was an attempt to get credit for a full consecration of what they possessed, on what was a partial dedication of their goods. They proposed to live a lie, and to tell one if necessary to cover the lie they proposed to live. When Ananias stood in the presence of the apostles, Peter put this very pointed question to him: "Why hath Satan filled thine heart to lie to the Holy Ghost?" * * * "Thou hast not lied unto men, but unto God."[A] To lie to the Holy Ghost is to lie to God, because the Holy Ghost is God. And frequently in the Scriptures the Holy Spirit is spoken of in this way.

[Footnote A: Acts 5.]

These three, the Father, Son, and the Holy Ghost, it is true, are spoken of in the most definite manner as being God; but the distinction of one from the other is also clearly marked in the scriptures. Take that circumstance to which I have already alluded—the baptism of Jesus. There we may see the three distinct personalities most clearly. The Son coming up out of the water from his baptism; the heavens opening and the Holy Spirit descending upon him; while out of heaven the voice of God is heard saying, "This is my beloved Son, in whom I am well pleased." Here three Gods are distinctly apparent. They are seen to be distinct from each other. They appear simultaneously, not as one, but as three, each one doing a different thing, so that however completely they may be one in spirit, in purpose, in will, they are clearly distinct as persons—as individuals.

In several instances in the scriptures these three personages are accorded equal dignity in the Godhead. An example is found in the commission which Jesus gave to his disciples after his resurrection, when he sent them out into the world to preach the gospel to all nations. He stood in the presence of the eleven, and said:

> All power is given unto me in heaven and in earth. Go ye, therefore and teach all nations, baptizing them in the name of the Father, and of the Son, and of the Holy Ghost.[A]

[Footnote A: Matt. 28:18-20.]

Each of the three is here given equal dignity in the Godhead. Again, in the apostolic benediction:

> May the grace of our Lord Jesus Christ, the love of God, and the communion of the Holy Ghost be with you all.

In one particular, at least, Jesus came very nearly exalting the Holy Ghost to a seeming superiority over the other personages in the Godhead; for he said:

> All manner of sin and blasphemy shall be forgiven unto men; but the blasphemy against the Holy Ghost shall not be forgiven unto men. And whosoever speaketh a word against the Son of Man, it shall be forgiven him: but whosoever speaketh against the Holy Ghost, it shall not be forgiven him, neither in this world, neither in the world to come.[A]

[Footnote A: Matt. 12:31,32.]

I take it, however, that this seeming superior dignity accorded to the Holy Ghost by the Son of God, is owing to the nature of the third personage in the Trinity, and the kind of testimony he can impart unto the soul of man because of his being a personage of spirit—a testimony that is better than the seeing of the eye, more sure than the hearing of the ear, because it is spirit testifying to spirit—soul communing with soul—it is the soul of God imparting to the soul of man; and if men, after receiving that Witness from God shall blaspheme against him, farewell hope of forgiveness for such a sin, in this world or in the world to come!

These three personages then are of equal dignity in the Godhead, according to the teachings of the New Testament, which teachings, I pray you keep in mind, we most heartily accept.

This simple Christian teaching respecting the Godhead, gave birth to what in ecclesiastical history is called "The Apostles' Creed." A vague tradition hath it that before the Apostles dispersed to go into the world to preach the gospel they formulated a creed with respect of the Church's belief in God. Whether that tradition be true or not, I do not know, and for matter of that, it makes little difference. Suffice it to say that the so-called "Apostles' Creed," for two centuries expressed the faith of the early Christians upon the question of God. It stands as follows:

> I believe in God, the Father, Almighty; and in Jesus Christ, his only Begotten Son, our Lord, who was born of the Virgin Mary by the Holy Ghost, was crucified under Pontius Pilate, buried, arose from the dead on the third day, ascended to the heavens, and sits at the right hand of the Father, whence he will come, to judge the living and the dead; and in the Holy Ghost.

This was the first formulated Christian creed upon the subject of the Godhead, so far as known; and the ancient saints were content to allow this expression of their belief to excite their reverence without arousing their curiosity as to the nature of God. Happy, perhaps, for this world, certainly it would have contributed to the honor of ecclesiastical history, had this simple formula of the New Testament doctrine respecting God been allowed to stand sufficient until it should please God to raise the curtain yet a little more and give definite revelation with respect of himself and especially of his own nature. But this did not satisfy the so-called Christians at the close of the third and the beginning of the fourth century. By a succession of most bitter and cruel persecutions, the great, strong characters among the Christians by that time had been stricken down; and, as some of our historians record it, only weak and timorous men were left in the church to grapple with the rising power of "science, falsely so-called."[A] For a long time the paganization of the Christian religion had been going on. The men who esteemed themselves to be philosophers must needs corrupt the simple truth of the "Apostles' Creed" respecting the three persons of the Godhead, by the false philosophies of the orient, and the idle speculations of the Greeks; until this simple expression of Christian faith in God was changed from what we find it in the "Apostle's Creed" to the "Athanasian Creed," and those vain philosophizings and definitions which have grown out of it, and which reduce the dignity of the Godhead to a mere vacuum—to a "being" impersonal, incorporeal, without body, without parts, without passions; and I might add also, without sense or reason or any attribute—an absolute nonentity, which they placed in the seat of God, and attempted to confer upon this conception divine powers, clothe it with divine attributes, and give it title, knee and adoration—in a word, divine honors!

[Footnote A: See Mosheim's Eccl. Hist. Cent. iv. bk. ii, ch. i, (note.)]

Let us now consider the form of God. In those scriptures which take us back to the days of creation, when God created the earth and all things therein—God is represented as saying to someone:

> Let us make man in our image, after our likeness. * * * So God created man in his own image, in the image of God created he him, male and female created he them.

Now, if that were untouched by "philosophy," I think it would not be difficult to understand. Man was created in the image and likeness of God. What idea does this language convey to the mind of man, except that man, when his creation was completed, stood forth the counterpart of God in form? But our philosophers have not been willing to let it stand so. They will not have God limited to any form. They will not have him prescribed by the extensions of his person to some line or other of limitation. No; he must needs be in his person, as well as in mind or spirit, all-pervading, filling the universe, with a center nowhere, with a circumference everywhere. We must expand the person of God out until it fills the universe. And so they tell us that this plain, simple, straightforward language of Moses, which says that man was created in the image of God—and which everybody can understand—means, not the image of God's personality, but God's "moral image!" Man was created in the "moral image" of God, they say.

It is rather refreshing in the midst of so much nonsense that is uttered upon this subject, in order to hide the truth and perpetuate the false notions of a paganized Christianity, to find now and then a Christian scholar who rises out of the vagaries of modern Christianity and proclaims the straightforward truth. Let me read to you the words of such an one—the Rev Dr. Charles A. Briggs; and this note will be found in the Manual that your Improvement Associations will use the coming winter. It may be said, of course, by our Presbyterian friends, that Dr. Briggs is a heretic; that he has been cast out of their church. Grant it; but with open arms, he has been received by the Episcopal church, and ordained into its priesthood; and has an influence that is considerable in the Christian world, notwithstanding the door of the Presbyterian church was shut in his face. But however heretical Dr. Briggs' opinions may be considered by his former Presbyterian brethren, his scholarship at least cannot be challenged. Speaking of man being formed in the image and likeness of God, he says:

> Some theologians refer the form to the higher nature of man [that is, to that "moral image" in likeness of which it is supposed man was created]; but there is nothing in the text or context to suggest such an interpretation. The context urges us to think of the entire man as distinguished from the lower forms of creation,—that which is essential to man, and may be communicated by descent to his seed.—The bodily form cannot be excluded from the representation.[A]

[Footnote A: Messianic Prophecy, p. 70.]

I say it is rather refreshing to hear one speak like that whose scholarship, at least, is above all question. And yet still another voice; and this time from one who stands high in scientific circles, one who has written a work on the "Harmony of the Bible and Science," which is a most valuable contribution to that branch of literature. The gentleman I speak of is a Fellow of the Royal Astronomical Society, and principal of the College at Highbury New Park, England. On this subject of man being created in the image of God, he says:

I think the statement that man was made in the Divine image is intended to be more literal than we generally suppose; for judging from what we read throughout the scriptures, it seems very clear that our Lord, as well as the angels, had a bodily form similar to that of man, only far more spiritual and far more glorious; but which, however, is invisible to man unless special capabilities of sight are given him, like that experienced by Elisha's servant when, in answer to the prophet's prayer, he saw the heavenly hosts surrounding the city of Dothan.

After discussing this question at some length, and bringing to bear upon it numerous Biblical illustrations, this celebrated man—Dr. Samuel Kinns—whose scientific and scholarly standing I have already referred to, speaks of the effect of this belief upon man, and thus concludes his statement on that head:

> I am sure if a man would only consider a little more the divinity of his human form, and would remember that God has indeed created him in his own image, the thought would so elevate and refine him that he would feel it his duty to glorify God in his body as well as in his spirit.

But, as a matter of fact, I care not a fig for the statements of either learned divines or scientists on this subject; for the reason that we have higher and better authority to which we can appeal—the scriptures. And here I pass by that marvelous appearance of God unto Abraham in the plains of Mamre, when three "men" came into his tent, one of whom was the Lord, who conversed with him, and partook of his hospitality, and disclosed to him his intention with reference to the destruction of Sodom and Gomorrah.[A]

[Footnote A: Gen. 18.]

I pass by also that marvelous revelation of God to Joshua, when Joshua drew near to Jericho and saw a person in the form of a man standing with sword in hand. Joshua approached him and said: "Art thou for us, or for our adversaries?" "Nay," replied the person, "but as captain of the host of the Lord am I now come." And Joshua bowed himself to the very earth in reverence, and worshiped that august warrior. Do not tell me that it was an "angel;" for had it been an angel, the divine homage paid by Israel's grand old warrior would have been forbidden. Do you not remember the time when John, the beloved disciple, stood in the presence of an angel and awed by the glory of his presence he bowed down to worship him, and how the angel quickly caught him up and said: "See thou do it not; for I am thy fellow-servant, and of thy brethren the prophets, and of them which keep the sayings of this book: worship God!"[B] The fact that this personage before whom Joshua bowed to the earth received without protest divine worship from him, proclaims trumpet-tongued that he indeed was God. Furthermore, he bade Joshua to remove the shoes from his feet, for even the ground on which he stood was holy.

[Footnote A: Joshua 5:13,14.]

[Footnote B: Rev. 22:8,9. Also Rev. 19:10.]

I also pass by that marvelous vision given of the Son of God to the pagan king of Babylon. This king had cast the three Hebrew children into the fiery furnace, and lo! before his startled vision were *"four men"* walking about in the furnace, "and," said he, "the form of the fourth is like the Son of God."[A] I pass by, I say, such incidents as these, and come to more important testimony.

[Footnote A: Dan. 3:25.]

The great Apostle to the Gentiles writing to the Colossian saints, speaks of the Lord Jesus Christ, "in whom we have redemption through his blood, even the forgiveness of sins," as being in the "image of the invisible God."[A] Again, writing to the Hebrew saints, and speaking of Jesus, he says:

[Footnote A: Col. 1:15.]

> Who being the brightness of his [the Father's] glory, and the express image of his [the Father's] person, and upholding all things by the word of his power, when he had by himself purged our sins, sat down on the right band of the Majesty on high.

[Footnote A: Heb. 1:1,2.]

In the face of these scriptures, will anyone who believes in the Bible say that it is blasphemy to speak of God as being possessed of a bodily form? We find that the Son of God himself stood among his fellows a man, with all the limitations as to his body which pertain to man's body; with head, trunk, and limbs; with eyes, mouth and ears; with affections, with passions; for he exhibited anger as well as love in the course of his ministry; he was a man susceptible to all that man could suffer, called by way of pre-eminence the "man of sorrows," and one "acquainted with grief;" for in addition to his own, he bore yours and mine, and suffered that we might not suffer if we would obey his gospel. And yet we are told that it is blasphemy to speak of God as being in human form—that it is "heathenism." In passing, let me call your attention to the fact that our sectarian friends are pretending to the use of gentle phrases now. They do not propose to hurt our feelings at all by harshness. We are to be wooed by gentle methods. And yet they denounce a sacred article of our faith as "heathenism." I think if we were to use such language with reference to them, or their creeds, they could not commend it for its gentleness.

But I have a text to propose to them:

"What think ye of Christ?"

I suppose that thousands of sermons every year are preached from that text by Christian ministers. And now I arraign them before their favorite text, and I ask them, What think ye of Christ? Is he God? Yes. Is he man? Yes—there is no escaping it. His resurrection and the immortality of his body as well as of his spirit that succeeds his resurrection is a reality. He himself attested it in various ways. He appeared to a number of the apostles, who, when they saw him, were seized with fright, supposing they had seen a spirit; but he said unto them, "Why are ye troubled? And why do thoughts arise in your hearts? Behold my hands and my feet, that it is I myself: handle me and see; for a spirit hath not flesh and bones, as ye see me have."[A] Then, in further attestation of the reality of his existence, as if to put away all doubt, he said, "Have ye here any meat?" And they brought him some broiled fish and honeycomb, and "he did eat before them." Think of it! A resurrected, immortal person actually eating of material food! I wonder that our spiritually-minded friends do not arraign him for such a material act as that after his resurrection! A Scotch Presbyterian is particularly zealous for a strict observance of the Sabbath. One who was a little liberal in his views of the law pertaining to the Sabbath was once arguing with an orthodox brother on the subject, and urged that even Jesus so far bent the law pertaining to the Sabbath that he justified his disciples in walking through the fields of corn on the Sabbath, and rubbing the ears of corn in their hands, blowing away the chaff, and eating the corn. "O weel," says Donald, "mebbe the Lord did that; but it doesna heighten him in my opeenion." And so this resurrected, second personage of the Godhead ate material food after his resurrection; but I take it that the fact does not "heighten" him in the opinion of our ultra spiritually-minded folk. It comes in conflict, undoubtedly, with their notions of what life ought to be after the resurrection.

[Footnote A: Luke 24:36-39.]

[Footnote B: Luke 24:41-43.]

But not only did he do this, but with his resurrected hands he prepared a meal on the sea shore for his own disciples, and invited them to partake of the food which he with his resurrected hands had provided.[A] Moreover, for forty days he continued ministering to his disciples after his resurrection, eating and drinking with them;[B] and then, as they gathered together on one occasion, lo! he ascended from their midst, and a cloud received him out of their sight. Presently two personages in white apparel stood beside them and said: "Ye men of Galilee, why stand ye gazing up into heaven? This same Jesus, which is taken up from you into heaven, shall so come in like manner as ye have seen him go into heaven."[C] What! With his body of flesh and bones, with the marks in his hands and in his feet? Shall he come again in that form? The old Jewish prophet, Zechariah, foresaw that he would. He describes the time of his glorious coming, when his blessed, nail-pierced feet shall touch the Mount of Olives again, and it shall cleave in twain, and open a great valley for the escape of the distressed house of Judah, sore oppressed in the siege of their great city Jerusalem. We are told that "They shall look upon him whom they have pierced, and they shall mourn for him as one mourneth for his only son," and one shall look upon him in that day and shall say, "What are these wounds in thy hands and in thy feet?" and he shall answer, "These are the wounds that I received in the house of my friends."[D]

[Footnote A: John 21:9-13 and Acts 10:41.]

[Footnote B: Acts 10:31, and Acts 1:2,3.]

[Footnote C: Acts 1:11.]

[Footnote D: Zech. the 12th, 13th, and 14th chapters.]

What think ye of Christ? Is he God? Yes. Is he man? Yes, Will that resurrected, immortal, glorified man ever be distilled into some bodiless, formless essence, to be diffused as the perfume of a rose is diffused throughout the circumambient air? Will he become an impersonal, incorporeal, immaterial God, without body, without parts, without passions? Will it be? Can it be? What think ye of Christ? Is he God? Yes. Is he an exalted man? Yes; in the name of all the Gods, he is. Then why do sectarian ministers arraign the faith of the members of the Church of Jesus Christ of Latter-day Saints because they believe and affirm that God is an exalted man, and that he has a body, tangible, immortal, indestructible, and will so remain embodied throughout the countless ages of eternity? And since the Son is in the form and likeness of the Father, being, as Paul tells, "in the express image of his [the Father's] person"—so, too, the Father God is a man of immortal tabernacle, glorified and exalted: for as the Son is, so also is the Father, a personage of tabernacle, of flesh and of bone as tangible as man's, as tangible as Christ's most glorious, resurrected body.

II.
THE ONENESS OF GOD.

There are some expressions of scripture to consider which speak of the "oneness" of God. Speaking of the question which agitated the early Christian Church about eating meats which had been offered to idols, Paul says: "We know that an idol is nothing in the world, and that there is none other God but one."[A] Moreover, Jesus himself made this strange remark— that is, strange until one understands it: "I and my Father are one;" and so much one are they that he said: "He that hath seen me hath seen the Father. * * * Believest thou not that I am in the Father, and the Father in me? the words that I speak unto you I speak not of myself; but the Father that dwelleth in me, he doeth the works. Believe me that I am in the Father, and the Father in me."[B] Consequently our philosophers, especially those who lived when the present Christian creeds concerning God were forming, thought that by some legerdemain or other they must make the three Gods—the Father, the Son, and the Holy Ghost—just one person—one being; and therefore they set their wits at work to perform the operation.

[Footnote A: I Cor. 8:4.]

[Footnote B: John 14.]

Let us seek out some reasonable explanation of the language used. I refer again to the passage I just quoted from the writings of Paul with reference to there being "none other God but one." Immediately following what I read on that point comes this language:

> For though there be that are called Gods, whether in heaven or in earth (as there be Gods many, and Lords many). But to us there is but one God, the Father, of whom are all things, and we in him; and one Lord, Jesus Christ, by whom are all things, and we by him.[A]

[Footnote A: I Cor. 8:4-6.]

Now I begin to understand. "To us," that is, *pertaining* to us, "there is but one God." Just as to the English subject there is but one sovereign, so "to us" there is but one God. But that no more denies the existence of other Gods than the fact that to the Englishman there is but one sovereign denies the existence of other rulers over other lands. While declaring that "to us there is but one God," the passage also plainly says that there "be Gods many and Lords many," and it is a mere assumption of the sectarian ministers that reference is made only to heathen gods.

Again, we shall find help in the following passage in the 14th chapter of John:

> At that day ye shall know that I am in the Father, and ye in me, and I in you.

Observe this last scripture, I pray you. "I in you," and "ye in me," as well as Jesus being in the Father. This oneness existing between God the Father and God the Son can amount to nothing more than this: that Jesus was conscious of the indwelling presence of the Spirit of the Father within him, hence he spoke of himself and his Father as being one, and the Father within him doing the works. But mark you, not only are the disciples to know that the Father is in him, that is, in Christ, and that Jesus is in the Father, but the disciples also are to be in Jesus. In what way? Jesus himself has furnished the explanation. When the solemn hour of his trial drew near, and the bitter cup was to be drained to the very dregs, Jesus sought God in secret prayer, and in the course of that prayer he asked for strength of the Father, not only for himself, but for his disciples also. He said:

> And now I am no more in the world, but these [referring to his disciples] are in the world, and I come to thee. Holy Father, keep through thy name those whom thou hast given me, that they may be one, *as we are*.[A]

[Footnote A: John 17.]

Now I begin to see this mystery of "oneness." What does he mean when he prays that the disciples that God had given him should be one, as he and the Father are one? Think of it a moment, and while you are doing so I will read you this:

> Neither pray I for these alone, but for them also which shall believe on me through their word; that they all may be one: as thou, *Father, art in me, and I in thee, that they also may be one in us.* [A]

[Footnote A: John 17.]

Does that mean that the persons of all these disciples, whose resurrection and individual immortality he must have foreknown, shall all be merged into one person, and then that one fused into him, or he into that one, and then the Father consolidated into the oneness of the mass? No; a thousand times, no, to such a proposition as that. But as Jesus found the indwelling Spirit of God within himself, so he would have that same Spirit indwelling in his disciples, as well as in those who should believe on him through their testimony, in all time to come; and in this way become of one mind, actuated by one will. It must have been thoughts such as these that prompted Paul to say to the Ephesians:

For this cause I bow my knees unto the Father of our Lord Jesus Christ, of whom the whole family in heaven and earth is named, that he would grant you, according to the riches of his glory, to be strengthened with might by his spirit in the inner man: that Christ may dwell in your hearts by faith; that ye, being rooted and grounded in him, may be able to comprehend with all saints what is the breadth, and length, and depth, and height; and to know the love of Christ, which passeth knowledge, that ye might be filled with all the fullness of God.[A]

[Footnote A: Eph. 8:14-19.]

So then, this oneness is not a oneness of persons, not a oneness of individuals, but a oneness of mind, of knowledge, of wisdom, of purpose, of will, that all might be uplifted and partake of the divine nature, until God shall be all in all. This is the explanation of the mystery of the oneness both of the Godhead and of the disciples for which Jesus prayed.

III.
THE PLURALITY OP GODS.

There are several other items in this branch of the subject that would be of interest to discuss; but I must pay a little attention to the indictment brought against us by sectarian ministers on the question of a plurality of Gods.

We have already shown that the Father, the Son, and the Holy Ghost are three separate and distinct persons, and, so far as personality is concerned, are three Gods. Their "oneness" consists in being possessed of the same mind; they are one, too, in wisdom, in knowledge, in will and purpose; but as individuals they are three, each separate and distinct from the other, and three is plural. Now, that is a long way on the road towards proving the plurality of Gods. But, in addition to this, I would like to know from our friends—the critical sectarian ministers who complain of this part of our faith—the meaning of the following expressions, carefully selected from the scriptures:

"The Lord your God is God of Gods, and Lord of Lords." That is from Moses.[A]

[Footnote A: Deut. 10:17.]

"The Lord God of Gods, the Lord God of Gods, he knoweth, and Israel he shall know." That is from Joshua.[A]

[Footnote A: Josh. 22:22.]

"O give thanks unto the God of Gods! * * O give thanks to the Lord of Lords!" That is David.[A]

[Footnote A: Psalm 137:2,3.]

"And shall speak marvelous things against the God of Gods." That is Daniel.[A]

[Footnote A: Daniel 11:36.]

"The Lamb shall overcome them: for he is Lord of Lords, and King of Kings." That is the beloved disciple of Jesus—John the Revelator.[A]

[Footnote A: Rev. 17:14.]

Had I taken such expressions from the lips of the pagan kings or false prophets who are sometimes represented as speaking in the scriptures, you might question the propriety of making such quotations in support of the doctrine I teach; but since these expressions come from prophets and recognized servants of God, I ask those who criticize our faith in the matter of a plurality of Gods to explain away those expressions of the scriptures. Furthermore, there is Paul's language, in his letter to the Corinthians, already quoted, where he says, "that there be Gods many and Lords many, whether in heaven or in earth." Had his expression been confined to those that are called gods in earth it is possible that there might be some good ground for claiming that he had reference to the heathen gods, and not true Gods; but he speaks of those that "are Gods in heaven" as well as gods in earth. Right in line with this idea is the following passage from the Psalms of the Prophet David: "God standeth in the congregation of the mighty; he judgeth among the Gods."[A] These, undoubtedly, are the Gods in heaven to whom Paul alludes, among whom the God referred to stands; among whom he judges. This is no reference to the heathen gods, but to the Gods in heaven, the true Gods.

[Footnote A: Psalm 82:1.]

In this same Psalm, too, is the passage which seems to introduce some telling evidence from the Lord Jesus Christ himself, *viz*: "I have said ye are Gods, and all of you are the children of the Most High." You remember how on one occasion the Jews took up stones to stone Jesus, and he called a halt for just a moment, for he wanted to reason with them about it. He said:

> Many good works have I shown you from the Father; for which of these works do ye stone me?

Their answer was:

> For a good work we stone thee not; but for blasphemy; and because that thou, being a man, makest thyself God.

What an opportunity here for Jesus to teach them that there was but one God! How easily too, had he been so disposed, he could have explained about his "human nature" and his "divine nature," and shown to them the distinction; for these words have become part of the phraseology of Christian polemics. But he did not do that. On the contrary, he affirmed the doctrine of a plurality of Gods. He said to them:

> *Is it not written in your law, I said, Ye are Gods?* If he called them Gods, unto whom the word of God came, *and the scripture cannot be broken;* say ye of him, whom the Father hath sanctified and sent into the world, Thou blasphemest; because I said, I am the Son of God? If I do not the works of my Father, believe me not. But if I do, though ye believe not me, believe the works.

Higher authority on this question cannot be quoted than the Son of God himself. While there is much more that could and doubtless ought to be said on that branch of the subject, I must leave it here, because I have still another matter to present to you, on another branch of the subject; and that is, our belief that there is a possibility, through development, through growth, through doing what Jesus admonished his disciples to do—"Be ye perfect, even as your Father in heaven is perfect"—that the sons of God, somewhere and some time, may rise to a dignity that the Father and our Elder Brother have already attained unto.

IV.
The Future Possibilities for Man.

Is there any doubt about men being the sons of God? If I thought there was any in your minds, I would like to read to you the words of an authority upon this question. Paul, in speaking of the unknown God to whom the Athenians had erected an altar, said to them:

> God that made the world and all things therein * * * hath made of one blood all nations of men for to dwell on all the face of the earth, and hath determined the times before appointed and the bounds of their habitation; that they should seek the Lord, if haply they might feel after him, and find him, though he be not far from every one of us: for in him we live, and move, and have our being; as certain also of your own poets have said, For we are also his offspring. Forasmuch then as we are the offspring of God, we ought not to think that the Godhead is like unto gold, or silver, or stone, graven by art and man's device.[A]

[Footnote A: Acts 17:24-29.]

Why ought they not to think that the Godhead is like unto gold or silver, graven by art and man's device? Because the very divinity within them, their own kinship with God, ought to have taught them better than to bow down to images of wood and stone, the creation of man's hands. "Ye are the offspring of God," said the apostle. And David, as quoted a moment ago, said: "I have said: Ye are Gods, and all of you are children of the Most High." Upon which passage, it must be remembered, Jesus fixed the seal of his approval, as shown a moment ago, where he quotes it in controversy with the Jews.

Is it a strange and blasphemous doctrine, then, to hold that men at the last shall rise to the dignity that the Father has attained? Is it "heathenish" to believe that the offspring shall ultimately be what the parent is? My soul, I wonder why men at all conscious of the marvelous powers within themselves should question this part of our faith. Think for a moment what progress a man makes within the narrow limits of this life. Regard him as he lies in the lap of his mother, a mere piece of organized, red pulp—a new-born babe! There are eyes, indeed, that may see, but cannot distinguish objects; ears that may hear, but cannot distinguish sounds; hands as perfectly fashioned as yours or mine, but helpless, withal; feet and limbs, but they are unable to bear the weight of his body, much less walk. There lies a man in embryo, but helpless. And yet, within the span of three score years and ten, by the marvelous working of that wondrous power within that little mass of pulp, what a change may be wrought! From that helpless babe may arise one like Demosthenes or Cicero, or Pitt, or Burke, or Fox, or Webster, who shall compel listening senates to hear him, and by his master mind dominate their intelligence and their will, and compel them to think in channels that he shall mark out for them. Or from such a babe may come a Nebuchadnezzar, or an Alexander, or a Napoleon, who shall found empires or give direction to the course of history. From such a beginning may come a Lycurgus, a Solon, a Moses, or a Justinian, who shall give constitutions and laws to kingdoms, empires and republics, blessing happy millions unborn in their day, and direct the course of nations along paths of orderly peace and virtuous liberty. From the helpless babe may come a Michael Angelo, who from some crude mass of stone from the mountain side shall work out a heaven-born vision that shall hold the attention of men for generations, and make them wonder at the God-like powers of man that has created an all but living and breathing statue. Or a Mozart, a Beethoven, or a Handel, may come from the babe, and call out from the silence those melodies and the richer harmonies that lift the soul out of its present narrow prison house and give it fellowship for a season with the Gods. Out from that pulp-babe may arise a master mind who shall seize the helm of the ship of state, and give to a nation course and direction through troublesome times, and anchor it at last in a haven of peace, prosperity and liberty; crown it with honor, too, and give it a proud standing among the nations of the earth; while he, the savior of his country, is followed by the benedictions of his countrymen.

And all this may be done by a man in this life! Nay, it has been done, between the cradle and the grave—within the span of one short life. Then what may not be done in eternity by one of these God-men? Remove from his path the incident of death; or, better yet, contemplate him as raised from the dead; and give to him in the full splendor of manhood's estate, immortality, endless existence, what may we not hope that he will accomplish? What limits can you venture to fix as marking the boundary of his development, of his progress? Are there any limits that can be conceived? Why should there be any limits thought of? Grant immortality to man and God for his guide, what is there in the way of intellectual, moral, and spiritual development that he may not aspire to? If within the short space of mortal life there are men who rise up out of infancy and become masters of the elements of fire and water and earth and air, so that they well-nigh rule them as Gods, what may it not be possible for them to do in a few hundreds or thousands of millions of years? What may they not do in eternity? To what heights of power and glory may they not ascend?

It is idle today to ask men to be satisfied with the old sectarian notions of man's future life, where at best he is to be but one of a minstrelsy twanging harps and singing to the glory of an incorporeal, bodiless, passionless, immaterial incomprehensible God. Such conceptions of existence no longer satisfy the longings of the intelligent or spiritual-minded man.[A]

[Footnote A: On this subject Sir Robert Ball, the great English astronomer and man of science, and who is feelingly spoken of as "a man with singular capacity for popularizing science without debasing it"—has the following passage:

> "The popular notion that man, once escaped from the confinement of the body, does nothing except sit on a cloud and sing psalms to the glory of a God, whose glory is so perfect without him that he was content when man was not in being, rests upon no evidence, whether of reason or revelation, and seems to us derived either from man's long experience of overtoil and misery and his enjoyment, therefore, of their absence, or from the inherent Asiatic dislike of exertion. Why should we not work forever as well as now? If man can live again, and grow in that new life, and

exert himself to carry out the always hidden, but necessarily magnificent purpose of the Creator, then indeed, his existence may have some importance, and the insignificance of his place of origin be forgotten. For he has an inherent quality which does not belong, so far as the mind can see what must always remain partially dark, even the Divine; he is capable of effort, and in the effort and through the effort, not only of growing greater than before, but of adding force to an inanimate thing like his own body. What if that power of effort should be slowly aggrandized until man, now a little higher than the monkey, became a really great being?" ("Self Culture" for March, 1899.)]

Growth, enlargement, expansion for his whole nature, as he recognizes that nature in its intellectual, moral, spiritual and social demands, are what his soul calls for; and the systems of theology that rise not to the level of these hopes are unworthy man's attention.

Keep these thoughts in mind for a moment, I pray you. That is, remember the powers in man, what he has attained to in this life, and what it is conceivable for him to attain unto after the resurrection of the dead, when death shall have been removed from his pathway. Keep this in mind, while I bring to bear on the theme under consideration another line of facts.

Let us consider, just for a moment, and in a very simple manner, the universe in which man lives. And let us start with what we know, and keep well within those lines. First of all, then, as to the earth itself: Thanks to the knowledge man now has respecting the earth it is no longer regarded as the center of the universe, around which revolve sun and moon and stars, that in the ages of darkness were thought to have been created for the sole purpose of giving light by day and by night to the earth. No; man has learned the true relation of the earth to these other objects in the universe. He knows that the earth is but one of a number of planets—one of a group of eight major planets, and a larger number of minor ones, that revolve regularly around the sun—and one of the smallest of the group of major planets at that. Outside of this group of planets, with whose motions and laws man has become familiar, is a vast host of what are called "fixed stars;" that is, stars that apparently have no motion, but which really do move, only their orbits are so immense that man with the unaided eye can not discern their movements—hence we call them "fixed stars."[A] Our astronomers have learned that these "fixed stars" are not like the planets which move in their orbits about our sun, but, on the contrary, are like the sun itself, self-luminous bodies, and doubtless like the sun the center of opaque planetary groups; or at least we may say that reasoning from analogy, that is regarded as a very probable fact.

[Footnote A: "To the unassisted eye, the stars seem to preserve the same relative positions in the celestial sphere generation after generation. If Job, Hipparchus, or Ptolemy should again look upon the heavens, he would, to all appearance see Aldebaran, Orion, and the Pleiades exactly as he saw them thousands of years ago, without a single star being moved from its place. But the refined methods of modern astronomy, in which the telescope is brought in to measure spaces absolutely invisible to the eye, have shown that this seeming unchangeability is not real, but that the stars are actually in motion, only the rate of change is so slow that the eye would not, in most cases, notice it for thousands of years. In ten thousand years, quite a number of stars, especially the brighter ones, would be seen to have moved, while it would take a hundred thousand years to introduce a very noticeable change in the aspect of the constellations." (Newcomb's Astronomy, pp. 464-5.)]

Sir Robert Ball in speaking of these worlds and the probability of their being inhabited says:

> We know of the existence of thirty millions of stars or suns, many of them much more magnificent than the one which gives light to our system. The majority of them are not visible to the eye, or even recognizable by the telescope, but sensitized photographic plates—which are for this purpose eyes that can stare unwinking for hours at a time—have revealed their existence beyond all doubt or question, though most of them are almost inconceivably distant, thousands or tens of thousands of times as far off as our sun. A telegraphic message, for example, which would reach the sun in eight minutes, would not reach some of these stars in eighteen hundred years. The human mind, of course, does not really conceive such distances, though they can be expressed in formula which the human mind has devised, and the bewildering statement is from one point of view singularly depressing. It reduces so greatly the probable importance of man in the universe. It is most improbable, almost impossible, that these great centers of light should have been created to light up nothing, and as they are far too distant to be of use to us, we may fairly accept the hypothesis that each one has a system of planets around it like our own. Taking an average of only ten planets to to each sun, that hypothesis indicates the existence, within the narrow range to which human observation is still confined, of at least

three hundred millions of separate worlds, many of them doubtless of gigantic size, and it is nearly inconceivable that those worlds can be wholly devoid of living and sentient beings upon them. Granting the to us impossible hypothesis that the final cause of the universe is accident, a fortuitous concourse of self-existent atoms, still the accident which produced thinking beings upon this little and inferior world must have frequently repeated itself: while if, as we hold, there is a sentient Creator, it is difficult to believe, without a revelation to that effect, that he has wasted such glorious creative power upon mere masses of insensible matter. God cannot love gases. The high probability, at least, is that there are millions of worlds—for, after all, what the sensitized paper sees must be but an infinitesimal fraction of the whole—occupied by sentient beings.[A]

[Footnote A: Self Culture for March, 1899.]

On this subject Richard A. Proctor, in his "Other Worlds Than Ours," also remarks:

To sum up what we have learned so far from the study of the starry heavens—we see that, besides our sun there are myriads of other suns in the immensity of space; that these suns are large and massive bodies capable of swaying by their attraction systems of worlds as important as those which circle around our own sun; that these suns are formed of elements similar to those which constitute our own sun, so that the worlds which circle round them may be regarded as in all probability similar in constitution to this earth; and that from these suns all forms of force which we know to be necessary to the existence of organized beings on our earth are abundantly emitted. It seems reasonable to conclude that these suns are girt round by dependent systems of worlds. Though we cannot, as in the case of the solar system, actual see such worlds, yet the mind presents them before us, various in size, various in structure, infinitely various in their physical condition and habitudes.[A]

[Footnote A: "Other Worlds Than Ours," p. 240.]

With the unaided eye there is ordinarily within the range of our vision some five or six thousand of these "fixed stars." With the aid of the telescope, however, there is brought within the range of man's vision between forty and fifty millions of fixed stars; with the probability existing that all these, as well as those fixed stars of sufficient magnitude to be within the range of our unaided vision, are, like our own sun, the centers of groups of opaque planets, which, because they are opaque, cannot be seen by us. But this is but the beginning of the story of the universe. Immense as are the numbers of "fixed stars" to which I have called attention, and their distances so great that in some cases it would take a ray of light a million years to reach us from them, though light moves through space at such speed that it will travel some eight times around the earth in a single second—immense, I say, as are these numbers of "fixed stars" revealed to man by the telescope, they are after all but as the first "street lamps" of God's great universe—but a few of the motes in God's sunbeam. Let me explain. You have seen a ray of sunlight dart into a room through the half drawn curtains, and have observed that it reveals the existence of innumerable motes floating about in the sunbeam. You know that if the sunbeam should shift into another part of the room it will reveal the existence of motes in that part of the room also—millions of them. So you know that the atmosphere in the whole room is filled with such motes; that the atmosphere in every room in your house is in the same condition—that is, filled with motes; so all the rooms in all the houses of your friends, or in the city; so also the whole circumambient air of the whole earth. Well, what man has discovered in space pertaining to the existence of "fixed stars"—great, selfluminous bodies, unquestionably the centers of planetary systems the same as our sun is—all this, I say, is but as the sunbeam revealing the existence of a few of the motes that exist in some little corner of a room: for out on the farthest edge of space explored by man's vision aided by the most powerful helps he can devise, man in contemplation can stand and conceive of still greater stretches of space filled by still more numerous suns, the centers of planetary systems, than has yet come within the range of his vision. And standing thus in the midst of the universe, he begins to comprehend that great truth uttered by Joseph Smith when he contemplated the creations of the Gods: "There is no space where there is no kingdom [created world], and there is no kingdom where there is no space, either a greater or a lesser space."[A] But this is beside the subject.

[Footnote A: Doc. & Cov. sec. 88:36,37.]

What I want you to do is to think how small and insignificant this earth of ours is, even in comparison with some of the planets of our own system, some of which are hundreds of times larger than our earth.[A] And then the sun, the center of the system, itself—what a speck it is in the universe! Though outweighing the combined mass of all the planets of which he is the center seven hundred and thirty times over, still he is but a point in the universe! To quote the words of an eminent author:

[Footnote A: The planet Jupiter, for example, has a diameter of about 85,000 miles, while the earth's diameter is but about 8,000 miles. In volume Jupiter exceeds our earth about 1,300 times, while in mass it exceeds it 213 times. (See "Newcomb's Astronomy," p. 339.)]

> As there are other globes like our earth, so, too, there are other worlds like our solar system. There are self-luminous suns exceeding in number all computation. The dimensions of this earth pass into nothingness in comparison with the dimensions of the solar system, and that system, in its turn, is only an invisible point if placed in relation with the countless hosts of other systems which form, with it, clusters of stars. Our solar system, far from being alone in the universe, is only one of an extensive brotherhood, bound by common laws and subject to like influences. Even on the very verge of creation, where imagination might lay the beginning of the realms of chaos, we see unbounded proofs of order, a regularity in the arrangement of inanimate things, suggesting to us that there are other intellectual creatures like us, the tenants of those islands in the abysses of space. Though it may take a beam of light a million of years to bring to our view those distant worlds, the end is not yet. Far away in the depths of space we catch the faint gleams of other groups of stars like our own. The finger of a man can hide them in their remoteness. Their vast distances from one another have dwindled into nothing. They and their movements have lost all individuality; the innumerable suns of which they are composed blend all their collected lights into one pale milky glow.
>
> Thus extending our view from the earth to the solar system, from the solar system to the expanse of the group of stars to which we belong, we behold a series of gigantic nebular creations rising up one above another, and forming greater and greater colonies of worlds. No numbers can express them, for they make the firmament a haze of stars. Uniformity, even though it be the uniformity of magnificence, tires at last, and we abandon the survey, for our eyes can only behold a boundless prospect and conscience tells us our own unspeakable insignificance.[A]

[Footnote A: Draper's "Intellectual Development of Europe," vol. 2, p. 292.]

And the earth itself, then, what of that? What an insignificant thing it is in the creations of God! With all its islands and continents, its rivers, lakes and mighty oceans; its mountains and its valleys; its towns, cities and all the tribes of men, together with all their hopes and fears and petty ambitions—all is but a mote in God's sunbeam—less than a single grain of sand on the sea shore!

What I want to ask in the light of these reflections is this: Is it such a wonderful thing to believe that at the last, one of God's sons shall preside over this little earth as the God-president or God of it? That our Father Adam, the "Grand Patriarch" of our race—the "Ancient of Days"—"Michael, the Archangel"—give him what title you will out of the many which are his—is it so hard to believe that he will eventually attain to the dignity of the governorship of this earth, when it is redeemed and sanctified and becomes one of the glorified spheres of God?

Some of the sectarian ministers are saying that we "Mormons" are ashamed of the doctrine announced by President Brigham Young to the effect that Adam will thus be the God of this world. No, friends, it is not that we are ashamed of that doctrine. If you see any change come over our countenances when this doctrine is named, it is surprise, astonishment, that any one at all capable of grasping the largeness and extent of the universe—the grandeur of existence and the possibilities in man for growth, for progress, should be so lean of intellect, should have such a paucity of understanding, as to call it in question at all. That is what our change of countenance means—not shame for the doctrine Brigham Young taught.

I feel that I must have wearied you with so long a discourse; I know very well I have wearied myself; and yet I am loth to quit this splendid field for thought. The subject, and our conception of it, must ever be grander than it is within our ability to express. It is beyond our power to grasp it and make it plain in words, I can see in this "Mormon" doctrine of God the highest spirituality that the mind of man is capable of grasping. If our sectarian friends think, that in us there is any drifting away from the teachings of our prophets upon this subject, any shadow of turning, and that we of modern days are growing more spiritual than were they, it is not that we are changing, or leaving the old moorings of our faith; but it is because they themselves are giving a little more careful attention to our doctrines, and begin to catch their first sight of the grand spirituality which all the while has pervaded our belief in the Gods and their government, and the heights of glory to which men—the offspring of the Gods—may finally attain.

CHAPTER II

REPLY TO ELDER ROBERTS' MORMON VIEWS OF DEITY,[A] BY REV. C. VAN DER DONCKT, OF THE CATHOLIC CHURCH, POCATELLO, IDAHO.

[Footnote A: The following note preceded Rev. Van Der Donckt's reply, when published in the *Improvement Era*: "In the first two numbers of the present volume of the *Era*, an article on the Characteristics of the Deity from a 'Mormon' View Point, appeared from the pen of Elder B. H. Roberts. It was natural that ministers of the Christian denominations should differ from the views there expressed. Shortly after its appearance, a communication was received from Reverend Van Der Donckt, of the Catholic church, of Pocatello, Idaho, asking that a reply which he had written might be printed in the *Era*. His article is a splendid exposition of the generally accepted Christian views of God, well written and to the point, and which we think will be read with pleasure by all who are interested in the subject. We must, of course, dissent from many of the deductions with which we cannot at all agree, but we think the presentation of the argument from the other side will be of value to the Elders who go forth to preach the Gospel, as showing them what they must meet on this subject. It is therefore presented in full; the *Era*, of course, reserving the right to print any reply that may be deemed necessary.—Editors."]

I.

I am very grateful for the privilege of being allowed space in your magazine to reply to Mr. B. H. Roberts' defense of the "Mormon Views of the Deity."

1. First, Mr. Roberts asserts: "Jesus came with no abstract definition of God." He certainly gave a partial definition of God when declaring: "God is a spirit" (John 4:24). Now, although we must believe whatever God reveals to us upon one single word of his, just as firmly as upon a thousand, nevertheless, I will add that St. Paul, who solemnly testifies that he *received of the Lord that which he delivered unto the Christians,* (I Cor. 11:23) also states: "The Lord is a spirit" (II Cor. 3:17).

I am well aware that the Latter-day Saints interpret those texts as meaning a spirit clothed with a body, but what nearly the whole of mankind, Christians, Jews, and Mohammedans, have believed for ages cannot be upset by gratuitous assertions of a religious innovator of this last century. Again, the context of the Bible admits of no such interpretation. And if anyone should still hesitate to accept the universally received meaning of the word *spirit*, our risen Savior settles the matter. As his disciples, upon first seeing him after his resurrection, were troubled and frightened, supposing they beheld a spirit, Jesus reassured them, saying, "*A spirit hath not flesh and bones* as you see me to have" (Luke 24:37-39).

2. Another very strong and explicit statement is: "Blessed art thou, Simon Bar-Jona [son of John] because *flesh and blood* hath not revealed it to thee, but my *Father* who is in heaven" (Matt. 16:17). As Christ has asked, "What do men say the Son of Man is" (Matt. 16:13). There is an evident antithesis and contrast between the opinion of men and the profession of Peter, which is based upon revelation. The striking opposition between *men, flesh and blood*, and the Father, evidently conveys the sense that God hath not flesh and blood like man, but is a spirit.

3. That God is a spirit is proved moreover by the fact that he is called invisible in the Bible. All material beings are visible. Absolutely invisible beings are immaterial or bodiless: God is absolutely invisible, therefore God is immaterial or bodiless.

Moses' unshaken faith is thus described by St. Paul: "He was strong *as seeing him that is invisible*" (Heb. 11:27).

"No man hath seen God at any time" (1 John 4:12).

"The King of kings—whom no man hath seen nor can see." (I Tim. 15:16).

In the light of these clear, revealed statements, how shall we explain the various apparitions of God mentioned in the Bible? Tertullian, (A. D. 160-245), Ambrose (330-397), Augustine (354-430) and other Fathers, whose deep scholarship is acknowledged by Protestants and Catholics alike, informs us that God the Father is called invisible because he never appeared to bodily eyes; whereas the Son manifested himself as an angel, or through an angel, and as man after his incarnation. He is the eternal revelation of the Father. It is necessary to remark that whenever the eternal Son of God, or angels at God's behest, showed themselves to man, they became visible only through a body or a material garb assumed for the occasion (see Cardinal Newman's "Development of Christian Doctrine," 9th edition, pp. 136 and 138).

I am well aware of St. Paul's, "We now see as through a glass darkly, but then face to face." (I Cor. 12:13.) "In thy light we shall see light." (Ps. 35:10.)

The first and chief element of the happiness of heaven will consist in the beatific vision; that is, in seeing God face to face, unveiled as he really is. The "face to face" however is, literally true only of our blessed Savior who ascended into heaven with his sacred body. Otherwise, as God is a spirit, he has no body and consequently no face. In paradise, spirits (angels and our souls) see spirits. We shall see God and angels, not with the eye of the body, nor by the vibrations of cosmic light, but with the spiritual eye, with the soul's intellectual perception, elevated by a supernatural influx from God. As in ordinary vision, the image of an object is impressed on the retina, so in the beatific vision, the perfect image of God will be reflected on the soul, impressing on it a vivid representation of him. We shall thus enjoy an intellectual possession of him, very different from our possession of earthly things.

4. That angels as well as God are bodiless beings, is also clearly proved by Holy Writ. To which of the angels said he at any time: "Sit on my right hand till I make thy enemies thy footstool? Are they not all ministering *spirits* sent to minister for them who shall receive the inheritance of salvation?" (Heb. 1:13, 14.) Again, *"Our* wrestling *is not against flesh and blood,* but against the rulers of the world of this darkness, against the spirits of wickedness" (Eph. 6:12).

Could plainer words be found to teach that angels, both good and bad, are spirits, devoid of bodies? Now, the Creator is certainly more perfect than his creatures, and pure minds are more perfect than minds united to bodies (men). ["The corruptible body is a load upon the soul, and the earthly habitation presseth down the mind" (Wis. 9:15.) "Who shall deliver me from this body of death?" (St. Paul).] Therefore, the Creator is a pure spirit.

5. It is a well known fact that all men, after the example of the inspired Writings, make frequent use of the figure called anthropomorphism, attributing to the Deity a human body, human members, human passions, etc.; and that is done, not to imply that God is possessed of form, limbs, etc., but simply to make spiritual things or certain truths more intelligible to man, who, while he tarries in this world, can perceive things and even ideas only through his senses or through bodily organs.

That even the Latter-day Saints thus understand such expressions is evident from their catechism (chapter 5: Q. 9). Yet it is from certain expressions of the same inspired Book that they conclude that God has a body. Now I contend that, if we must understand the Bible literally in those passages God created man in his own image, (Genesis 1:27, and Genesis 32:24, etc., and Exodus 24:9, etc.) from which they attempt to prove that God has a body, we must interpret it literally in other similar passages: so that if Moses, etc., really saw the feet of God (Exodus 24:10), then we must hold that the *real hand* of God is meant by David in (Psalm 138) (Hebrew Bible Ps. 139; 13:9; 9; 10): "If I take my wings early in the morning, and dwell in the uttermost part of the sea, even there shall *thy hand* lead me, and *thy right hand* shall hold me." And as the Psalmist says also: "Whither shall I flee from *thy face*? If I ascend into heaven, thou art there; if I descend into hell, thou art there" (Psalm 139:7, 8). Have we then according to "Mormon" standards, not the right to infer that God has such a long hand as to extend to the uttermost parts of the sea, and such an extremely long face, reaching from heaven to hell? To this, I am sure, even the gloomiest Protestants would object. By the way, should we not also conclude that David had wings? ("If I take my wings early in the morning, and fly," etc.) unless we admit that the royal Prophet anticipated our modern scientists, the Brazilian Santos-Dumont, Professor Zahm of Notre Dame, Ind., etc., in experimenting with flying machines.

6. A sixth proof of the truth that God has not a body, and therefore is not an exalted man, is the fact of the incarnation of the Son of God. The "Mormons" admit that Jesus Christ is the Great I Am, (from all eternity to all eternity) therefore, God (Doctrine and Covenants section 39). By the by, I see no mention of this fundamental Christian truth of the incarnation, in the sacred books of the Latter-day Saints, not even in their catechism. Yet what is more capable of winning cold hearted, careless people to the love of God than the exposition of this mystery which has been hidden for ages and generations, but now is made manifest to his saints: (Col. 1:26) "God so loved the world as to give us his only begotten Son, that whosoever believeth in him may not perish but may have everlasting life" (John 3:16.)

So the "Mormons" admit that Jesus Christ is God for all eternity. The Bible teaches that Jesus Christ became a man at a specified time; therefore, Jesus Christ, or God was not man before that specified time.

"In the beginning was the Word, and the Word was with God and the Word was God. *And the Word was made flesh* and dwelt among us" (John 1:1-14). It is plain that the Son of God became flesh only at the time of his sojourn on earth. Now, had he been flesh, or man, before, as "Mormons" hold, how could he become what he was already from all eternity? No; not from the beginning of the world, but only now once, at the end of ages, he (Jesus) hath appeared for the destruction of sin, by the sacrifice of himself. When he came into the world, he said: "Sacrifice and oblation thou wouldst not, *but a body thou hast fitted to me."* Then said I: "Behold I come" (Heb. 9:26 and 10:5, 7). "Let this mind be in you which was also in Christ Jesus, *who being in the form* (nature, glory, majesty) *of God*, thought it not robbery to be equal with God (deemed it not fitting to assume to his human nature the glory and majesty due him without labor and suffering) but emptied (stripped) himself, *taking the form of a servant, being made in the likeness of men and in habit* (in his whole exterior) *found as a man"* (Philip. 2:5), etc. Again: *"In him* (Christ) dwelleth all the fulness of the Godhead *corporeally"* (Col. 2:9). Had God a body (*Latin corpus*) what sense would there be in St. Paul's corporally or bodily? All save "Mormons," understand St. Paul to mean that in Christ the true God manifested himself in the flesh, or as man.

"Because the children are partakers of flesh and blood, he also himself in like manner hath been partaker of the same, that through death he might destroy him who hath the empire of death. For nowhere doth he take hold of the angels, but the seed of Abraham, he taketh hold, wherefore, it behooved him in all things to be made like unto his brethren" (Heb. 2:14-16). "Every spirit which confesseth that Jesus Christ is come in the flesh is of God" (I John 4:2). "Many seducers are gone out into the world who confess not that Jesus Christ is come in the flesh" (II John 1:7). Why do the New Testament writers lay so much stress upon the taking of flesh by Jesus Christ? Evidently we must see in those expressions (the Word was made flesh, etc.) more than a Hebraism, for "He became man" (Gen. 6:12; Is. 40:5). The inspired authors want to teach us humility by impressing upon our minds the excessive abasement of the Eternal Son of God in uniting his Divinity, not to the nature of an angel, but to that of an inferior creature, as man is. They have still the further aim of impuning the heretics, of the early days of the Church the Docetae, Cerinthus, Ebion, etc., who, attributing the flesh to an evil principle, and therefore holding it as utterly polluted, maintained that Christ had not a real body of flesh but only an apparent body. This we learn from SS. Irenaeus, Jerome, Clem. of Alex., etc.

7. Another proof that God is not an exalted man; that is, that he was not what we are now, and became perfected into God, is the direct statement of the Bible: "God is not as a man that he should lie, *nor as the Son of man that he should be changed"* (Num. 23:19). "I will not execute the fierceness of my wrath because I am God and not man" (Psalm 11:19).

8. Another most striking proof is to be found in God's immutability. The Latter day Saints teach that God was once imperfect, as man is; the Bible teaches the very opposite: *"Thou art always the self-same"* (Psalm 101:26). *"I am the Lord and I change not"* (Mal. 3:6). *"The Father of lights with whom*

there is no change nor shadow of alteration." (The Latin *alter* means other. So the Lord is never other from all eternity.) (James 1:17.)

9. Finally, the Latter-day Saints' theory of the Man-God supposes a past and present with God. The Bible excludes that succession of time, and speaks of God as the Everlasting Present "I Am Who Am." "Before Abraham was, I am." "From eternity and to eternity thou art God" (Psalm 89:2). "His power is an everlasting power" (Daniel 7:14).

PHILOSOPHICAL PROOFS OF GOD'S SIMPLICITY OR SPIRITUALITY.

The "Mormons" admit that God existed from all eternity; consequently, there was no time at which God did not exist. Therefore, the Eternal Being, or God, must be simple.

A compound is, at least by nature, posterior to its component parts. If God is a compound, he is posterior to his component parts. Therefore, he would not be eternal; therefore, not God.

Illustration. The Latter-day Saints believe that God creates the souls of men, long before their conception. Man is a composite being, spirit and flesh being the component parts. Man is evidently posterior to his elements; in other words, before a human being can exist, there must first be a spirit, a soul; and in the second place there must be the embryo (or foetus); and, thirdly, both of these existing elements must be united before a human being comes into existence. No need of more illustration. Fancy a clock, an engine, a shoe, or any composite being. The parts must exist before the whole. Then to have the compound, some one or something must do the compounding, or put the ingredients or elements together. Who then did compound the Eternal? Not himself, as no one can work before he exists: not another being, as no other being existed before it was created by God. God is the necessary Being; *i. e.* who could not not exist. Something exists; therefore, there exists the Necessary Being. Everything that exists is produced or unproduced. Now all things cannot be produced; for *whatever is produced or made is produced by another,* (otherwise it would have made itself, which is impossible, as nothing can act before it exists). *This other* (the producer) *is either a necessary being or a produced being.* If produced, it must have been produced by another. Thus we must finally come to a being that was not produced, or a necessary being. That necessary being (who was not made and who always existed) is God.

If God were an aggregate of parts, these parts would be either necessary beings or contingent (that do not necessarily exist); or some would be necessary and some contingent. None of these suppositions are tenable, therefore, God is not an aggregate of parts.

First supposition: If the parts of God were necessary beings there would be several independent beings, which the infinity of God precludes. God would not be infinite, if there were even one other being independent of him, as his power, etc., would not reach that being.

Second supposition: The Necessary Being would be the aggregate of several contingent beings. An unreasonable supposition: contingent beings cannot by their addition or collection lose their essential predicate of contingency; in other words, the nature of the parts clings to the whole.

The third supposition is equally absurd, for if some part exit necessarily, it must be infinite in every perfection; therefore, it would of itself be sufficient to constitute God, and could not be improved by the addition of other parts.

The Necessary Being must be infinite, or illimitable. Nothing is done without a cause. No cause of limitation to the Necessary Being can be found.

If finite, or limited, he must be limited by his own essence, or by another, or by himself.

a. He cannot be limited by his own essence, for his essence, is actual Being or existence: *I Am Who Am.* No perfection is repugnant to that essence; for every perfection is some existence, something that *is*. No defect necessarily flows from that essence, for defect is in a thing only in as much as that thing is not in some sense or regard; now in the notion or in the concept of him who is Being itself (I Am Who Am) is not contained the concept that he is not in some regard; for something is limited not because it is, but because it is this or that, for instance, a stone, a plant, a man.

b. He cannot be limited by another, because he depends on no other, and has not received his being from another.

c. He could not be limited by himself as he is not the cause of his existence, but the sufficient reason thereof.

The Infinite Being is most simple, or not compound. Were he compound, his parts would be either all finite, or infinite, or one infinite and the others finite. None of these suppositions are possible, therefore, he is not compound.

1. Several finite things cannot produce an infinite or an illimitable, as there would always be a first and a last.

2. Many infinite beings are inconceivable; for, if there were several, they would have to differ from each other by some perfection. Now from the

moment one would have a perfection, the other one lacks, the latter would not be infinite. Therefore, God cannot be a compound of infinite parts.

3. If one is infinite, nothing can be added to it. Finite parts could not belong to the infinite essence, else they would communicate their limitations to God.

Therefore, the Infinite Being is not composite, but simple or spiritual. Therefore, he is not, nor ever was, a man, who is a composite being.

II.

Above, I proved God's *immutability* from the Bible; now I prove it from philosophy, or the light of reason.

Mutation or change is the passing from one state into another. The Infinite Being is not liable to change, as change implies an imperfection in the being susceptible of it, as that being had not in the previous state what it has in the subsequent, or *vice versa*. God having all perfections must be unchangeable. Therefore, he is not a man grown into a God.

The Necessary Being is such that he could not exist, nor exist otherwise. He cannot receive his existence, nor lose it. So he cannot change with regard to his existence; nor can he change with regard to his mode of existence. His perfections being infinite cannot increase; nor can they wane or decrease, else there would be an imperfection in him, and he would no longer be infinite, or God. Therefore, God is unchangeable. Therefore, he never was what we are.

God is pure essence (I Am Who I Am), pure actuality or act.

Change implies potentiality, liability to become what it is not.

As God is infinitely perfect, all potentiality is excluded from him; in other words, there is no room for growth or more perfection. Consequently, no possibility of change. Therefore, God was never without the fullness of the Godhead, consequently, never a man.

NOR CAN MAN EVER BECOME A GOD.

Man is finite or limited in everything, ever changeable and changing, ever susceptible of improvement. What is finite can never become infinite. Supposing man grown or improved for billions of years; after that immense period, he could begin over again improving for billions of years, and yet ever remain short of infinite perfection, as no number of finite things can make the infinite. There is and always shall be a first and a last, to which could be added more and more. "When a man hath done, then he shall begin, and when he leaveth off, he shall be at a loss" (Ecclesiasticus 18:2).

A being cannot be at the same time infinite and finite, necessary and contingent, compound and simple, unchangeable and changeable, eternal and temporary, omnipotent and weak, actual being and potentiality, etc., etc.

Now if God were an exalted man, he would have all those contradictory attributes at the same time, which is absurd. Therefore, it is an utter impossibility that God should be an exalted man.

As to man becoming God, the idea is absurd. With far more reason might we contend that the gnat will develop into a lion, and the animalcules which we swallow in a sip of water will grow into gigantic giraffes and colossal elephants, as there is infinitely less distance or difference between those respective animals than between the most perfect creature and the Creator, the finite and the infinite. Bring all the scientists of the world together, the Darwins, the Huxleys, the Tyndalls, the Pasteurs, the Kochs, the Teslas, the Edisons, etc., etc., supply them with the most ingenious machinery, and the most complicated instruments, and with unlimited material, let them make, I will not say an imitation sun or moon, but simply a little worm as we often unconsciously crush under our feet, or let them produce not the magnificent lily or rose, but a tiny blade of grass. Before such a task, apparently so insignificant, those profound mathematicians, naturalists and chemists, will throw up their hands in utter impotence. Expert mixers can indeed make wines in their laboratories, but will President Roosevelt or Emperor William, or other sovereigns, ever give them an order to manufacture a little bunch of grapes or a few of the commonest berries?

What frequent accidents are there on our railroads, despite most careful and most attentive trainmen! Yet a collision never occurred between the millions of suns, stars and planets that whirl, rush, tear and bound wildly along their prescribed pathways for thousands or millions of years, at the rate of over one thousand miles a minute (our earth), and three thousand miles a minute (the planet Arcturus). Notwithstanding the bewildering speed of their movements, the stars and planets float through space with such regularity and precision, and along such well defined paths, deviating neither to the right nor to the left, that astronomers can foretell to a nicety — to within a minute — at what point in the heavens they may be found at any future time, say, next month, next year, or even next century. They can indeed predict transits and eclipses; but suppose astronomers from New Zealand on their way to America to observe this fall's moon eclipse, meet with an accident in mid-ocean, would they at once send this wireless telegram to the United States' star-gazers assembled say at Lick Observatory: "Belated by leak. Please retard eclipse two hours that we may not miss it." As well might all the telescopemen in the world combined, attempt to fetch down the rings of Saturn for the construction of a royal-race track as pretend to control movements of the heavenly bodies.

The helpless babe of yesterday may indeed rival Mozart, Hayden and Paderewski, but tomorrow he may rise with lame hands and pierced eardrums; and millions of worshipers of the shattered idol are powerless to restore it to the musical world. Still Jesus healed the blind, the deaf and the palsied, by a mere act of his will, even without speaking a word.

"We have this treasure in earthen vessels" (II Cor. 4:7).

"Seeing I have once begun, I will speak to my Lord whereas I am dust and ashes" (Genesis 18:27). "In the morning man shall grow up like grass and flourish, in the evening he shall fall, grow dry and wither" (Psalm 89:6). *"Can man be compared with God,* even though he were of perfect knowledge" (Job 22:2). "None is good but God alone" (Luke 18:19). "Of his greatness there is no end" (Psalm 144: 3). "All nations are before him as if they had no being at all, and are counted to him as nothing and vanity. To whom then have you likened God, or what image will you make for him? It is he that sitteth upon the globe of the earth, and the inhabitants thereof are as locusts: he that stretcheth out the heavens as nothing, and spreadeth them out as a tent to dwell in. All flesh is grass, and all the glory thereof as the flower of the field. The grass is withered, and the flower is fallen because the wind of the Lord had blown upon it. Indeed, the people is grass" (Isaiah 40:17, 18, 22, 6, 7). "He that bringeth the searches of secrets to nothing, that hath made the judges of the earth as vanity—hath measured the waters in the hollow of his hand, and weighed the heavens with his palm? Who hath poised with three fingers the bulk of the earth, and weighed the mountains in scales, and the hills in a balance" (Isaiah 40:23-12).

An Ingersoll might sneer and cry out: Surely Isaias had no idea of the size of the earth. Even though he did not know that the globe is such an immense ball, and that the volume of the sun is one million two hundred thousand times greater than the earth, and three hundred thousand times its weight, God who inspired the prophet knew infinitely more about it than our conceited astronomers.

I fear Mr. B. H. Roberts will be inclined to think God jealous because he gives man no show for comparison with him. This would certainly be a less blunder of the Utah man ("I will not give my glory to another") (Isaiah 42:8) than his contention, which is a mere echo of Satan's promise in Paradise; "You shall be as gods." (Genesis 3:5).

Man is indeed capable of progress, but his forward movement is slow, and in some matters his attainments remain stationary; for instance, nothing has been added to philosophy since the days of Aristotle, and nothing to geometry since Euclid. Both of these geniuses lived over three hundred years before Christ. Conclude we, then, with the Psalmist: "All my bones shall say: Lord, who is like to thee?" (Psalm 34:10).

THE UNITY OF GOD.

1. The first chapter of the Bible reveals the supreme fact that there is One Only and Living God, the Creator and moral Governor of the universe. As Moses opened the sacred Writings by proclaiming him, so the Jew in all subsequent generations, has continued to witness for him, till from the household of Abraham, faith in the one only living and true God has spread through Jerusalem, Christianity and Mahometanism well-nigh over the earth.[A]

[Footnote A: "Hours with the Bible," by Geikie, vol. 1, chapters 1, 2.]

Primeval revelations of God had everywhere become corrupted in the days of Moses, save among the chosen people. Therefore, the first leaf of the Mosaic record, as Jean Paul says, has more weight than all the folios of men of science and philosophers.

While all nations over the earth have developed a religious tendency which acknowledged a higher than human power in the universe, Israel is the only one which has risen to the grandeur of conceiving this power as the One Only Living God. If we are asked how it was that Abraham possessed not only the primitive conception of the Divinity, as he had revealed himself to all mankind, but passed through the denial of all other gods, to the knowledge of the One God, we are content to answer, that it was by a special *divine revelation*.[A]

[Footnote A: "Chips from a German Workshop," by Max Muller, vol. 1, pp. 345-372.]

The record of this divine revelation is to be found in the Bible: "Hear, Israel: Our God is one Lord." "I alone am, and there is no other God besides me" (Deut. 6:4 and 32:39). "I am the first and I am the last, and after me there shall be none" (Isaiah 44:6; 43:10.) "I will not give my glory to another" (Isaiah 42:8; 45:5, etc., etc.).

And as Mr. Roberts admits that our conception of God must be in harmony with the New Testament, it as well as the Old witnesses continually to One True God. Suffice it to quote: "*One* is good, *God*" (Matthew 19:17;) "Thou shalt love the Lord thy God" (Luke 10:27); "My Father of whom you say that he is your God" (John 8:54). Here Christ testified that the Jews believed in only one God.

"The Lord is a God of all Knowledge" (I Kings 2). ("Mormon" Catechism v. Q. 10 and Q. 11.)

"Of that day and hour *no one knoweth*, no not the angels of heaven, but *the Father alone"* (Matthew 24:36).

No one knoweth who the Son is *but the Father* (Luke 10:22).

Therefore, no one is God but one, the Heavenly Father.

In another form: The All-knowing alone is God. The Father alone is all-knowing. Therefore the Father alone is God.[A]

[Footnote A: To the exclusion of another or separate divine being, but not to the denial of the distinct Divine Personalities of the Son and the Holy Ghost in the One Divine Being.]

From these clear statements of the Divine Book it is evident that all the texts quoted by Mr. Roberts do not bear the inference he draws from them; on the contrary, they directly make against him, plainly proving the unity of God.

First, then, if God so emphatically declares, both in the Old and in the New Testament, that there is but one God, has anyone the right to contradict him and to say that there are several or many Gods? But Mr. Roberts insists that the Bible contradicts the Bible; in other words, that God, the author of the Bible, contradicts himself. To say such a thing is downright blasphemy.

The liability to self-contradiction is characteristic of human frailty. It is incompatible with God's infinite perfections. Therefore, I most emphatically protest that there is no *real* contradiction in the Bible, though here and there may exist an *apparent* one.

Let me premise that the name God, Elohim, is applied (1) to the one true God; (2) to false gods and idols; (3) to representatives of God, such as angels, judges, kings; (4) to the devil, at least in this phrase: the god of this world.

I beg to observe, first, that whenever the plural *gods* occurs in Holy Writ, it is in sense (2) or (3); i. e., it is meant of false gods or representatives of God; secondly, that plural is generally put in opposition to the singular Jehovah or Lord, who is emphatically mentioned as the sovereign of the gods in every instance, alleged or allegable.[A]

[Footnote A: "There is none like thee among the gods, O Lord" (Psalm 85:8). "Our God is not like their gods" (Deut. 32:31). "Who is God besides the Lord" (Psalm 17:32). "Their gods have no sense" (Baruch 6:41). "The

Lord is terrible over all the Gods: because all the gods of the gentiles are devils; but the Lord hath made the heavens" (Psalm 95:4, 5). "Neither is there any nation so great that hath gods so nigh them as our God is present to all our petitions" (Deut. 4:7).]

Now, all these Bible expressions point to the clear inference that this Sovereign or Supreme God is the only true God. Consequently, these very texts, instead of proving Mr. Roberts' contention, plainly disprove it, demonstrating that there is but one God. "Thou alone art God" (Psalm 85:11).

Two of these texts, for instance, have the significant qualification: Being *called* gods. A man must not be a lawyer to know that the fact that not a few quacks and clowns are *called* doctors does not make them such. "Although there be that are called gods either in heaven or on earth (for there be gods many and lords many); yet to us there is but one God" (I Corinthians 8:5, 6). Jesus answered, referring to Psalm 82:6, "Is it not written in your law: I said you are Gods? If he *called* them gods to whom the word of God was spoken" * * * (John 10:34, 35). Neither Christ nor Paul say that they *are* or *were gods*, but simply that they are called gods. Bear with me for further quoting: "I have said you are gods, and all of you the sons of the Most High. *But you shall die like men,*" etc. (Psalm 82:6, 7). How unlike the true God, the *Immortal* King of ages.

Wherever Elohim occurs in the Bible in sense 1, (meaning the True God) it is employed with singular verbs and singular adjectives.

Had the "Mormon" Church leaders known Hebrew, the original language of the Book of Moses, and nearly the whole of the Old Testament, they would not have been guilty of the outrageous blunders perpetrated by the writers of the Pearl of Great Price and of the Catechism, as appears on pages 24, 25, 26, 27, of the latter book: "They organized and formed (that is, the Gods,) the heavens and the earth * * * and the Spirit of the Gods was brooding upon * * * What did the *Gods* do on the second day? etc. The Gods said, Let there be light * * * *and they [the Gods] comprehended the light, for it was bright.*" (Whoever heard of a dark light? But even had the light lacked brightness, would the gods have been powerless to comprehend it?) The original had singular verbs in all these sentences and, unlike our imperfect English, which has the same form in the singular and in the plural, the Hebrew, the Greek, the Latin, the Syriac, etc., have different terminations in the plural from the singular.

Had Joseph Smith and his partners not been ignorant of those ancient languages in which were written the original text and the oldest versions of the Bible, their revelations would, at least in reference to the Creator have tallied with the revelations of Moses.

One of the strongest and clearest proofs of the unity of God, is God's solemn revelation of himself as Jehovah, prefaced by the emphatic statement: "*I am* Who Am. Thou shalt say to the sons of Israel: I Am sent me to you, (that is: The one who said, I Am Who Am, sent me to you)" (Exodus 3:14). "Jehovah, the God of your fathers—I am Jehovah" (Exodus 6:2).

If there ever was an occasion on which God should have disclosed his unity or his plurality, it was certainly then when Moses ventured to demand the credentials of his mission. God used singular verbs whenever referring to himself. He said: *I am*, not *we are*. He calls himself by the singular noun *Jehovah*, which, unlike the plural *Elohim*, is applied only to the one true God. This name Jehovah occurs one hundred and sixty times in Genesis alone.[A]

[Footnote A: J. Corluy S. J. *"Spicilegium,"* Volume 1. Com. 2. See also Smith's Bible Dictionary, word God.]

II. *The Father, the Son and the Holy Ghost are one and the same identical Divine Essence or Being.*

A. "I and the Father are one" (John 10-30). Christ asserts his physical, not merely moral, unity with the Father.

"My sheep hear my voice * * * and I give them everlasting life; and they shall not perish forever, and *no man shall pluck them out of my hand*."

The following argument by which Christ proves that no man shall pluck his sheep from his hand, proves his consubstantiality, or the unity of his nature or essence with his Father's:

My Father who gave me the sheep is greater than all men or creatures, (v. 29) and therefore no one can snatch the sheep or aught else from his hand. (Supreme or almighty power is here predicated of the Father.)

Now, I and the Father are one (thing, one being) v. 30. (*Therefore, no one can snatch the sheep or aught else from my hand.*)

To perceive the full meaning and strength of Jesus' argument, one must read and understand the original text of St. John's Gospel, that is, the Greek; or the *Latin* translation: *Ego et Pater unum sumus.*

If Christ had meant *one* in mind or *one morally* and not *substantially*, he would have used the masculine gender, Greek *eis*, (*unus*)—and not the neuter *en*, (*unum*)—as he did. No better interpreters of our Lord's meaning can be found than his own hearers. Had he simply declared his moral union with the Father, the Jews would not have taken up stones in protest against his making himself God, and asserting his identity with the Father. Far from retracting his statement or correcting the Jews' impression, Jesus insists that as he is the Son of God, he has far more right to declare himself God than the Scripture had to call mere human judges gods, and he corroborates his affirmation of his *physical* unity with his Father by saying: "The Father is in me, and I am in the Father," which evidently signifies the same as verse 30: I and the Father are one and the same individual being, the One God.

The preceding argument is reinforced by John 14, 8-11: "Philip saith to him: Lord, show us the Father, * * * Jesus saith: So long a time have I been with you and thou hast not known me. Philip, *he that seeth me seeth the Father also.* How sayest thou: Show us the Father. Do you not believe that *I am in the Father and the Father in me? The words that I speak I speak not of myself. But the Father who abideth in me, he doth the works.* Believe me that I am in the Father and the Father is in me. What things soever the Father doth, these the Son also doth likewise" (John 5:19).

These words are a clear assertion of the *physical* unity of the Son and the Father. It is plain from the context that Christ means more than a physical *resemblance*, no matter how complete, between him and his Father. Of mere resemblance and moral union could never be said that one is the other, and that the words uttered by one are actually spoken by the other.

To see the Son and the Father at the same time in the Son, the Son and the Father must be numerically one Being. Now Christ says: "He that seeth me seeth the Father." Therefore, he and the Father are numerically one Being.

Again, if the speech and the acts of the Son are physically the words and the works of the Father, the Son and the Father are physically one; indivisible, inseparably one principle of action, therefore, one Being. Now Christ tells us that his words and works are physically the words and works of his Father. Therefore, the Son and the Father are one indivisible, inseparable principle, and therefore identical Being: Let no one object: Is not the word and the deed of the agent, the word and the deed of his master or employer? Christ is more than his Father's agent. An agent could indeed say that his utterances and his actions are dictated or prompted by his master, but he could never say what Christ said: The words I utter are actually, physically spoken by my Father while I speak them; and the works I perform are actually, physically, performed by my Father. Is the Son, then, like the phonograph or the machine, the instrument of the Father? Nay, he is more than that. Being together with his Father, the one equally intelligent and equally efficient principle of action, the words and works are simultaneously both the Son's and the Father's.

There remains to prove that the Holy Ghost is inseparably one with the Father and the Son. *There are three who give testimony in heaven, and these three are one* (1 John 5:8).

As Christ proved his identity and unity with the Father by texts quoted: "*The words that I speak I speak not of myself. But the Father who abideth in me he doth the works,*" so he now shows his unity with the Holy Ghost by almost the selfsame sentences: "When the Spirit of Truth will have come, he will teach you all truth; for *he will not speak or himself, but he will speak whatever he will hear,* and will announce to you the things to come. He will glorify me, because *he will receive* of mine and announce to you: *whatever the Father hath are mine.*[A] Therefore I said: because he will receive of mine and announce it to you" (John 16:13-15).

[Footnote A: In the Old Testament, the foreknowledge of future events was ever spoken of as an incommunicable attribute of Jehovah (Isaiah 41:22, 23; 44:7; 45:11; Daniel 2:22, 47; 13; 42, etc.) As whatever the Father hath is the Son's, therefore, also, the knowledge of the future.]

That the Holy Ghost is one with the Son, or Jesus, is proved also by the fact that the Christian baptism is indiscriminately called the *Baptism of the Holy Ghost, the Baptism in or with the Holy Ghost and the Baptism of or in Jesus*: "He [Christ] shall baptize *in the Holy Ghost and fire*" (that is the Holy Ghost acting as purifying fire) (Matthew 3:11); "have you received the Holy Ghost? *We have not so much as heard whether there be a Holy Ghost.*" He said: "*In what then* [in whose name then] *were you baptized?*" Who said: "In John's baptism * * * Having heard these things *they were baptized in the name of the Lord Jesus*" (Acts 9:2, 5). "All we who are *baptized in Christ Jesus*" (Romans 6:3).

B. Although the systematic doctrine of the Blessed Trinity, that is, of three Divine Persons (not three Gods) in one God, is a gradual development in the Church, nevertheless the distinction of the human and divine natures in Christ is found in the writings of St. Ignatius, disciple of the Apostle St. John, and Bishop of Antioch, who, because of his faith, was devoured by lions by order of Trajan, A. D. 107. Fifty and sixty years later, different Fathers, among whom Tertullian ("Adv. Marc" IV. 25, and "Adv. Wax." 2), Athenagoras ("Leg" 10: 24, 44), and Clement of Alexandria ("Strom" III: 12) are the most famous, taught there are three Divine Persons in one God; that these three, the Father, the Son and the Holy Ghost, are equal to each other and are one in substance.[A]

[Footnote A: The manifestation of the three Divine Persons at our Lord's baptism could be interpreted as if there were three distinct beings in God, or three Gods, if such interpretation were not precluded by God's emphatic revelation of his Divine Unity. There was, on that memorable occasion, a twofold divine witnessing to Christ as Son of God come in the flesh to redeem mankind. In order to find in that event anything in support of the "Mormon" tenets, there should have appeared above the Son two glorious exalted men both pointing to him; whereas, only a voice was heard, and a dove was seen. Nor can we argue from the voice that the Father must have a mouth, and therefore a body; with greater reason might we maintain that the Holy Ghost is a pigeon, as a dove was visible; whereas, the organ of the voice was not.]

III. *Pagan Witness to the Unity of the Christian's God.*

As the Roman historian Tacitus, in his account of the Jews, wrote: "The Jews have no notion of any more than one Divine Being, and that known only to the mind." Other pagans bore similar testimony concerning the unity of God. In his letter to the Emperor Trajan, (A. D. 98-117) Pliny governor of Pontus, said among other things: "They [the Christians] assemble on certain days before sunrise to sing hymns of praise to Christ, their God. * * They submit to torture and death rather than invoke the gods."

And Celsus, the forerunner of our modern infidels, thus slandered the early Christians: "Confessing that these are worthy of *their God*, they desire to convert but fools, and vulgar and stupid and slavish women and boys."

One more. Caecilius wrote: "What monstrous notions * * * they [the Christians] fabricate that that *God* of theirs, whom they can neither show nor see, should be inquiring diligently into the characters, the acts, nay the words and secret thoughts of all men! * * * Most of you are in want, cold, toil, hunger, and *your God* suffers it."

CHAPTER III

A REJOINDER TO REV. C. VAN DER DONCKT'S REPLY.

I have read with great interest and I trust with due care the Rev. C. Van Der Donckt's Reply to my discourse on "Mormon Doctrine of Deity." With regard to his Reply in general, I observe three things: first, the Reverend gentleman labors with some pains to demonstrate that "Mormon" views of Deity with respect to the form and nature of God are at variance with the Catholic and even the orthodox Protestant views on that subject; second, the "Mormon" views of Deity are in conflict with the accepted Christian philosophy; third, that "Mormon" doctrines stand in sharp contrast to both Catholic and Protestant ideas respecting the unity of God. All this is easily proved; and would have been conceded cheerfully without proofs. "Mormons" not only admit the variances but glory in them. The foregoing, however, is not the issue between Mr. Van Der Donckt and myself. After the variances referred to are admitted, these questions remain: Which is most in agreement with what God has revealed concerning his form and nature, "Mormon" or orthodox Christian doctrine? Which is most in harmony with sound reason and the scriptures, "Mormon" doctrine, or the commonly accepted Christian philosophy? Which in their teaching presents the true doctrine of God's unity, "Mormons" or orthodox Christians? These are the issues; and so far as the Reverend gentleman has maintained the orthodox Christian doctrine against the "Mormon" doctrine, I undertake to controvert his arguments.

I.
THE FORM OF GOD.

Following the order of my treatise, the gentleman first deals with the form of God. His first premise is that *"God is a Spirit,"* quoting the words of the Savior (John 4:24;) and Paul's words, "The Lord is a spirit," (II Cor. 3:17.) He then argues that a spirit is different from a man, and quotes the remark of Jesus to his disciples, when he appeared to them after his resurrection: "A spirit hath not flesh and bones as ye see me have" (Luke 24:37-39). Also the words of Jesus to Peter, "Flesh and blood hath not revealed it [that is, that Jesus is the Christ] unto thee, but my *Father* who is in heaven." (Matt. 16:17.) The gentleman in all this sees a striking contrast between *men, flesh and blood,* and the *Father;* which "conveys the sense that God hath not flesh and blood like man, but is a spirit."

That God is a spirit Mr. V. holds is proved also from his being called "invisible" in the Bible; and from this premise argues: "All material beings are visible. Absolutely invisible beings are immaterial, or bodiless:" and therefore, to help the gentleman out a little, not like man in form.

With reference to the passage—"Flesh and blood hath not revealed it unto thee, but my Father who is in heaven," and the Reverend gentleman's remarks thereon, I wish to say, in passing, that the antithesis between man and God in the passage extends merely to the fact that the source of Peter's revelation was God, not man; and is no attempt at defining a difference between the nature of God and the nature of man. Here also I may say that the Latter-day Saints do not hold that God is a personage of *flesh* and *blood,* but a personage of *flesh and bone,* inhabited by a spirit, just as Jesus was after his resurrection. Joseph Smith taught concerning the resurrection that "all [men] will be raised by the power of God, having *spirit* in their bodies, and not *blood.*"[A] Again, in speaking of the general assembly and church of the first born in heaven (Heb. 12:23), he said: "Flesh and blood cannot go there; but flesh and bones, quickened by the Spirit of God, can."[B] So that it must be remembered throughout this discussion that the Latter-day Saints do not believe that God is a personage of flesh and blood; but a personage of flesh and bone and spirit, united.

[Footnote A: Discourse delivered at Nauvoo, March 20, 1842. *Mill. Star,* Vol. xix, p. 213.]

[Footnote B: Discourse delivered at Nauvoo, Oct. 9, 1843. *Mill. Star,* Vol. xxii, p. 231.]

I would remind the reader, also, that while Jesus said, "God is a spirit," and that a spirit "hath nor flesh and bone as ye see me have," he nowhere says that a spirit is immaterial or not substance. That is a conclusion drawn by the theologians from the false philosophy of the ancient pagans.

But let us examine these premises and arguments of Mr. Van Der Donckt, more in detail. The inspired apostle says: "*Our God is a consuming fire*" (Heb. 12:29). "Now," to use the words of Mr. V., "although we must believe whatever God reveals to us upon one single word of his, just as firmly as upon a thousand; nevertheless, I will add" that Moses, who solemnly received the word from God which he delivered unto Israel, also says, "*The Lord thy God is a consuming fire*" (Exod. 4:24). Is Mr. V. ready to believe on these solemn assertions of scripture—hence of the Lord—that God is a fire, and therefore that fire is God? Or would he insist upon interpreting these passages by others, and by reason? Would he not want to quote Moses again where he says, "Thy God is * * * *as* a consuming fire" (Ex. 9:3), and accept this as a reasonable interpretation of the passage stating so definitely that "God is a fire"?

Again, "God is light" (I John 1:5). Would Mr. V. from that definition of God believe and teach that God is light, mere cosmic light? Or would he find an interpretation, or explanation necessary? And still again, "God is love" (I John 4:7, 16). Love is an attribute of mind, of spirit; must one conclude then from this definition that God is a mere attribute of mind? These reflections will demonstrate that these definitions of God, so far as they are such, together with the one with which Mr. V. commences his argument, "God is a Spirit," need defining. He endeavors to anticipate the "Mormon" answer to this argument by saying:

> I am well aware that the Latter-day Saints interpret those texts as meaning a spirit clothed with a body, but what nearly the whole of mankind, Christians, Jews, and Mohammedans, have believed for ages, cannot be upset by the gratuitous assertions of a religious innovator of this last century.

At this point I will not appeal to or quote the "gratuitous assertions of a religious innovator of this last century"—meaning Joseph Smith. There is no need of that. If I were an unbeliever in the true Deity of Christ, I might take up the gentleman's argument in this way: You say God is a spirit, and hence bodiless, immaterial? His answer must be, "Yes." But Jesus says, "a spirit hath not flesh and bones as ye see me have"—hence Jesus is not God, because he is a personage of flesh and bone, in the form of man—not bodiless or immaterial. This, of course, is not *my* point. I merely refer to it in the beaten way of good fellowship, and by way of caution to my Catholic friend, who, I am sure, in his way, is as anxious to maintain the true Deity of the Nazarene as I am; but his method of handling the text, "God is a spirit," might lead him into serious difficulty in upholding the truth that Jesus was and is true Deity, if in argument with an infidel.

But now for the "Mormon" exposition of the text. Is Jesus Christ God? Was he God as he stood there among his disciples in his glorious and, to use Mr. V.'s own word, "sacred," resurrected body? There is but one answer that the Reverend Catholic gentleman or any orthodox Protestant can give, and that is in the affirmative—"yes, Jesus is God."[A] But "God is a spirit!" True, he is; but Jesus is a spirit inside a body—inside an immortal, indestructible body of flesh and bone; therefore, if Jesus is God, and God is a spirit, he is an embodied spirit, just as the Latter-day Saints teach.

[Footnote A: "His acts proved his Deity; Jesus is Jehovah, and therefore we sing unto him as the Lord." "Treasury of David" (Spurgeon). Vol. iv, p. 371.]

Now let it be understood that Latter-day Saints are not so foolish as to believe that so much phosphate, lime, carbon, hydrogen, and oxygen as may compose the body of a perfected man, is God. They recognize the fact that the body without the spirit is dead, being alone; but the spirit having through natural processes gathered to itself a body, and that body having been purified by the power of God—who has promised in holy scripture that he will "change our vile body, that it may be fashioned like unto his glorious body, according to the working whereby he is able even to subdue all things unto himself" (Phil. 3:20, 21)—when this is done, even the body takes upon it some of the divine nature. It indeed becomes "sacred," and something more than "sacred"—it becomes incorporated with and forever united to, a spirit that is divine, and henceforth becomes an integral part of God. Of which process, of a divine spirit taking on a body of flesh and bone, Jesus Christ is the most perfect example.

At this point, I shall pass for the present a few items that stand next in order in Mr. Van Der Donckt's argument, that I may consider some statements and arguments of his made further on in the "Reply," because they are immediately related to what has just been said. Mr. V. holds that it is proved by Holy Writ that "angels as well as God are bodiless beings." After quoting passages of scripture in support of this statement, he then adds: "Could plainer words be found to teach that angels, both good and bad, are spirits, devoid of bodies? Now, the Creator is certainly more perfect than his creatures, and pure minds are more perfect *than minds united to bodies* [A] (men)." In support of which he quotes the following: "The corruptible body is a load upon the soul, and the earthly habitation presseth down the mind" (Wisdom 9:15)[B]; and Paul's saying, "who shall deliver me from this body of death?"[C] (Rom. 6:24). *Therefore the Creator is a pure spirit.*

[Footnote A: Italics are mine.]

[Footnote B: This is a book received by the Catholic Church on alleged apostolical tradition, but not found in the Hebrew Bible nor Protestant versions of the Bible.]

[Footnote C: Quoted thus by Mr. V. In both Catholic and Protestant Bibles it stands: "Who shall deliver me from the body of this death?"]

I fear Mr. V. in these statements has run into more difficulty. Let us see. According to his doctrine, "Angels as well as God are bodiless beings." "Angels, both good and bad, are spirits, devoid of bodies. The Creator is more perfect than his creatures, *and pure minds* [minds separated from bodies] *are more perfect than minds united to bodies.* * * * Therefore the Creator is a pure spirit." But where does this leave Jesus?

Was and is Jesus God—true Deity?

Yes.

But Jesus is a spirit and body united into one glorious personage. His mind was and is now united to and dwelling in a body. Our Catholic friend says, "pure minds [i. e. minds not united to bodies] are more perfect than minds united to bodies." He also says, "Angels, both good and bad, are spirits (i. e. minds) devoid of bodies." Therefore, it must follow from his premises and argument that angels are superior to Jesus since his spirit is united to a body, while they are minds *not* united to bodies! I will not press the point, that the same conclusions could be drawn from his premises and argument with reference even to bad spirits, whom he says are bodiless, and hence, upon his theory, superior to minds or spirits united to bodies, for that would be ungenerous upon my part, and would lay upon his faulty argument the imputation of awful blasphemy, which I am sure was not intended and would be as revolting to him as it would be to myself. Mr. V., I am sure, would contend as earnestly as I would that Jesus is superior to the angels, though it is perfectly clear that he is a spirit united to a body. "When he had by himself purged our sins, [Jesus] sat down on the right hand of the majesty on high; being made so much better than the angels, as he hath by inheritance obtained a more excellent name than they. * * * And again, when he bringeth in the first begotten into the world, he saith, and let all the angels of God worship him. And of the angels he saith, who maketh his angels spirits, and his ministers a flame of fire. *But unto the Son he saith, Thy throne, O God, is for ever and ever*" (Heb. 1:3-8). In this passage the superiority of Jesus over the angels is manifested in four ways: first, by the direct affirmation of God, that he was made "better" than the angels; second, that by inheritance he obtained a more exalted name; third, that the angels are commanded to worship him; fourth, God, the Father, addressing Jesus, said, "Thy throne, O God, is for ever and ever." In this passage the Father directly addresses Jesus by the title "God." And as God is exalted above all angels, Jesus must be superior to angels, for he is "God," if we may believe the words of the Father—whom to disbelieve would be blasphemy.

Mr. Van Der Donckt admits in his argument,'of course, that Jesus is God; and also admits the persistence of him in the physical condition in which he left the earth with his resurrected body. For in explaining the scripture passage about seeing God "face to face," he remarks:

The first and chief element of the happiness of heaven will consist in the beatific vision; that is, in seeing God face to face, unveiled, as he really is. The "face to face," however, is literally true only of our blessed Savior, who ascended into heaven with his sacred body. Otherwise, as God is a spirit, he has no body, and, consequently, no face.

From this it is clear that, in the mind of the Reverend gentleman, Jesus not only ascended into heaven with his "sacred body," but now dwells there spirit and body united; and the blessed, who shall inherit heaven will see him there literally "face to face."[A] Otherwise than this "face to face" view of Jesus—according to Mr. V.—we shall only see God, since he is a spirit, "with the spiritual eye; with the soul's intellectual perception, elevated by a supernatural influx from God!" This admission with reference to Jesus and his existence as an immortal personage of flesh and bone, and our literal view of him in heaven "face to face," draws with it some consequences which my Catholic friend evidently overlooked. In the creed usually named after St. Athanasius, it is said: "*Such as the Father is, such is the Son.*" I take it that this, in the view of those who accept the Athanasian creed, has reference to the "substance of the Father," as well as to other things pertaining to him; for, according to that creed, the "substance" of the Father and Son is one and undivided. "We worship one God in Trinity, and Trinity in Unity," says the creed; "neither confounding the persons nor *dividing the substance.*" It must be, therefore, according to Mr. V.'s creed, that all the "substance" of God there is, is in Jesus Christ, as well as the attributes of God. The terms of the creed forbid us believing that part of the "substance" of God was enclosed in the flesh and bone body of Jesus, and the remainder existed outside of that body; for that would be dividing the "substance" of God, a thing the Athanasian creed forbids: therefore, all the "substance" of God inhabits the body of Jesus Christ, and he is wholly God. In this view of the subject, there is no God except the Deity enclosed in the flesh and body of Jesus Christ. But that would place our Catholic friend—after all he has said about God being a spirit, and about the superiority of pure minds (i. e. spirits not united to bodies) over minds united to bodies—under the necessity of accepting as God, the Supreme, the Almighty, a personage that is a spirit and body united in one glorious personage, and in form like man—a thing most abhorrent to our friend's principles.

[Footnote A: In an article for the *Improvement Era,* on the Doctrines and Claims of the Catholic Church, Bishop Scanlan, of Salt Lake City, also said of the Divinity of Christ; "The Catholic Church teaches that Jesus Christ is not a mere elect child or special creation of God, or in any sense or manner a creature, but that he is the eternal and only Son of God, God of God, Light of Light; the expression of the Eternal Father, with whom he is one in nature and substance, and to whom he is equal in all divine attributes, power and glory." —*Improvement Era*, vol. i, p. 14.]

On the other hand, if it be contended that besides the Son of God, Jesus, a personage of flesh and bone and spirit, there exists God, a spirit, then there is likely to arise again the conception of the "substance" being divided, and the existence of two individual Gods instead of one. The one a spirit unembodied, and the other a spirit enclosed in a body of flesh and bone—the glorified, exalted Man, Christ. This danger is also increased by the part of the creed now being considered, *viz.*, "Such as the Father is, such is the Son;" for it must follow, if this be true that such as the Son is, such is the Father also. And this, must hold with reference to God, wholly; to his substance, essence, personality, form, as well as to all attributes possessed, or else it is not true at all. And if true, since we know that Jesus is an immortal being of flesh and bone and spirit united into one glorious personage (and Mr. V. admits that, and also that the blessed in heaven shall see him as such a personage, literally "face to face"), then God the Father must be the same, a personage of flesh and bone and spirit united—a thing most abhorrent to Mr. V.'s principles.

At this point, I must complain of the gentleman's argument a little. However able and fair his article may be considered on the whole, I think, on the question of the "form of God," I am justified in charging that he has not dealt at all with my strong scripture proofs relative to that matter. He makes but the very slightest reference to the passage:

> And God said, Let us make man in our image, after our likeness. * * * So God created man in his own image, in the image of God created he him; male and female created he them (Genesis 1:26, 27).

And he considered nowhere the very definite passage:

> God * * hath in these last days spoken unto us by his Son. * * * who, being the brightness of his glory *and the express image of his person*, and upholding all things by the word of his power, when he hath by himself purged our sins, sat down on the right hand of the Majesty on high (Heb. 1:3).

"Now," to use the solemn words of the Reverend gentleman himself, "we must believe whatever God reveals to us upon one single word of his, just as firmly as upon a thousand"—I shall hold that it was incumbent upon Mr. V. to deal with these passages, and set forth in what way they are to be understood, if *not* to be understood as they read.[A] I can think of no language that could express the truth more forcibly, that man was created in the form of God and, therefore, that God in form is like man, than the language of these two passages. When the word of God says: "God created man in his own image, in the image of God created he him;" and then again, in speaking of Jesus, who certainly bore all the semblance, figure and stature of a man—who was a man—when the divine Spirit, I say, in speaking of him, says that *he was the express image of God's person*—I shall despair of human language expressing any fact whatsoever, if this language does not say that in form God and man are alike. And what the word of God in plainness teaches—so plain that he who "runs may read," so plain that "wayfaring men though fools need not err therein"—"is not to be set aside by the gratuitous assertions" of "religious innovators" of early Christian centuries who corrupted the plain meaning of God's word by their vain philosophies, and oppositions of science, falsely so called. Mr. Van Der Donckt makes no reference to this plain passage in Hebrews 1:3; and I am under the necessity of thinking that in respect of this passage and the one in Genesis, he had no means at his command by which he could satisfactorily explain away their force. They stand, therefore, with their strength unimpaired, in proof of the doctrines taught in the discourse at which Mr V. leveled his Reply.

[Footnote A: The meaning of this language from the 26th verse of the first chapter of Genesis is made perfectly clear when compared with the third verse of the 5th chapter of Genesis where it is written: "And Adam lived an hundred and thirty years, and begat a son in his own likeness, after his image; and called his name Seth." What do these words imply but that Seth was like his father in features and also doubtless in intellectual and moral qualities? And if when it is said Adam begat a son in his "own likeness, after his image," it simply means that Seth in form and features and intellectual and moral qualities was like his father—then there can be no other conclusion formed upon the passage that says God created man in his own image and likeness than that man, in a general way, in form and feature and intellectual and moral qualities was like God.]

Of God Being Invisible.

Mr. Van Der Donckt thinks he sees further proof of God's being a "Spirit," and therefore immaterial or bodiless, in the fact that he is spoken of in the Bible as being "invisible." Moses "was strong as seeing him that is invisible," (Heb. 11:27;) "No man hath seen God at any time" (I John 4:12;) "The King of kings—whom no man hath seen nor can see," (I Tim. 6:16); are the passages he relies upon for the proof of his contention.

Of course, Mr. V. is aware of the fact—for he mentions it—that these passages are confronted with the explicit statement of scripture that God has been seen by men. Moses saw him. At one stage of his experience, the great Hebrew prophet was told that he could not see God's face; "for," said the Lord, "there shall no man see me and live." But even at that time, Moses was placed in a cleft of the rock, "and thou shalt see my back parts," said the Lord to him; "but my face shall not be seen" (Exodus 23:18-23). On another occasion, Moses, Aaron, Nadab and Abihu, and seventy of the elders of Israel, saw God.

> And they saw the God of Israel; and there was under his feet as it were a paved work of sapphire stone, and as it were the body of heaven in his clearness. And upon the nobles of the children of Israel he laid not his hand: also they saw God, and did eat and drink (Ex. 24:9-11).

Isaiah saw him: "I saw the Lord sitting upon a throne, high and lifted up, and his train filled the temple." At the same time the seraphims proclaimed his holiness, saying, "Holy, holy, holy is the Lord of hosts; the whole earth is full of his glory." Then said Isaiah: "Woe is me! for Iam undone; because I am a man of unclean lips, and I dwell in the midst of a people of unclean lips; for mine eyes have seen the King, the Lord of hosts" (Isaiah 6:1-5).

To harmonize these apparitions of God to men with his theory of the invisibility of God, Mr. V. appeals to the writings of some of the Christian fathers, and Cardinal Newman, from whose teachings he concludes that God the Father is called "invisible" because "he never appeared to bodily eyes; whereas the Son manifested himself as an angel, and as a man after his incarnation. * * * Whenever the Eternal Son of God, or angels at God's behest, showed themselves to man, they became visible only through a body, *or a material garb assumed for the occasion!*"

Surely Tertullian, Ambrose, Augustine, the great English Cardinal of the Roman church, and Mr. V. are in sore straits when they must needs take refuge in the belief of such jugglery with matter as this, in order to reconcile apparently conflicting scriptures. And what a shuffling off and on of material garbs there must have been, as from time to time hosts of angels and spirits appeared unto men!

It is but the materialization of the spiritualist mediums on a little larger scale. But there is a better way of harmonizing the seeming contradictions; and better authority for the conclusion to be reached than the Christian fathers and Cardinal Newman. I mean the scriptures themselves.

Take this expression of the scripture, "No man hath seen God at any time" (I John 4:12). Standing alone, it seems emphatic and conclusive. And in the same connection this also, from the testimony of John: "No man hath seen God at any time; the only begotten Son which is in the bosom of the Father, he hath declared him" (St. John 1:18). But consider these texts in connection with what the Master himself said on the same subject: "It is written in the prophets, And they shall be all taught of God. Every man, therefore, that hath heard, and hath learned of the Father, cometh unto me. Not that any man hath seen the Father, *save he which is of God, he hath seen the Father*" (St. John 6:45, 46). Now we have the key to the matter. "No man hath seen God at any time, *save* [except] *he which is of God, he hath seen the Father.*" If any one shall contend that this *"he which is of God"* has reference to Jesus only, the complete answer to that will be found in the account of the Martyr Stephen's glorious view of the Father and the Son together and at one time: "But he [Stephen] being full of the Holy Ghost, looked up steadfastly into heaven, *and saw the glory or God, and Jesus standing on the right hand of God, and said, "Behold, I see the heavens opened, and the ton of Man standing on the right hand of God."* (Acts 7:55-6). Undoubtedly, for reasons that are wise, God the Father has been "invisible" to men except under very special conditions; for the most part the "Only Begotten hath declared him," and stood as his representative; and in the absence of those special conditions, no man hath seen God the Father; no man in the absence of these conditions can see his face and live. He must be *"of God,"* as Stephen was, then he may see God, even the Father, as that martyr evidently did. Here, too, may be cited a passage from one of the revelations of the Lord to Joseph the Prophet, which throws more light upon the subject. Speaking of the Higher or Melchizedek Priesthood, the Lord says:

> This greater Priesthood administereth the gospel and holdeth the key of the mysteries of the kingdom, even the knowledge of God; therefore, in the ordinances thereof, the power of godliness is manifest; and without the ordinances thereof, and the authority of the Priesthood, the power of godliness is not manifest unto men in the flesh; *for without this no man can see the face of God, even the Father, and live* (Doc. and Cov. sec. 84:19-22).

God, then, in the Bible, is called "invisible," not because he is absolutely so by reason of his nature, because he is "immaterial or bodiless," but because he is not to be seen by men except under very special conditions. The special conditions complied with, however, certain holy men have seen God; the Father, and have borne witness of the fact. Of course, it follows that the "invisibility" of God as here set forth does not carry with it the idea that God is immaterial or bodiless; nor would it follow that God is immaterial, even if absolutely invisible to human eyes in our present existence. Mr. V. advances a strange doctrine when he says that "All *material* beings are visible. Absolutely invisible beings are *immaterial* or bodiless." I take it that his assertion is equivalent to saying that all material things are visible;

and that absolutely invisible things, like "invisible beings," are immaterial or bodiless. Is that true? Is the atmosphere visible? No. But it is material. "It is composed of atoms of matter whose weight is such that the pressure upon every square inch amounts to fifteen pounds; and upon the body of an ordinary-sized man some fourteen tons; but notwithstanding this, man could not construct a microscope sufficiently powerful to render these atoms visible."[A] What of the ether extending throughout the universe, in which millions of suns and their attendant planets move as motes in a sunbeam; is that visible? No; but it is material nevertheless. So with many things that, notwithstanding they are absolutely invisible, are material for all that, and have some of the qualities in common with grosser matter. We know but little of substances, as yet; less of their essence; but since there are many material substances absolutely invisible to us, is it unreasonable to believe that there are also beings consisting of substances more refined, pure and glorious than the material that is visible to our limited and imperfect vision?—beings invisible to us, unless our eyes be quickened by the power of God, yet material, and having form, and limitations and relations to other beings and things; and also possessed of many other qualities common to matter. In view of these facts, is not Mr. Van Der Donckt a little reckless, and too dogmatic, in stating the *datum* from which he argues for the absolute invisibility of God, and hence also his supposed immateriality, or bodiless state?

[Footnote A: Samuel Kinns' "Harmony of the Bible and Science," p. 338.]

Mr. Van Der Donckt argues that angels and spirits are also bodiless or immaterial. Was it a bodiless or immaterial angel that wrestled with Jacob until the breaking of the day; and who, when he could not prevail against the patriarch, touched the sinew of his thigh that it forthwith shrank? (Gen. 32:23-32). Were they immaterial or bodiless angels who called at the tent-home of the patriarch Abraham, on the plains of Mamre, for whom Sarah baked cakes, and Abraham's servant prepared a roast of veal; and, when all things were made ready, the patriarch stood by, and the three heavenly personages—one of them is called "the Lord"—"did eat" (Gen. 18)—were they immaterial or bodiless? Perhaps the Reverend gentleman will say, however, that these cases, and a score of others of similar nature that might be quoted, are answered by his statement—made on the authority of some Christian fathers and Cardinal Newman—that when angels "showed themselves to man they became visible [hence materialized, according to my friend's theory of visible and invisible beings] only through a body, or material garb assumed for the occasion!" For which theory, as whimsical as it is nonsensical, I venture to tell the Reverend gentleman there is no warrant of divine authority; nothing but the assumptions and speculations of churchmen seeking to harmonize Christian doctrine with the vain speculations of old pagan philosophers. I know nothing that equals this theory for absurdity, except it be the idea of Epicurus, who, after affirming that the gods were of human form, explained—"Yet that form is not body (i. e. material), but something *like* body; nor does it contain any blood, but something *like* blood!"[A] Or may I say that Mr. Van Der Donckt's absurdity is really equalled by that of Heracleitus, who taught that the sun was extinguished every evening and made new every morning?

[Footnote A: *Tuscul. Dispt.* Cicero, p. 227 (Younge's translation).]

As for the rest of Mr. V.'s theory of immateriality and invisibility of angels and spirits, I shall trust to what I have said on these subjects in dealing with the invisibility of God, to be a sufficient answer.

Of Anthropomorphism and understanding the Bible Literally.

I must say a word upon Mr. V.'s remarks respecting the plain anthropomorphism of the Bible, and the matter of understanding that sacred book literally. With reference to the first he says:

> All men after the example of the inspired writings, make frequent use of the figure called anthropomorphism, attributing to the Deity a human body, human members, human passions, etc., and that is done, not to imply that God is possessed of form, limbs, etc., but simply to make spiritual things or certain truths more intelligible to man.

I would like to know upon what authority Mr. V. adjudges the "inspired writings" not to imply that God is really possessed of form, limbs, passions, etc., after attributing them to him in the clearest manner. The "inspired writings" plainly and most forcibly attribute to Deity a form like man's, with limbs, organs, etc., but the Bible does not teach that this ascription of form, limbs, organs and passions to God, is unreal, and "simply to make spiritual things or certain truths more intelligible to man." On the contrary, the Bible emphasizes the doctrine of anthropomorphism by declaring in its very first chapter that man was created in the image of God: "So God created man in his own image, in the image of God created he him." The explanation is offered that it was necessary to attribute human form, members and passions, to God, in order to make spiritual things intelligible to man; *but what is the reason for ascribing the divine form to man,* as in the passage just quoted? Was that done to make human beings or certain truths more intelligible to God? Or was it placed in the word of God because it is simply true?

The truth that God in form is like man is further emphasized by the fact that Jesus is declared to have been in "the express image" of the Father's person (Heb. 1:3); and until Mr. V. or some other person of his school of thought, can prove very clearly that the word of God supports his theory of the unreality of the Bible's description of form, organs, proportions, passions and feelings, to God and other heavenly beings, the truth that God in form is like man will stand secure on the foundation of the revelations it has pleased God to give of his own being and nature.[A]

[Footnote A: Dean Mansel administers a scathing reproof to the German philosophers Kant and Fichte (and also to Professor Jowett in his note xxii in Lecture 1.) for what he calls "that morbid terror of what they are pleased to call anthropomorphism, which poisons the speculation of so many modern philosophers, when they attempt to be wise above what is written, and seek for a metaphysical exposition of God's nature and attributes." These philosophers, while holding in abhorrence the idea that God has a form such as man's—or any form whatsoever—parts, organs, affections, sympathies, passions or any attributes seen in man's spirit, are, nevertheless, under the necessity of representing God as conscious, as knowing, as determining; all of which, as pointed out by Dean Mansel in the passage which follows, are, after all, qualities of the human mind as well as attributes of Deity; and hence the philosophers, after all their labor, have not escaped from anthropomorphism, but have merely represented Deity to our consciousness, shorn of some of the higher qualities of the human mind, which God is represented in the scriptures as possessing in their perfection—such as love, mercy, justice. As orthodox Christian ministers, both Catholic and Protestant alike, including Mr. V., are afflicted with the same madness, I see no reason why the Dean's reproof should not be made to apply to them, and hence quote the passage *in extenso*: "They may not forsooth, think of the unchangeable God as if he were their fellow man, influenced by human motives, and moved by human supplications. They want a truer, juster idea of the Deity as he is, than that under which he has been pleased to reveal himself; and they call on their reason to furnish it. Fools, to dream that man can escape from himself, that human reason can draw aught but a human portrait of God. They do but substitute a marred and mutilated humanity for one exalted and entire: they add nothing to their conception of God as he is, but only take away a part of their conception of man. Sympathy, and love, and fatherly kindness, and forgiving mercy, have evaporated in the crucible of their philosophy; and what is the *caput mortuum* that remains, but only the sterner features of humanity exhibited in repulsive nakedness? The God who listens to prayer, we are told, appears in the likeness of human mutability. Be it so. What is the God who does not listen, but the likeness of human obstinacy? Do we ascribe to him a fixed purpose? Our conception of a purpose is human. Do we speak of him as continuing unchanged? Our conception of continuance is human. Do we conceive him as knowing and determining? What are knowledge and determination but modes of human consciousness? and what know we of consciousness itself, but as the contrast between successive mental states? But our rational philosopher stops short in his reasoning. He strips off from humanity just so much as suits his purpose; 'and the residue thereof he maketh a God less pious in his idolatry than the carver of the graven image, in that he does not fall down unto it and pray unto it, but is content to stand off and reason concerning it. And why does he retain any conception of God at all, but that he retains some portions of an imperfect humanity? Man is still the residue that is left; deprived indeed of all that is amiable in humanity, but in the darker features which remain, still man. Man in his purposes; man in his inflexibility; man in that relation to time from which no philosophy, whatever its pretensions, can wholly free itself; pursuing with indomitable resolutions a preconceived design; deaf to the yearning instincts which compel his creatures to call upon him. Yet this, forsooth, is a philosophical conception of the Deity, more worthy of an enlightened reason than the human imagery of the Psalmist: 'The eyes of the Lord are over the righteous, and his ears are open unto their prayers.' Surely downright idolatry is better than this rational worship of a fragment of humanity. Better is the superstition which sees the image of God in the wonderful whole which God has fashioned, than the philosophy which would carve for itself a Deity out of the remnant which man has mutilated. Better to realize the satire of the eleatic philosopher, (Xenophanes) to make God in the likeness of man, even as the ox or the horse might conceive gods in the form of oxen or horses, than to adorn some half-hewn Hermes, the head of a man joined to a misshapen block. Better to fall down before that marvelous compound of human consciousness whose elements God has joined together, and no man can put asunder, than to strip reason of those cognate elements which together furnish all that we can conceive or imagine of conscious or personal existence, and to deify the emptiest of all abstractions, a something or nothing, with just enough of its human original left to form a theme for the disputation of philosophy, but not enough to furnish a single ground of appeal to the human feelings of love, of reverence, and of fear. Unmixed idolatry is more religious than this. Undisguised atheism is more logical." (Limits of Religious Thought, Mansel, pp. 56-58).

Notwithstanding this passage, however, it should be remarked that Dean Mansel holds on the very next page of this treatise that there is a principle of truth of which this philosophy is the perversion. "Surely," he remarks, "there is a sense in which we may not think of God as though he were a man; as there is also a sense in which we cannot help so thinking of him. * * * * * We feel that there is a true foundation for the system which denies human attributes to God; *though the superstructure, which has been raised upon it, logically involves the denial of his very existence.*" The position of the Dean, as is well known, is that such are the limitations of the human mind—such the limitations of religious thought, that man may not hope to understand the divine nature, but as an act of faith must accept what is revealed concerning that nature.]

But the strangest part of the Reverend gentleman's contention on the matter now in hand is that the Latter-day Saints understand the anthropomorphic expressions in the scriptures as he explains them; and cites our catechisms (chapter 5, question 9) in proof of it![A] I quote the reference given:

[Footnote A: This is a thing so astonishing for Mr. Van Der Donckt to say, that lest the reader should think I had misunderstood him. I place before him in this note Mr. Van Der Donckt's statement at length. "It is a well known fact that all men after the example of the inspired writings, make frequent use of the figure called anthropomorphism, attributing to the Deity a human body, human members, human passions, etc.; and that is done, not to imply that God is possessed of form, limbs, etc., but simply to make spiritual things or certain truths more intelligible to man, who, while he tarries in this world, can perceive things and even ideas only through his senses, or through bodily organs.

"That even the Latter-day Saints thus understand such expressions is evident from their catechism (chapter 5: question 9), etc., etc."]

> 9. Q. If God is a person, how can he be everywhere present?
> A. His person cannot be in more than one place at the same time, but he is everywhere present by his Holy Spirit.

This is preceded by the following passages from the same book and chapter:

> 1. Q. What kind of a being is God?
> A. He is in the form of a man.
> 2. Q. How do you learn this?
> A. The scriptures declare that man was made in the image of God. * * *
> 3. Q. Have you any further proof of God's being in the form of a man?

A. Yes, Jesus Christ was in the form of a man, and was at the same time in the image of God's person. * * *

4. Q. Is it not said that God is a spirit?

A. Yes; the scriptures say so. (John 4:24.) * * *

5. Q. How, then, can God be like man?

A. Man has a spirit, though clothed with a body, and God is similarly constituted.

6. Q. Has God a body then?

A. Yes; like unto man's body in figure.

7. Q. Is the person of God very glorious?

A. Yes; infinitely glorious.

8. Q. Is God everywhere present?

A. Yes; He is in all parts of the universe.

Then follows, of course, question nine and its answer, quoted above and by Mr. V.; and yet the gentleman, in the very face of these explicit statements concerning the reality of God's form in our faith, would have it believed that the Latter-day Saints understand the expressions of scripture ascribing human forms, limbs and organs to God as he explains them— not to imply that God is possessed of form, limbs, etc., but simply to make spiritual things more intelligible to man! This is a splendid illustration of Mr. V.'s ability to misunderstand.

Mr. V. next takes up the subject of understanding the language of the Bible literally. He says it is from anthropomorphic passages of the Bible that the Latter-day Saints conclude that God has a body—such passages as speak of the face, hands feet and other limbs and organs of God. He holds these passages to be figurative. "I contend," he remarks, "that if we must understand the Bible literally in those passages ('God created man in his own image') from which they attempt to prove that God has a body, we must interpret it literally in *other similar passages*."[A] I assent to that. It is well known that the language of the Bible is highly figurative, almost extravagantly so in places, and much allowance must be made for the inclination to imagery of prophetic natures, which, like poetic temperaments, are given to imagery; and hyperbole is the vice of oriental speech. But Mr. V. is not true to this canon of interpretation he lays down, *viz., the same rule of interpretation must be applied to passages that are similar in character.* After laying down this principle of interpretation, he proceeds to depart from it by placing for comparison very *dissimilar passages*. What similarity is there, for example, in the plain, matter of fact statement, "God created man in his own image, in the image of God created he him;" and the passage he quotes from Psalms: "If I take my wings early in the morning, and dwell in the uttermost part of the sea, even there shall thy hand lead me, and thy right hand shall hold me"? And this also: "Whither shall I flee from thy face. If I ascend into heaven, thou art there; If I descend into hell thou art there?" Has not the Reverend gentleman placed for comparison here the most dissimilar passages that perhaps could be found in the whole Bible? Yet he insists that the prosy passage from Genesis must be regarded as equally figurative with David's poetry, and insists that if "Mormons" believe literally that God made man in his own image and likeness, or that Moses and seventy elders saw the God of Israel, as plainly declared by Moses, then "They must believe that God had such a very long hand as to extend to the uttermost parts of the sea;" and "such an extremely long face, reaching from heaven to hell;" and "conclude that David had wings!" Further remarks on this head are not necessary. One is under no obligation to seriously discuss nonsense.

[Footnote A: Italics are mine—R.]

Of the Incarnation or the Son or God.

Another case of misapprehension of "Mormon" ideas will be found in what Mr. Van Der Donckt says with reference to the Latter-day Saints' sacred books not teaching the Christian truth of the incarnation of Deity in the person of Jesus Christ. The sacred books of the Latter-day Saints may not contain the verbiage of so-called Christian literature on the subject; but if full recognition of the fact that Jesus was in the beginning with the Father—was the "Word," and, moreover, the "Word" that "was God," and afterwards was made flesh and dwelt among men—is to believe in the incarnation of the Son of God, then the sacred books of the Latter-day Saints teach this doctrine, for over and over again in our sacred books will passages to that effect be found (especially section 93 of the Doctrine and Covenants). Moreover, the Reverend gentleman should remember that "Mormons" include among their sacred books the Holy Bible, and all the doctrine of incarnation taught in that book is our doctrine. I think the main difference between the Latter-day Saints and "Christians" on the subject of incarnation, is that the Latter-day Saints believe that incarnation does not stop with the Lord Jesus Christ. Our sacred books teach that not only was Jesus Christ in the beginning with God, but that the spirits of all men were also with him in the beginning, and that these sons of God, as well as the Lord Jesus Christ, became incarnated in bodies of flesh and bone (Doctrine and Covenants, section 93). But Mr. V. thinks he discovers in this doctrine of incarnation a proof that "God has not a body and therefore is not an exalted man," "It is plain," says he, "that the Son of God became flesh only at the time of his sojourn on earth. Now had he been flesh or man before, as the 'Mormons' hold, how could he become what he was already from all eternity?" This is another instance of Mr. V.'s misapprehension of what "Mormons" teach. We nowhere teach that Jesus Christ, the Son of God, was flesh and bone from all eternity.

When seeking to make "Mormonism" appear inconsistent with itself, the Reverend gentleman is in duty bound to keep in mind our whole doctrine on any particular subject he is treating. He should remember that our theology holds that the Father, Son and Holy Ghost are distinct and separate personages, in the sense that they are three distinct individuals; and that the Father is a personage of flesh and bone, as Jesus now is; but previous to Messiah's birth into the world, he was a spirit, the First Born of the hosts of the spirits in heaven, and was with the Father in the beginning of the creation of our earth and its heavens. Indeed, under the direction of the Father, he was the creator of them (Heb. 1:3; Col. 15:17; John 1:3); but he came to the earth to receive a tabernacle, that in all things he might become as his Father is—a divine spirit inseparably united to a sacred and glorified body—one glorious spiritual personage. As much of Mr. V.'s argument on this head is built on a misapprehension of our doctrine, it will not be necessary for me to follow him through the interminable windings of his argument with reference to it. "There is never a proper ending to reasoning which proceeds on a false foundation" (Cicero).

Mr. V. next brings as proof against God's being an exalted man, what he calls the direct statement of the Bible, that God is not man: "God is not a man, that he should lie; neither the son of man, that he should be changed" (Numbers 23:19). "I am God and not man" (Psalm). These passages simply present the contrast between man as he is now, and with all his imperfections on his head, and God. The Latter-day Saints do not teach that man in his present state and condition is God; on the contrary, they hold that there is a very, very wide difference between them, all the difference indicated by the Bible: but they do believe that through the eternities that will pass over man's head, and with God for guide and teacher, he may become as his Father in heaven is, and that such is his destiny.[A] It follows that when man shall attain to that destiny, the contrast now so striking between man and God will not exist. The contrast noted in the scriptures by Mr. V. is not between *perfected* men and God, but between very imperfect men—men who lie, and are changeable—and God; and since the Latter-day Saints do not hold that man while imperfect is God, or like God, or God like him, the argument of the gentleman, based on the passages quoted, is of no force. It could be said of some grandly developed, noble, high-minded man, such as a Gladstone, a Bismarck, or a Washington: He is not a child that he should halt in reason, or falter in action, or be frightened by phantoms of the dark.

But such a contrast does not include the idea that the child may not change his status, and finally become all that the great man is with whom he is now contrasted. Clearly, the contrast is one of conditions, more than of natures, and at its very highest value is the contrast between a perfected nature and one not yet perfected.

[Footnote A: In a discourse in which much of the "Mormon" doctrine concerning the Deity is unfolded by the Prophet Joseph Smith—the King Follett discourse (see chapter 5)—in a passage dealing with the time in which man may attain to some of the contemplated exaltations in the future, he remarks: "When you climb up a ladder, you must begin at the bottom and ascend step by step, until you arrive at the top; and so it is with the principles of the Gospel—you must begin with the first, and go on until you learn all the principles of exaltation. *But it will be a great while after you have passed through the vail [of death] before you will have learned them. It is not all to be comprehended in this world: it will be a great work to learn our salvation and exaltation, even beyond the grave.*"]

The same answer applies to the Reverend gentleman's contention based on the passage, "Thou art always the selfsame;" "I am the Lord and change not;" "The Father of lights, with whom there is no change nor shadow of alteration." These passages teach what the Reverend gentleman calls the "immutability of God," which he holds to preclude the idea that God rose from a state of imperfection to that of perfection—since he is always the "selfsame." Before answering at length, I couple with this Mr. Van Der Donckt's final argument on this division of the subject—the scriptural evidences and arguments on the form and nature of God—namely, "The Latter day Saints' theory of the Man-God supposes a past and present with God. The Bible excludes that succession of time," says the Reverend gentleman, "and speaks of God as the everlasting present; 'I Am Who am,' 'From eternity to eternity thou art God.'" Against this argument, based upon God's reputed unchangeableness, and being always as he now is, from all eternity to eternity, I wish to say, first, that the *God-nature* is doubtless always the same, without reference to those who may attain unto it; and speaking of the God-nature, it is always the "Selfsame," from eternity to eternity; but after that statement, against the Reverend gentleman's argument bottomed on God's immutability and eternity—and, in fact, against all his arguments, from first to last, respecting the form and nature of God, I place Jesus of Nazareth, the Messiah, the revelation of God to man, I place him as my premises, and my argument against all the reverend gentleman has said, or can say, on this division of the subject. I call attention to the fact that neither in my discourse which brought forth Mr. Van Der Donckt's Reply nor in this Rejoinder, have I turned to those numerous passages of the Bible that speak of the face, limbs or organs of God. Not that I mistrust the force of those passages as evidence, but because I have thought it unnecessary to appeal to them, so long as I had in Jesus, the Messiah, a full length and complete representation of God, not only as to the *reality* of his being, but as to the *kind* of being God is. And now I ask, as I did in my discourse, *is Jesus God*? Is he a manifestation of God—a revelation of him? If so, there must be in him an end of controversy; for whatever Jesus Christ was and is God must be, or Jesus Christ is no manifestation, no revelation of God. Is Jesus Christ in form like man? Is he possessed of a body of flesh and bone which is eternally united to him—and now an integral part of him? Does he possess body, parts and passions? There can be but one answer to all these questions, and that is, "Yes; he possessed and now possesses all these things." Then God also possesses them; for even according to both Catholic and orthodox Protestant Christian doctrine, Jesus Christ was and is God, and the complete manifestation and revelation of God the Father.

Also the specific points of argument based upon God's unchangeability, and there being no succession of time with God—that, too, is answered in the person and experience of Jesus Christ. According to Catholic teaching, Jesus was a spirit, identical with God the Father in substance, before he became man; but at a certain time he became man, was not that a change? By it, he became something he was not before. His humanity, according to their teaching, was *added* to the Son of God when he received his tabernacle of flesh and bone; and he was certainly changed from an unembodied state to an embodied one; and there was a "before and after"—in reference to this great event, in the God Jesus' experience. Is it thinkable that this change was a deterioration? Was the Son of God's divinity debased to the human, or was so much of humanity as he took on raised to the divine nature, and henceforth made an integral part of it?

The orthodox doctrine of Christianity is—Catholic and Protestant alike—that Jesus Christ is God; that he always was and is God, according to both orthodox theology and Christian philosophy. Yet it is said of this Jesus that he *"increased in wisdom and stature, and in favor with God and man"* (Luke 2:52). Here is certainly a change in condition; here is succession of time with God—a before and after; here is being and becoming; for whereas, he was a spirit, he became man; and in becoming man, he passed through all the phases in life from infancy to manhood. It is significant also that it was not until Jesus had arisen from the tomb and stood in the presence of his disciples, a glorified personage, body and spirit united, that he exclaimed, *"All power is given unto me in heaven and in earth."* If *"given,"* there must have been a time when he did not possess all power in heaven and in earth; and hence, a change from possessing some power to the condition of possessing "all power," a fullness of power—"for it pleased the Father that in him should all fullness dwell" (Col. 1:19). But more of this when I come to deal with Mr. Van Der Donckt's philosophical proofs on the subject, I shall close this part of my rejoinder with the following summary of the facts maintained thus far in my argument:

First:—While the scriptures declare that God is a spirit, it does not follow that he is necessarily an unembodied spirit; on the contrary, it is clear that he is an embodied spirit; for Jesus Christ is God, and he, we know, is a spirit and body united; and he is said to be the express image of his Father's person; therefore, the Father of Jesus Christ, or God the Father, must be just what Jesus is—a spirit embodied in a tabernacle of flesh and bone.

Second:—Although the Bible says that God is a spirit, and speaks of angels as spirits also, and points out some differences between the nature of men and spirits, it does not follow that spirits are immaterial beings, and therefore without form. On the contrary, the evidence of scripture is to the effect that angels are very substantial personages. One wrestled bodily with Jacob and lamed him; while three others "did eat" of the substantial meal provided by Abraham; and there are many other proofs of angels being substantial, material personages.

Third:—It is an assumption absolutely unwarranted by authority of the word of God to say that when spirits, or angels, or Jesus—before his incarnation—showed themselves to men, they merely assumed the material garb for the occasion.

Fourth:—Although the Bible in sundry passages speaks of God the Father as "invisible," it does not follow that he is absolutely so, nor invisible from the nature of his being; on the contrary, it is clear from what has been set forth that under certain special conditions, God the Father as well as Jesus—before his incarnation—and certain angels, have been seen; and hence, the invisibility of God the Father, arises from his being invisible to men in their normal condition, unquickened by, and unclothed with, the power of God.

Fifth:—The doctrine that all absolutely invisible beings are immaterial is simply untrue, being contradicted by the fact that a number of absolutely invisible things are known to be material, and yet possess some of the properties of grosser matter; and it is reasonable to believe that the same truth holds as to spiritual beings.

Sixth:—The Bible distinctly ascribes to God and angels the form, limbs, organs, feelings and passions of men; and the Bible nowhere leads us to believe that this ascription of bodily form and organs and passions to God is simply to "make spiritual things, or certain truths more intelligible to man;" nor does it follow because *some* passages of the Bible are figurative, and hence not to be taken literally, that *all* the passages ascribing human form, organs and feelings to God are figurative, and hence not to be taken literally. It is only when anthropomorphic passages and expressions are similarly used as other clearly figurative passages and expressions are, that they are to be adjudged as figurative and *not* to be taken literally.

Seventh:—And lastly, beside all premises and arguments to the effect that God is an unembodied spirit, without form, without limbs, organs, features, human feelings, or passions, such as love, compassion, pity, etc., etc.,—beside all this, I place the Lord Jesus, the Image of God the Father's person, the full length representation and revelation of God to men, as an all sufficient answer, and say that whatsoever Jesus Christ was and is, so, too, has been and is God, the Father; for such is the teaching of holy scripture.

II.
MR. VAN DER DONCKT'S "PHILOSOPHICAL PROOFS" OF THE FORM AND NATURE OF GOD.

Mr. Van Der Donckt, at the beginning of his argument under his "philosophical proofs of God's simplicity or spirituality," again exhibits the fact that he misapprehends the doctrines of the Latter-day Saints. He says: "The Latter-day Saints believe that God created the souls of men long before their conception." That is not the belief of the Latter-day Saints; and his misapprehension of what their doctrine is relative to man and God leads the gentleman to make statements, and indulge in lines of argumentation he would not have followed had he apprehended aright the teachings of the Church of Jesus Christ of Latter-day Saints. Since his philosophical argument has proceeded from a wrong basis, it becomes necessary to state what the "Mormon" doctrine is relative to the subject in hand, and then consider so much of his argument as may apply to the facts.

Latter-day Saints believe that the "soul of man" consists of both his spirit and his body united. "The spirit and the body is the soul of man; and the resurrection from the dead is the redemption of the soul" (Doc. and Cov. sec. 88:15, 16). This, I am aware, is not the usually accepted sense of the word "soul;" for it generally stands for what is regarded as the incorporeal nature of man, or the principle of mental and spiritual life of him. It is used variously in the scriptures. In one place, the Savior uses it in contrast with the body: "Fear not them which kill the body, but are not able to kill the soul: but rather fear him which is able to destroy both soul and body in hell" (Matt. 10:28). But the word as used in the passage above quoted from the Doctrine and Covenants also has warrant of scriptural authority: "And the Lord God formed man of the dust of the ground, and breathed into his nostrils the breath of life; and man became a living soul" (Gen. 2:7). Here body and "breath of life," the spirit, constitute the soul of man.

Of course, Mr. Van Der Donckt uses the phrase "souls of men" as we perhaps would use the phrase "spirits of men," and evidently makes reference to our doctrine of the pre-existence of spirits, that is, the doctrine of the actual existence of the spirits of men long ages before they tabernacled in the flesh, when he says: "The Latter-day Saints believe that God creates the souls of men long before their conception." But again explanation is necessary, as that statement does not quite meet our belief. Our doctrine is that "Intelligences are begotten spirits," which spirits are in form like men, and are really, substance, that is, matter, but of a more subtle and finer nature than the matter composing man's tabernacle of flesh and bone.[A] Christians believe that "the Word," that is, Jesus Christ, was in the beginning with God; and not only that "the Word" was with God, but also that "the Word was God" (John 1:1, 2), Latter-day Saints not only believe Jesus was in the beginning with God, but it is their doctrine that man was "also in the beginning with the Father, that which is spirit" (Doc. and Cov. sec. 93:23). And again: "Man was also in the beginning with God. Intelligence, or the light of truth *was not created or made, neither indeed can be.* * * * * Every man whose spirit receiveth not the light is under condemnation *for man is spirit.* The elements are eternal, and spirit and element, inseparably connected, receive a fullness of joy; and when separated, man cannot receive a fullness of joy. The elements are the tabernacle of God; yea man is the tabernacle of God, even temples" (Doc and Cov. sec. 93:29, 32-35). The point to be observed is that intelligences—whence the spirits of men—are not created or made, nor indeed can they be, for they are eternal—eternal as God the Father, and God the Son are. "The mind of man—the immortal spirit—where did it come from?" asks the Prophet Joseph Smith, in a discourse delivered at Nauvoo;[B] and then answers:

[Footnote A: The Prophet Joseph teaches that "all spirit is matter, but it is more fine or pure [than the gross matter tangible to our senses] and can only be discerned by purer eyes. We cannot see it, but when our bodies are purified, we shall see that it is all matter." (Doc. and Cov. sec 137.)]

[Footnote B: April 7th, 1844, Mill. Star, vol. xxiii p. 245, et seq.]

> All learned men, and doctors of divinity, say that God created it in the beginning; but it is not so; the very idea lessens man in my estimation. I do not believe the doctrine. I know better. Hear it, all ye ends of the world, for God has told me so.

If you don't believe me it will not make the truth without effect. * * * * We say that God himself is a self-existent being. Who told you so? It is correct enough, but who told you that man did not exist in like manner upon the same principle? God made a tabernacle and put his [man's] spirit into it, and it became a living soul. How does it read in Hebrew? It does not say in Hebrew that God created the spirit of man. It says, "God made man out of earth and put in him Adam's spirit, and so became a living body." The mind, or the intelligence which man possesses is co-eternal with God himself. * * * * * I am dwelling on the immortality of the spirit of man. Is it logical to say that the intelligence of spirits is immortal, and yet that it had a beginning? The intelligence of spirits had no beginning, neither will it have an end. That is good logic. That which has a beginning may have an end. There never was a time when there were not spirits, for they are co-eternal with our Father in heaven. I want to reason more on the spirit of man; for I am dwelling on the body and spirit of man—on the subject of the dead. I take my ring from my finger and liken it unto the mind of man—the immortal part, because it has no beginning. Suppose you cut it in two; then it has a beginning and an end; but join it again, and it continues one eternal round. So with the spirit of man. As the Lord liveth, if it has a beginning it will have an end. All the fools and learned and wise men from the beginning of creation, who say that the spirit of man had a beginning, prove that it must have an end: and if that doctrine is true, then the doctrine of annihilation would be true. But if I am right, I might with boldness proclaim from the house tops that God never had the power to create the spirit of man at all, God himself could not create himself. Intelligence is eternal, and exists upon a self-existent principle. It is a spirit from age to age, and there is no creation about it. * * * * The spirit of man is not a created being; it existed from eternity, and will exist to eternity. Anything created cannot be eternal: and earth, water, etc., had their existence in an elementary state, from eternity.

Mr. Van Der Donckt will recognize quite a difference between the doctrine here stated as to the spirits of men, and the one he states for us when he says, "Latter-day Saints believe that God creates the souls of men long before their conception." There is that in man, according to our doctrine, which is not created at all; there is in him an "ego"—a "spirit" uncreated, never made, a self-existent entity, eternal as God himself; and of the same kind of substance or essence with him, and, indeed, part of him, when God is conceived of in the generic sense.

With the doctrine of "Mormonism" relative to man and God thus stated, the question is, what part of Mr. Van Der Donckt's philosophical argument touches it?

Mr. Van Der Donckt, it must be remembered, bases his philosophical argument upon the absolute "simplicity or spirituality" of God. "I Am Who Am," is the definition of God about which circle all his arguments. God is "the Necessary Being," is his contention; infinite, illimitable; not limited by his own essence, by another, or by himself. From which I understand him to mean, after the philosophers of his school, that God, the very essence of him, is pure being-"Actual being or existence" are his own words.

This his premise; and the part of his argument which affects our doctrine is the following:

> If God were an aggregation of parts, these parts would be either necessary beings or contingent (that do not necessarily exist), or some would be necessary and some contingent. None of these suppositions are tenable, therefore God is not an aggregate of parts. * * * * If the parts of God were necessary beings, there would be several independent beings, which the infinity of God precludes. God would not be infinite, if there were even one other being independent of him, as his power, etc., would not reach that being.
>
> The infinite being is most simple, or not compound. Were he compound, his parts would be either all finite, or all infinite, or one infinite and the others finite. None of these suppositions are possible, therefore he is not compound.
>
> Several finite things cannot produce an infinite or an illimitable, as there would always be a first and last.
>
> Many infinite beings are inconceivable, for, if there were several they would have to differ from each other by some perfection. Now, from the moment one would have a perfection the other one lacks, the latter would not be infinite. Therefore, God cannot be a compound of infinite parts.
>
> If one is infinite, nothing can be added to it. Finite parts could not belong to the infinite essence, else they would communicate their limitations to God.

Therefore, the infinite Being is not composite, but simple or spiritual. Therefore he is not, nor ever was, a man, who is a composite being.

Of Mr. Van Der Donckt's Premise.

I have to do first of all with Mr. Van Der Donckt's premise—"the simplicity or spirituality" of God.

So far as it is possible to make language do it, the gentleman teaches that God is "pure being," "most [therefore absolutely] simple—not compound." He is not only infinite, then, but infinity. It follows that he is without quality, other than being—mere existence—"I Am Who Am;" without attributes; not susceptible of division, or of relation; for if he possessed quality or attribute or was susceptible of division or of relation, his absolute simplicity—that tremulously precarious thing on which, according to Mr. V.'s philosophy, his very existence and all his excellence depends—would be destroyed. It was doubtless these considerations that led the Church of England—which, by the way, is at one with the Roman Catholic Church in the doctrine of God—to say of the "one true and living God," that he is *without body, parts or passions*.[A] With which also the Westminster Confession of Faith agrees, by saying: "There is but one only living and true God, who is infinite in being and perfection, a most pure spirit, invisible, *without body, parts or passions*, immutable, immense, eternal, incomprehensible," etc.[B]

[Footnote A: Bk. Com. Prayer, Articles of Religion, Art. 1.]

[Footnote B: Westminster Confession, Art. 2, Sec. 1.]

The German school of philosophy of the eighteenth and nineteenth centuries, which ends in inevitable agnosticism, went but one step further than these creeds; a step made inevitable by the creeds themselves. The creeds postulate God as "pure being"—"existence" "the one who could not *not* exist," Mr. V.'s interpretation of "I Am Who Am." But "existence," says Fichte, "implies origin," and "God is beyond origin"—i. e. beyond "being," "existence." Schelling reached substantially the same conclusion when, by a pathway but little divergent from that followed by Fichte, he was led to regard God as neither "real or ideal;" "neither thought nor being." While Hegel, by similar subtleties, established the identity of "Being and Non-Being." This German philosophy, which but extends the philosophy of the orthodox creeds to its legitimate conclusion, leaves us with the paradox on our hands of regarding God at once as the most real existence, and as the most absolute non-existence. The conclusions from the premise are just; and Mr. V.'s "most simple," "infinite being," he who is "pure existence itself," vanishes amid the metaphysical subtleties of the learned Germans.[A]

[Footnote A: "Existence itself, that so-called highest category of thought, is only conceivable in the form of existence modified in some particular manner. Strip off its modification, and the apparent paradox of the German philosopher becomes literally true;—*pure being is pure nothing*. We have no conception of existence which is not existence in some particular manner; and if we abstract from the manner, we have nothing left to constitute the existence. Those who, in their horror of what they call anthropomorphism, or anthropopathy, refuse to represent the Deity under symbols borrowed from the limitations of human consciousness, are bound in consistency, to deny that God exists; for the conception of existence is as human and as limited as any other" (Limits of Religious Thought, Mansel, pp. 95, 96).]

Let us examine the effect of this Deity-destroying postulate in England. Mr. Van Der Donckt's "Infinite being," "most simple or not compound," is identical with the "absolute," the "unconditioned;" the "first cause," hence the "uncaused." These terms, it is well known, Mr. Herbert Spencer seized upon, in his volume on "First Principles," and ran them down to logical absurdity, showing them to be "unthinkable," and that ultimate religious ideas (arising from the postulates of orthodox creeds) lead to the "Unknown!" In reaching this conclusion he was wonderfully helped by Henry L. Mansel, some time Dean of St. Paul's, who in his celebrated Bampton Lecture arrives at substantially the same conclusion—with an exception to be noted later. Indeed, so nearly at one are the churchman and the philosopher, in their methods of thought, in their deductions, that the latter reaches his conclusions from the data and reasoning of the former, whom he quotes with approval and at great length. I select from these writers a few typical passages tending to show the absurdity of God's "simplicity," or "spirituality," as held by Mr. Van Der Donckt, reminding the reader that Mr. V.'s "Infinite Being," "most simple or not compound," is identical with the "absolute," "unconditioned," the "first cause," the "uncaused" of both Mr. Mansel and Mr. Spencer.

Mr. Spencer, after showing that the First Cause cannot be finite, nor dependent, reaches the conclusion that it must be infinite and independent; and then proceeds:

> But to think of the First Cause as totally independent is to think of it as that which existed in the absence of all other existence; seeing that if the presence of any other existence is necessary, it must be partially dependent on that other existence, and so cannot be the First Cause. Not only, however, must the First Cause be a form of being which has no necessary relation to any other form of being, but it

can have no necessary relation within itself. There can be nothing in it which determines change, and yet nothing which prevents change. For if it contains something which imposes such necessities or restraints, this something must be a cause higher than the First Cause, which is absurd. Thus the First Cause must be in every sense perfect, complete, total; including within itself all power, and transcending all law. Or to use the established word, it must be absolute.[A]

[Footnote A: First Principles (Spencer) pp. 29, 30; 1896 edition, D. Appleton & Co., N. Y.]

Thus far the philosopher; and even Mr. Van Der Donckt, I think, could not complain that he has not stated the "simplicity" of the First Cause most clearly. But at this point the philosopher, Mr. Spencer, introduces the churchman, Dean Mansel, to abolish the structure of the "First Cause," the "simple" or "spiritual being," or "God," as held by Mr. V. and all orthodox Christians. I quote Mr. Mansel:

> But these three conceptions—the Cause, the Absolute, the Infinite—all equally indispensable, do they not imply contradiction to each other, when viewed in conjunction, as attributes of one and the same Being? A Cause cannot, as such, be absolute: *the Absolute cannot as such be a cause*. The cause, as such, exists only in relation to its effect; the effect is an effect of the cause. On the other hand, the conception of the Absolute implies a possible existence out of all relation. We attempt to escape from this apparent contradiction by introducing the idea of succession in time. The Absolute exists first by itself, and afterwards becomes a cause. But here we are checked by the third conception, that of the infinite. How can the infinite become that which it was not from the first? If Causation is a possible mode of existence, that which exists without causing is not infinite; that which becomes a cause has passed beyond its former limits. *
> * Supposing the Absolute to be a cause, it will follow that it operates by means of free will and consciousness. For a necessary cause cannot be conceived as absolute and infinite. If necessitated by something beyond itself, it is thereby limited by a superior power: and if necessitated by itself, it has in its own nature a necessary relation to its effect. The act of causation must therefore be voluntary, and volition is only possible in a conscious being. But consciousness again is only conceivable as a relation. There must be a conscious

subject and an object of which he is conscious. The subject is a subject to the object; the object is an object to the subject; and neither can exist by itself as the absolute. This difficulty, again, may be for the moment evaded, by distinguishing between the absolute as related to another and the absolute as related to itself. The absolute, it may be said, may possibly be conscious provided it is only conscious of itself. But this alternative is, in ultimate analysis, no less self-destructive than the other. For the object of consciousness, whether a mode of the subject's existence or not, is either created in and by the act of consciousness, or has an existence independent of it. In the former case the object depends upon the subject, and the subject alone is the true absolute. In the latter case, the subject depends upon the object, and the object alone is the true absolute. Or, if we attempt a third hypothesis, and maintain that each exists independently of the other, we have no absolute at all, but only a pair of relatives; for coexistence, whether in consciousness or not, is itself a relation.

The corollary from this reasoning is obvious. Not only is the absolute, as conceived, incapable of a necessary relation to anything else, but it is also incapable of containing, by the constitution of its own nature, an essential relation within itself; as a whole, for instance composed of parts, or as a substance consisting of attributes, or as a conscious subject in antithesis to an object. For, if there is in the absolute any principle of unity, distinct from the mere accumulation of parts or attributes, this principle alone is the true absolute. If, on the other hand, there is no such principle, then there is no absolute at all, but only a plurality of relatives. The almost unanimous voice of philosophy, in pronouncing that the absolute is both one and simple, must be accepted as the voice of reason also, as far as reason has any voice in the matter. But this absolute unity, as indifferent and containing no attributes, can neither be distinguished from the multiplicity of finite beings by any characteristic feature, nor be identified with them in their multiplicity. Thus we are landed in an inextricable dilemma. The absolute cannot be conceived as conscious, neither can it be conceived as unconscious: it cannot be conceived as complex, neither can it be conceived as simple; it cannot be conceived by difference, neither can it be conceived by the absence of difference:

it cannot be identified with the universe, neither can it be distinguished from it. The One and the Many, regarded as the beginning of existence, are thus alike incomprehensible.

Let us, however, suppose, for an instance, that these difficulties are surmounted, and the existence of the Absolute securely established on the testimony of reason. Still we have not succeeded in reconciling this idea with that of a Cause: we have done nothing towards explaining how the absolute can give rise to the relative—the infinite to the finite. If the condition of causal activity is a higher state than that of quiescence, the Absolute, whether acting voluntarily or involuntarily, has passed from a condition of comparative imperfection to one of comparative perfection; and, therefore, was not originally perfect. If the state of activity is an inferior state to that of quiescence, the Absolute, in becoming a cause, has lost its original perfection. There remains only the supposition that the two states are equal, and the act of creation one of complete indifference. But this supposition annihilates the unity of the absolute, or it annihilates itself. If the act of creation is real, and yet indifferent, we must admit the possibility of two conceptions of the absolute—the one as productive, the other as non-productive. If the act is not real, the supposition itself vanishes. * * *

Again, how can the relative be conceived as coming into being? If it is a distinct reality from the absolute, it must be conceived as passing from non-existence into existence. But to conceive an object as non-existent is again a self-contradiction; for that which is conceived exists, as an object of thought, in and by that conception. We may abstain from thinking of an object at all; but, if we think of it, we cannot but think of it as existing. It is possible at one time not to think of an object at all, and at another to think of it as already in being; but to think of it in the act of becoming, in the progress from not being into being, is to think that which, in the very thought, annihilates itself. * * *

To sum up briefly this portion of my argument:

The conception of the absolute and the infinite, from whatever side we view it, appears encompassed with contradictions.

There is a contradiction in supposing such an object to exist, whether alone or in conjunction with others; and there is a contradiction in supposing it not to exist.

There is a contradiction in conceiving it as one; and there is a contradiction in conceiving it as many.

There is a contradiction in conceiving it as personal; and there is a contradiction in conceiving it as impersonal.

It cannot, without contradiction, be represented as active, nor, without equal contradiction, be represented as inactive.

It cannot be conceived as the sum of all existence; nor yet can it be conceived as a part only of that sum.[A]

[Footnote A: First Principles (Spencer) pp. 40-44. Limits of Religions Thoughts, lecture II, first American edition, 1875.]

After thus running to absurdity the prevalent conceptions of the "Infinite," the "Absolute," the "Uncaused," Mr. V.'s "Most simple or not compound" "Being," the churchman does what all orthodox Christians do, he commits a violence against all human understanding and good sense—he arbitrarily declares, in the face of his own inexorable logic and its inevitable deductions, that, "*it is our duty to think of God as personal; and it is our duty to believe that he is infinite;*" that is, it is our duty to think of the infinite as at once limited and unlimited; as finite and infinite—"which," to use a phrase dear to Mr. Van Der Donckt, "is absurd," and therefore not to be entertained. At this point, the philosopher and the churchman reach the parting of the ways, and this is the exception, in the conclusion of the two, noted a few pages back.

Some do indeed allege [says Mr. Spencer] that though the Ultimate Cause of things cannot really be thought of by us as having specified attributes, it is yet incumbent upon us to assert these attributes. Though the forms of our consciousness are such that the Absolute cannot, in any manner or degree, be brought within them, we are nevertheless told that we must represent the Absolute to ourselves under these forms! * * * That this is not the conclusion here adopted, needs hardly be said. If there be any meaning in the foregoing arguments, duty requires us neither to affirm nor deny personality. Our duty is to submit ourselves with all humility to the established limits of our intelligence, and not perversely to rebel against them. Let those who can, believe there is eternal war between our intellectual faculties and our moral obligations. I, for one, admit no such radical vice in the constitution of things.[A]

[Footnote A: First Principles]

Yet Mr. Mansel, in the inconsistent and illogical course he pursues, is not more inconsistent, illogical, and unphilosophical than all orthodox Christians. The postulates of their creeds concerning the nature of God leads them to affirm what they call his "Spirituality," "Infinite Being," "Simplicity," etc. (which are but the equivalents of the philosopher's "absolute," "infinite," and the "uncaused"); and yet the necessities of their faith in revelation make it imperative that they regard him as existing in some relation to the universe and to man, which destroys his alleged "simplicity." To ascribe to him attributes is to destroy that simplicity[A] which orthodox creeds affirm, and for which Mr. Van Der Donckt so stoutly argues. Nor does it help matters when it is said that these attributes are existences—the attitude of Mr. V., for he says: "Every perfection [goodness, mercy, justice, etc.—attributes of God] is some existence, something that is." If this be granted, then it follows that God must be the sum of all these existences, therefore a compound, not "simple." And not only does orthodox belief in revelation compel those who follow it to concede the existence of attributes in God, but personality also. But if God be conceived as a personality, his "simplicity" or "spirituality," as held by Mr. V., vanishes, because, when recognized as personality, God is no longer "being"—but *a* being.

[Footnote A: "The rational conception of God is that *he is*, nothing more. To give him an attribute is to make him a relative God. * * * We cannot attribute to him any quality, for qualities are inconceivable apart from matter." *"Origin and Development of Religious Beliefs—Christianity."* —(S. Baring-Gould, p. 112.) It was held by well nigh the whole medieval school of theologians that God was unknowable because "the absolute simplicity of the divine essence was incompatible with the existence of distinctions therein." (See art. "Theism," *Ency. Brit.*, and the references there given.)]

Mr. Van Der Donckt himself says: "Something is limited, not because it *is* [i. e. exists]: but because it is *this or that*; for instance, a stone, a plant, a man"—*or a person*, I suggest. For if God has personality, he is a person, a some-thing, and hence limited, according to Mr. V.'s philosophy; if limited, as he must be when conceived of as *this or that*, as a person, for instance, then of course not infinite being; and thus my friend's doctrine of God's "simplicity" is destroyed the moment he ascribes personality to Deity. Nor does the difficulties of Mr. Van Der Donckt and all orthodox Christians end here. Not only does revelation as they view it demand belief in the personality of God, but it demands the belief that in God are *three persons*—the Father, the Son and the Holy Ghost. This further complicates the matter, and removes orthodox Christians still further from the postulate of "simplicity" they affirm of God; for if there are three persons in God, by no intellectual contortions whatsoever can this conception of "three" be harmonized with the orthodox Christian postulate of God's "simplicity." For the Son, if he exists at all, must exist in virtue of some distinction from the Father; so also the Holy Ghost must exist in virtue of some distinction from both the Father and the Son. Each must have something distinct from the other; must be what the other is not, in some particular;* and if each one has something the other has not, and each lacks something which the other has, how can it be said that each of these persons is God, and each infinite as he must be in order to be God, under Mr. V.'s doctrine?

[Footnote A: "Distinction is necessarily limitation; for, if one object is to be distinguished from another, it must possess some form of existence which the other has not, or it must not possess some form which the other has." Dean Mansel, "Limits of Religious Thoughts."]

If the three be conceived as one God—yet each with that about him which distinguishes him from the other—how can God be regarded as "simple," "not compound?" The orthodox creeds of Christendom, moreover, require us to believe that while the Father is a person, the Son a person, and the Holy Ghost a person, yet there are not three persons, but one person. So with each being eternal and almighty. So with each being God: "The Father is God, the Son is God, the Holy Ghost is God: and yet there are not three Gods but one God"[A] No wonder the whole conception is given up as "incomprehensible." "Their mode of subsistence [i. e., the subsistence of the three persons] in the one substance," says the *Commentary on the Confession of Faith*, "*must ever continue to us a profound mystery, as it transcends all analogy.*"[B] So the Douay Catechism (Catholic), ch. i:

[Footnote A: See the creed of St. Athanasius, a copy is published in the History of the Church, vol. I, Introduction, p. 87.]

[Footnote B: This Commentary is by Rev. A. A. Hodges, D.D., LL.D., p. 58.]

> Q. In what do faith and law of Christ consist? A. In two principal *mysteries,* namely, *the Unity and Trinity of God,* and the incarnation and death of our Savior.

"To think that God *is*, as we *think* him to be, is blasphemy," is the lofty assertion behind which some of the orthodox hide when hard pressed with the inconsistency of their creed; and if I mistake not, "A God understood is a God dethroned," has long been an aphorism of the Church of which Mr. Van Der Donckt is a priest.

But what is the sum of my argument thus far on Mr. Van Der Donckt's premise of God's absolute "simplicity" or "spirituality?" Only this:

First, his premise is proven to be unphilosophical and untenable, when coupled with his creed, which ascribes qualities, attributes and personality to God. Either the gentleman must cease to think of God as "infinite being," "most simple," "not compound," or he must surrender the God of his creed, who is represented by it to be three persons in one substance; and, moreover, persons possessed of attributes and qualities which bring God into relations with men and the universe, a mode of being which destroys "simplicity." Either one or the other of these beliefs must be given up; they cannot consistently be held simultaneously, as they destroy each other. If Mr. V. holds to the God of his creed, what becomes of all his "philosophy?" If he holds to his "philosophy," what becomes of the God of his creed.

Second, as affecting this discussion, the matter at this point stands thus: Since the gentleman's premise of God's absolute simplicity is proved to be illogical and unphilosophical, it affords no sound basis of argument against the Latter-day Saints' views of Deity, wherein they hold him to be something different from absolute "being"—more than a mere, and, I may say, bare and barren "existence," a metaphysical abstraction. Mr. V.'s premise of absolute simplicity affords no consistent basis of argument against our view that God is a person in the sense of being an individual, in form like man, and possessed of attributes which bring him within the nearest and dearest relations to men that it is possible to conceive.

Of the Doctrine of God's "Simplicity" Being of Pagan Rather than of Christian Origin.

The next step in my argument is to prove that this doctrine of God being "most simple," "not compound," "pure being"—without body (i. e., not material), parts or passions—hence, without attributes, is not a doctrine of the Christian scriptures, but comes from the old Pagan philosophies.

Clearly the data for this doctrine of God's absolute "simplicity" did not come from the Old Testament, for that teaches the plainest anthropomorphic ideas respecting God. It ascribes to him a human form, and many qualities and attributes possessed by man, which, in the minds of philosophers of Mr. V.'s school, limit him who must be, to their thinking, without any limit whatsoever; and ascribes relativity to him who must not be relative but absolute.

The data for the doctrine of God's absolute "simplicity"—contended for by Mr. V.—does not come from the New Testament, for the writers of that volume of scripture accept the doctrine of the Old Testament respecting

God, and even emphasize its anthropomorphic ideas, by representing that the man Christ Jesus was in the "express image" of God, the Father's, person; was, in fact, God manifest in the flesh (I Tim. 3:16); "the image of the invisible God" (Col. 1:5); "God, the Word, who was made flesh, and dwelt among men, who beheld his glory" (St. John 1:1-14). Hence Mr. Van Der Donckt's doctrine of God's "simplicity" cannot claim the warrant of New Testament authority.

Plato, in his *Timaeus*, (Jowett's translation, page 530,) incidentally referring to God, in connection with the creation of the universe, says:

> We say indeed that "he was," "he is," "he will be;" but the truth is that *"he is"* alone truly expresses him, and that "was" and "will be" are only to be spoken of generation in time.

Here, then, is Mr. V.'s "pure being," "most simple," "not compound." Again:

> We must acknowledge that there is one kind of being which is always the same, uncreated and indestructible, never receiving anything into itself from without, nor itself giving out to any other, but invisible and imperceptible by any sense, and of which the sight is granted to intelligence only (Ibid. p. 454).

Here Mr. V. may find his God, "who cannot change with regard to his existence, nor with regard to his mode of existence." Also his God who can only be seen with the "soul's intellectual perception, elevated by a supernatural influx from God." Dr. Mosheim, in his account of Plato's idea of God, says: "He considered the Deity, to whom he gave the supreme governance of the universe, as a being of the highest wisdom and power, and *totally unconnected with any material substance.*"[A]

[Footnote A: Mosheim's "Historical Commentaries on the State of Christianity, During the First Three Hundred Years", vol. 1. p. 37.]

To the same effect, also, Justin Martyr (second Christian century) generalizes and accepts as doctrine what may be gathered from the sixth book of Plato's "Republic," with reference to God. To the Jew, Trypho, Justin remarks:

> The Deity, father, is not to be viewed by the organs of sight, like other creatures, but he is to be comprehended by the mind alone, as Plato declares, and I believe him. * * * * Plato tells us that the eye of the mind is of such a nature, and was given Us to such an end, as to enable us to see with it by itself, when pure, that *Being* who is the source of whatever

is an object of the mind itself, *who has neither color, nor shape, nor size, nor anything which the eye can see,* but who is above all essence, who is ineffable, and undefinable, who is alone beautiful and good, and who is at once implanted into those souls who are naturally well born, through their relationship to and desire of seeing him.

Athanasius (third Christian century) quotes the same definition (Contra Gentes, ch. 2), almost *verbatim.* Turning again to the *Timaeus* of Plato, this question is asked:

What is that which always is and has no becoming; and what is that which is always becoming and has never any being? That which is apprehended by reflection and reason [God] always is; and is the same; that on the other hand which is conceived by opinion, with the help of sensation without reason [the material universe], is in a process of becoming and perishing but never really is. * * * Was the world [universe], always in existence and without beginning? or created and having a beginning? Created, I reply.

In this, the orthodox Christians and Mr. V. may find their God of pure "being," that never is "becoming," but *always is*; also the creation of the universe out of nothing. The fact is that orthodox Christian views of God are Pagan rather than Christian.

In his great work on the "History of Christian Doctrine," Mr. William G. T. Shedd says:[A] "The early Fathers, in their defenses of Christianity against their pagan opponents, contend that the better pagan writers themselves agree with the new religion in teaching that their is one Supreme Being. Lactantius (Institutiones, 1, 5), after quoting the Orphic poets, Hesiod, Virgil, and Ovid, in proof that the heathen poets taught the unity of the supreme deity, affirms that the better pagan philosophers agree with them in this. 'Aristotle,' he says, 'although he disagrees with himself, and says many things that are self-contradictory, yet testifies that one supreme mind rules over the world. Plato, who is regarded as the wisest philosopher of them all, plainly and openly defends the doctrine of a divine monarchy, and denominates the supreme being, not ether, nor reason, nor nature, but as he is, *God*; and asserts that by him this perfect and admirable world was made. And Cicero follows Plato, frequently confessing the deity, and calls him the supreme being, in his Treatise on the Laws.'"

[Footnote A: Vol 1, p 56.]

It is conceded by Christian writers that the Christian doctrine of God is not expressed in New Testament terms, but in the terms of Greek and

Roman metaphysics, as witness the following from the very able article in the *Encyclopedia Britannica* on Theism, by the Rev. Dr. Flint, Professor of Divinity, University of Edinburgh: "The proposition constitutive of the dogma of the Trinity—the propositions in the symbols of Nice, Constantinople and Toledo, relative to the immanent distinctions and relations in the Godhead—were not drawn directly from the New Testament, and could not be expressed in New Testament terms. *They were the product of reason speculating on a revelation to faith*—the New Testament representation of God as a Father, a Redeemer and a Sanctifier—with a view to conserve and vindicate, explain and comprehend it. They were only formed through centuries of effort, *only elaborated by the aid of the conceptions, and formulated in the terms of Greek and Roman metaphysics.*" The same authority says: "The massive defense of theism, erected by the Cambridge school of philosophy, against atheism, fatalism, and the denial of moral distinctions, was avowedly built on a Platonic foundation."

In method of thought also, no less than in conclusions, the most influential of the Christian fathers on these subjects followed the Greek philosophers rather than the writers of the New Testament.[A] "Platonism, and Aristotelianism," says the author of the *History of Christian Doctrine*, "exerted more influence upon the intellectual methods of men, taking in the whole time since their appearance, than all other systems combined. They certainly influenced the Greek mind, and Grecian culture, more than all the other philosophical systems. They re-appear in Roman philosophy—so far as Rome had any philosophy. We shall see that Plato, Aristotle, and Cicero, exerted more influence than all other philosophical minds united, upon the greatest of the Christian Fathers: upon the greatest of the Schoolmen; and upon the theologians of the Reformation, Calvin and Melanchthon. And if we look at European philosophy as it has been unfolded in England, Germany and France, we shall perceive that all the modern theistic schools have discussed the standing problems of human reason, in very much the same manner in which the reason of Plato and Aristotle discussed them twenty-two centuries ago. Bacon, Des Cartes, Leibniz, and Kant, so far as the first principles of intellectual and moral philosophy are concerned, agree with their Grecian predecessors. A student who has mastered the two systems of the Academy and Lyceum will find in modern philosophy (with the exception of the department of natural science) very little that is true, that may not be, found for substance, and germinally, in the Greek theism."[B]

[Footnote A: Especially compare Plato's methods of arising from the conception of the finite and variable, to the infinite and unchangeable; from the relatively beautiful and good, to the absolutely beautiful and good, in the sixth and seventh books of the "Republic," with St. Augustine's manner of arriving at the conception of *"That which is"* —God.—*Confessions St. Augustine*, book seven.]

[Footnote B: History of Christian Doctrine, by William G. T. Shedd; Vol. I, p. 52.]

It is hoped that enough is said here to establish the fact that the conception of God as "pure being," "immaterial," "without form," "or parts or passions," as held by orthodox Christianity, has its origin in Pagan philosophy, not in Jewish nor Christian revelation.

Of Jesus Christ Being Both Premise and Argument against Mr. Van Der Donckt's "Philosophical Argument."

And now as to the whole question of God being "existence," "pure being," "most simple," "not compound;" also his "immutability," as set forth in Mr. Van Der Donckt's "philosophical argument." What of it? This of it: Whatever "simplicity," "immutability," or other quality that is ascribed to God, *must be in harmony with what Jesus Christ is*: I meet Mr. V.'s "philosophical argument" as I meet his scriptural argument. I appeal to the being and nature of Jesus Christ, as a refutation of his philosophical conclusions. Is Jesus Christ God? "Yes," must be my friend's answer. Very well, this is my premise. Jesus is God in his own right and person, and he is a revelation of what God the Father is. He is not only a revelation of the *being* of God, but of the *kind* of being God is. And now I test Mr. V.'s argument by the revelation of what God is, as revealed in the person and nature of the Son of God. While I am doing so, let it be remembered that Jesus is now and will ever be what he was at the time of his glorious ascension from the midst of his disciples on Mount Olivet—God, possessed of all power in heaven and in earth, a glorious personage of flesh and bone and spirit. And now, is Jesus Christ without form? No; he is in form like man. Is Jesus Christ illimitable? Not as to his glorious body; that has limitations, dimensions, proportions. Is Jesus Christ without parts? Not as to his person; his body is made up of limbs, trunk, head; and parenthetically I may remark, a whole without parts is inconceivable. Then it follows that God's "infinity," so far as it is spoken of in scripture, does not refer to his person, but evidently to the attributes of his mind—to his intelligence, wisdom, power, patience, mercy, and whatsoever other qualities of mind or spirit he may possess. If it is argued that it is illogical and unphilosophical to regard God in his person as finite, but infinite in faculties, that is finite in one respect and infinite in another, my answer is that it is a conception of God made necessary by what the divine wisdom has revealed concerning himself, and it is becoming in man to accept with humility what God has been pleased to reveal concerning his own nature, being assured that in God's infinite knowledge he knows himself, and that which he reveals concerning himself is to be trusted far beyond man's philosophical conception of him.

But to resume our inquiry: Is Jesus Christ immutable, unchangeable? Is he Plato's "that which always is and has no becoming?" or Mr. Van Der Donckt's "necessary Being * * * that cannot change with regard to his existence, nor can he change with regard to his *mode* of existence," and therefore could never be anything other than he was from eternity? It is inconceivable how any being can be a son and not have a beginning as such. Whatever of eternity may be ascribed to the existence of the Lord Jesus, he must have had a beginning as a son; that term implies a relation, let it be brought about how it may, and that relation must have had a beginning. While there may never have been a time when Jesus was not in respect of his existence as an Intelligence, there must have been a time when he was not as "Son." So that he doubtless became "Son," hence changed his relation from not Son to Son; hence changed in his relations, in his mode of existence. We know there was a time when he was not man, that is, not man of flesh and bone made of the materials of this world; and he became man; another change. There was a time when he was mortal man, by which I mean, man subject to death; and he became, and is now, immortal man; another change. There was a time when all power in heaven and in earth was "*given*" to him; (Matt. 28:18) hence, there must have been a time when he did not possess it; hence another change, a change from the condition of holding *some* power to that of possessing *all* power. These facts attested by Holy Writ are against Mr. V.'s doctrine of God's "immutability," so far at least as relates to the impossibility of changing his mode of existence. And if Mr. V.'s doctrine of the "immutability" of God means that God cannot change in his relations, then I put these facts in the career of the Lord Jesus against his argument, and say that not only did Jesus pass through these changes of conditions and relations, but that God the Father could, and very likely did, pass through similar relations and changes. Else of what significance are the following passages?

> The Son can do nothing of himself, but what he seeth the Father do; for what things soever he doeth, these also doeth the Son likewise (St. John 5:19).

The Prophet Joseph Smith quoting the substance of St. John 5:26, also says:

> "As the Father hath power in himself, even so hath the Son power"—to do what? Why, what the Father did. The answer

is obvious—in a manner to lay down his body and take it up again. "Jesus, what are you going to do?" "To lay down my body as my Father did, and take it up again." Do you believe it? If you do not believe it, you do not believe the Bible.[A]

[Footnote A: *Millennial Star*, Vol. 23: p. 247.]

It is the accepted doctrine of the orthodox Christian creeds that Jesus Christ, the Son of God, is as the Father is—(Creed of St. Athanasius) that is, of the *same* nature and essence. Very well, then; as God, the Father, begot Jesus, the Son, may not the Son in time also beget a son or sons? Or, after ascribing to the Son the *same* nature and the *same power* as is ascribed to the Father, will our orthodox friends insist upon limiting the Son by denying him productive virtue, and contend that Jesus must endure without the exercise of it? If the existence of the Son was essential to the perfection of God, the Father—and it cannot be thought of in any other light—may it not be, since the Son is of the same nature as the Father, that the fact of fatherhood is necessary to the perfection of the Son? To deny him the power of attaining it would be to limit his power, which may not be done even according to orthodox Christian doctrine. Is it not likely, nay, would it not be so? that the same cause or impulse, or necessity, or what influence or consideration soever it was that led God, the Father, to beget a Son, create a world, and provide for its redemption, would impel the Son, since he is of the same nature as the Father, to do these same things? And where was the beginning of such proceedings? and where will be the end of them?

But now, to resume again our measuring of Mr. V.'s philosophy by Jesus Christ as God.

Is Jesus Christ without passions? No; his deathless love for his friends, so beautifully manifested by word and deed throughout his mortal life, together with his love for mankind, which led him to give his life for the world, as also his explicitly declared hatred of that which is sin and evil, forbid us thinking of him as without passions.[A] As in him dwelt "all the fulness of the Godhead bodily," so in him necessarily are gathered all these qualities, attributes and perfections that go to the making of God. Does possession of these qualities, together with Messiah's mode of existence in the form and person of Jesus Christ, come in conflict with the notion of God's "simplicity," "immutability," and "eternity," as conceived by philosophers? So much the worse, then, for the faulty and merely human conceptions of those qualities, as relating to God. Better mistrust the accuracy of metaphysical reasoning; better throw aside Plato and his philosophy as untrustworthy, than to be moved ever so slightly from the great truth of revelation that Jesus, the Messiah, is God; and that such as he is, God is, as to essence, attributes, existence, and the mode of existence. Jesus Christ, then, once accepted as God, and the manifestation of God to men, is a complete answer to Mr. Van Der Donckt's philosophical argument for the absolute "simplicity" or "spirituality" or "immutability" of God.

[Footnote A: God is angry with the wicked every day (Ps 7:11.)]

More of Mr. Van Der Donckt's "Philosophy."

I must not neglect Mr. Van Der Donckt's "philosophy" that forbids us believing that "several finite things" can "produce an infinite, or an illimitable, as there would always be a first and last." Also his "finite parts could not belong to the infinite essence, else they would communicate their limitations to God." Also, his "many infinite beings are inconceivable; for, if there were several, they would have to differ from each other by some perfection." And his "from the moment one would have a perfection, the other one lacks, the latter would not be infinite. Therefore, God cannot be a compound of infinite parts."

Can any one, can Mr. Van Der Donckt himself, be quite sure of all this? Who knows how the infinite is constituted? When men speak of the infinite, are they not treating of that which is beyond the comprehension of the mind of man, at least in his present state of limited intellectual powers; for whatever may be the heights to which the mind of man may rise, when freed from his present earth-bound conditions, here and now he must recognize his intellectual limitations: for, as in Christ's humiliation (i. e. in his earth-life) his judgement was taken away (Acts 8:33), that is, his divine, supreme, intellectual and spiritual powers were veiled—so with man, in this same world of trial and limitations. Whatever his power as an eternal Intelligence may have been, or what it may be hereafter, he is now compelled to admit that he sees but as through a glass darkly, and therefore imperfectly. Men, I hold, though they be philosophers, cannot comprehend the infinite, much less say how it is constituted. But let us reflect a little upon the several propositions Mr. V. submits to us:

1—"*Several finite beings cannot produce the infinite.*"

So far as it is possible for the human intellect to conceive the infinite, the material universe is infinite, eternal, without beginning and without end. It is inconceivable that the universe could have had a beginning, could have been produced from nothing. "All the apparent proofs," remarks Herbert Spencer, "that something can come out of nothing, a wider knowledge has one by one cancelled. The comet that is suddenly discovered in the heavens and nightly waxes larger, is proved not to be a newly created body, but a body that was until lately beyond the range of vision. The cloud which in course of a few minutes forms in the sky, consists not of substance that has just begun to be, but of substance that previously existed in a more diffused and transparent form. And similarly with a crystal or precipitate in relation to the fluid depositing it" (First Prin., p. 177.) Mr. Spencer holds it "impossible to think of *nothing* becoming *something*," for the reason that "nothing" cannot become an object of consciousness (*Ibid* pp. 161-2.) In like manner, he holds that matter is indestructible, and hence, that the universe cannot be annihilated. "The doctrine that matter is indestructible has become a common-place," he remarks. "The seeming annihilations of matter turn out, on close observation, to be only changes of state. It is found that the evaporated water, though it has become invisible, may be brought by condensations to its original shape." The indestructibility of matter, Mr. Spencer holds to be a datum of consciousness, which he thus illustrates:

> Conceive the space before you to be cleared of all bodies save one. Now imagine the remaining one not to be removed from its place, but to lapse into nothing while standing in that place. You fail. The place that was solid you cannot conceive becoming empty, save by the transfer of that which made it solid * * * However small the bulk to which we conceive a piece of matter reduced, it is impossible to conceive it reduced into nothing. While we can represent to ourselves the parts the matter as approximated, we cannot represent to ourselves the quantity of matter as made less. To do this would be to imagine some of the constituent parts compressed into nothing; which is no more possible than to imagine compression of the whole into nothing. Our inability to conceive matter becoming non-existent, is immediately consequent on the nature of thought. Thought consists in the establishment of relations. There can be no relation established, and therefore no thought framed, when one of the related terms is absent from consciousness. Hence, it is impossible to think of something becoming nothing, for the same reason that it is impossible to think of nothing becoming something. (First Prin., p. 181.)

The material universe, then, is eternal, it always existed, and how many changes soever it may pass through, it will never be annihilated. Not one atom can be added to the sum total of its substance, nor one blotted out of existence—it is everywhere existing, and, so far as the mind of man can conceive "infinity," it is infinite. Yet we know that this whole is made up of a great variety of substances and objects which are finite; and our philosophers, for the most part, hold that matter is divisible into ultimate atoms. Not that such a fact has been demonstrated or is demonstrable; but granted the existence of matter, its existence as an aggregation of such ultimate things as atoms seems to be a necessary truth. I say necessary truth, because the mind of man cannot conceive to the contrary, and hence, science assumes matter to be composed of atoms. But atoms are things—material things; and in the mind must necessarily be thought of as having dimensions—an upper and lower part, also a hither and thither side; or if spherical then a circumference and diameter; in other words, atoms are finite, material things, and in the aggregate constitute the material universe, which, so far as the wit of man can conceive, is infinite; and hence, we may say the infinite universe is composed of finite atoms; or, several finite things—Mr. V.'s philosophy to the contrary notwithstanding—produce the infinite.

2—"*Many infinite beings are inconceivable; for if there were several, they would have to differ from each other by some perfection. Now, the moment one would have a perfection the other one lacks, the latter would not be infinite.*"

That may be true in relation to absolute "infinity." But we have already seen that God cannot be considered as absolutely infinite, because we are taught by the facts of revelation that absolute infinity cannot hold as to God; as a person, God has limitations, and that which has limitations is not absolutely infinite. If God is conceived of as absolutely infinite, in his substance as in his attributes, then all idea of personality respecting him must be given up; for personality implies limitations. If the idea of personality in respect of God be retained, then the idea of absolute infinity regarding him must be abandoned. That "infinite" which does not include all things and all qualities is not absolutely infinite. The only persons who consistently hold to the absolute infinity of God are those who identify God with the universe—regarding God and the universe as one and the same. So long as orthodox Christians regard God as distinct from what they call the "material universe," that long they teach but a modified infinity respecting God. They really mean that God is only infinite "*after his kind.*" One of Spinoza's definitions may help us here. He says a thing is *finite* after its kind "*when it can be limited by another thing or the same nature,*" as one body is limited by another (Ethics Def. ii.) is not a thing *infinite* after its kind, then, when it is *not* limited by anything of the same nature? Is not this the necessary corollary of Spinoza's definition of the "finite after its kind?" and do not those who regard God as distinct from the universe, and at the same time ascribe infinity to him, mean only that he is infinite "after his kind?" There may be, then, many infinites after their kind; and this view is sustained by the fact that such infinites do exist. Duration or time is infinite after its kind, because not limited by anything of the same nature. Space is infinite after its kind, for the same reason; so, too, are force and matter. If there may be two or four things infinite after their kind, because not limited by anything of the same nature, are many infinites inconceivable? Moreover, when *infinity* is thus understood—and it can be understood when relating to God in no other way—the difficulty raised by the latter part of Mr. V.'s proposition, viz., that, if there were several infinite beings, they would differ from each other by some perfection, and when one would have a perfection that the other lacked, the latter would not be infinite, etc.—disappears; for when beings are infinite after their kind, they are only limited by things of a different nature, and therefore the perfections possessed by those beings of a different nature will constitute no limitation to their infinity.

3—"*If one is infinite nothing can be added to it.*"

This maybe true of the absolutely infinite; for that which is absolutely infinite must be the sum total of all existence. To say, therefore, that something existed in addition to this sum total, and could be added to it, would be illogical. But infinity in this conception cannot be ascribed to God; for we have seen that God is only infinite in faculties and power, not in person, hence not absolutely infinite; therefore, this statement in the gentleman's philosophy can have no bearing on the controversy in which we are engaged.

4—"*Finite parts could not belong to the infinite essence, else they would communicate their limitations to God.*"

When the Son of God, Jesus, took on a human body of flesh and bone, was not that which is finite, his body, added to the infinite in Jesus Christ? Did the finite body, taken on by the spirit of Jesus, communicate its limitations to God? And is Jesus, now in his resurrected, immortal body of flesh and bones, less "infinite" than before his spirit was united to his body? If one accepts Mr. V.'s doctrine of the absolute infinity of God, then one must believe that Jesus "the Word," who "was in the beginning with God," who "was God"—was not "made flesh;" that is, did not take on a body of flesh and bone; for the body of Jesus was finite; it had, in fact, all the limitations of a man's body, and Mr. V.'s doctrine tells us that "*if one is infinite, nothing can be added to it*"—therefore the "Word," who "was God," could not have been made flesh. If, on the other hand, one accepts the fact, so well attested by holy scriptures, *viz.*, that Jesus, "the Word," "who was God," *was* made flesh, *did* take on a body that was flesh and bones, even though that body was finite, then one must reject the philosophy of Mr. V., which says the infinite may not take on finite parts, for the reason that they would communicate their limitations to the infinite, and thus destroy its infinity.

It is not difficult to see that something is wrong with the philosophy of Mr. Van Der Donckt, which thus constantly brings us in conflict with the revelations of God in the scriptures, and especially in the revelation of God in Jesus Christ.

In what state do these considerations leave the argument? Mr. Van Der Donckt reaches the conclusion, from the premise that *several finite things cannot produce the infinite*, that God cannot be a compound of finite parts. Yet we have seen that what is called the material universe, so far as it is possible for the mind of man to apprehend infinity, answers to his conception of the infinite; and we know that the universe is made up of finite parts; and that in its last analysis, it is but the aggregation of finite atoms.

From the premise that *many infinite beings are inconceivable*, Mr. V. reaches the conclusion that God cannot be a compound of infinite parts. But upon principles of sound reason, we have seen that things are infinite after their kind when not limited by anything of the same nature; and his premise of a number of infinites being inconceivable is destroyed by the actual existence of a number of infinites after their kind, such as duration, space, matter, spirit, and hence the absolute infinite, if existing at all, must be composed of an aggregation of infinities after their kind.

From the premise that *if one is infinite nothing can be added to it*, the gentleman implies the conclusion that God is infinite and therefore nothing can be added to him. Still, since Jesus was the Word, and the Word was and is God, we have seen that something was added to whatever of infinity there was in God, the Word, *viz.*, what orthodox Christians call his "humanity" — that is, the pre-existent, divine spirit of Jesus took on a tabernacle of flesh — something finite was added to the infinite of God, the Word, and that, too, let me say, without communicating any limitations to the infinity possessed of God.

On these several premises, Mr. Van Der Donckt bases his general conclusion: —

> Therefore, the infinite Being is not composite, but simple or spiritual. Therefore, he is not, nor ever was, a man, who is a composite being.

But since the premises themselves have been shown to be utterly untenable, as relating to God, as revealed in the scriptures, and in the person and nature of Jesus Christ, the conclusions are wrong; and the facts established are that while God in mind, faculties and in power is doubtless infinite, in person he is finite; and as his spirit is united to a body, he is composite, not simple; and as Jesus Christ was God manifested in the flesh, the express image of God the Father's person, the counterpart of his nature, and yet at the same time was a man— it is neither unscriptural, nor unphilosophical to hold that God, even the Father, is also a perfected, exalted man.

III.
MR. VAN DER DONCKT'S CONTRASTS BETWEEN MAN AND GOD.

Of the Intellectual Powers of Man.

Mr. Van Der Donckt insists that man can never become a God, because he "is finite or limited in everything; ever changeable and changing, ever susceptible of improvement." Granting that man is ever susceptible of improvement, ought not the gentleman to proceed with some caution before dogmatically asserting that there are to be limitations to man's enlargement, to his progress, and to his attainments? Given the susceptibility to improve, never ending duration through which the processes of improvement shall continue, and God to direct such processes, who can dogmatize upon the limitations of the Intelligences now known as men? It is not enough to say in reply to this that the "finite can never become infinite;" nor to argue that if God were an exalted man he would possess contradictory attributes, such as being both finite and infinite, compound and simple. We have already seen that when one undertakes to treat of the infinite, he is dealing with the unknown, dealing with terms that stand for the names of things of which the mind can form no adequate or satisfactory conception. But so far as the Father and the Son are concerned—personages held out to us in the scriptures as Gods—we have seen that absolute infinity may not be predicted of them. In person, form and the general nature of their physical being, they have limitations; and whatever of infinity or simplicity is ascribed to them must be ascribed to mind and attributes, not to personality. Seeing then, that the revelation of God in the scriptures, and especially in the revelation of God in the person and character of Jesus Christ, forces upon us a conception of God that represents him as concrete rather than abstract, finite in some respects, and infinite in others; and as compound rather than simple—it follows that urging the apparent absurdity of such characteristics in Deity as these is of no avail against the facts in the revelations God has given of himself. And now, as the limitations found in man, as to his physical person, nature, etc.,—and which are supposed by Mr. V. to forever bar man from attaining divinity— are found also in God the Father and in God the Son, it is quite clear that these physical limitations may not be urged as insuperable obstacles to man attaining divinity. As for the spirit of man—the mind—who can say what its metes and bounds are, much less what they shall be? Who comprehends its powers? Who dare say that it is not potentially infinite? and shall be hereafter actually infinite after its kind? I have already called attention to the fact that it is said of Messiah that in his humiliation, his judgment was taken away, which doubtless means that in his earth-life his intellectual and spiritual powers were somewhat veiled; and with man doubtless it is the same; in his earth-life that intellectual excellence which he enjoyed as a spirit in the mansions of the Father is veiled; but veiled as it is, there is of its manifestations sufficient to inspire one with awe, and make him hesitate ere pronouncing dogmatically upon its nature or its limitations. To illustrate my thought: I am this moment sitting at my desk, and am enclosed by the four walls of my room—limited as to my personal presence to this spot. But by the mere act of my will, I find I have the power to project myself in thought to any part of the world. Instantly I can be in the crowded streets of the world's metropolis. I walk through its well remembered thoroughfares, I hear the rush and roar of its busy multitudes, the rumble of vehicles, the huckster's cries, the cab-man's calls, sharp exclamations and quick retorts in the jostling throngs, the beggar's piping cry, the sailor's song, fragments of conversation, broken strains of music, the blare of trumpets, the neighing of horses, ear-piercing whistles, ringing of bells, shouts, responses, rushing trains and all that mingled din and soul-stirring roar that rises in clamor above the great town's traffic.

At will, I leave all this and stand alone on mountain tops in Syria, India, or overlooking old Nile's valley, wrapped in the awful grandeur of solemn silence. Here I may bid fallen empires rise and pass in grand procession before my mental vision and live again their little lives: fight once more their battles; begin again each petty struggle for place, for power, for control of the world's affairs; revive their customs: live again their loves and hates, and preach once more their religions and their philosophies—all this the mind may do, and that as easily and as quickly as in thought it may leave this room, cross the street to a neighbor's home, and there take note of the familiar objects within his habitation. Nor does this begin to indicate all the power of the mind in these respects. Though the sun is ninety-two millions of miles away, on the instant, in thought, one may stand upon it within its resplendent atmosphere. In the same manner and with equal ease, one may project himself to the Pole Star, though it is so distant that it requires forty years for a ray of light to pass through the intervening space between that star and our earth, and still light travels at the rate of one hundred and eighty-six thousand miles per second! Nor is the end yet. In like manner and with equal ease one may instantly project himself in thought from within the four walls of his room to those more distant constellations of stars known to exist out in the depths of space, whence it would require a ray of light a million years to reach our earth; yet standing there in a world so distant from ours, one would find himself still centered in the universe, and out beyond him, in a straight line from the earth whence he has traveled, would extend other realms in splendor no less magnificent. From the vasty deep of these realms, he could call up other worlds, and people them with creatures of his thought, as one may call up empires to pass in mighty procession before him in the Nile or in the Ganges valley.

Distance, then, to the mind of man, is as nothing. The infinity of extension, and of duration also, is matched by the infiniteness of man's mind, though that mind has a local habitation and a name within a tabernacle of flesh and bone. This is but a glimpse at the infinite powers of the mind of man in one direction, and under circumstances that somewhat veil the splendor of his intellectual and spiritual glory; what those powers may be in all particulars when man shall be made free from the restricting and depressing environment of the present earth-life, no one may say; but enough may be seen from what is here pointed out to establish the firm belief that, as the intellectual powers in man rise to match the infinitudes of extension and duration, as indicated, so, too, in all other respects shall the mind of man, when free, rise to the harmony of all the infinities that make up the universe. And it is not inconceivable (in view of the great spiritual and intellectual powers even now discernible in him) that the time will come when man will not only be able to project himself in thought to any part of the universe, no matter how distant, but in his future immeasurably exalted state he may project both thought and consciousness equally to all points of the universe at once, steadfastly maintain them there, and thus be all-knowing, everywhere present in thought, in consciousness—in spirit in fact—as God now is; and if, as it is reasonable to believe will be the case, his power equals his knowledge; and his freedom of volition equals his knowledge and his power—then, indeed, will man be a spiritual and intellectual force immanent in the universe, both to will and to do, even as God.

Jesus prayed that his disciples might be one with each other even *as* he and the Father are one (St. John 17:11); that they all might be one; and as the Father was in Christ, and as Christ was in the Father, so also would Messiah have the disciples to be one in him and in the Father, that they might all be one with the Father and the Son, and with each other, even as the Father and the Son are one (St. John 17; 21,22.) But for the disciples to be "one" with the Father and the Son, in the complete sense in which the Messiah here prayed for that "oneness," necessarily means to be "like" the Father, and that "likeness" can rise to the full height of its perfection only when it reaches equality with those with whom the disciples are to be "one" or "like." If man may not rise to the height of divinity, how shall this prayer of the Christ be realized? Or must we believe that the divine wisdom in the Son of God exercised itself in praying for that which is unattainable, that which is not only absurd but impossible? It is unthinkable that the divine nature shall be brought down to be "one" with men; so that if the "oneness" which also involves "likeness," be realized, in fulfilment of Messiah's prayer, it must be by men rising to divinity, Mr. Van Der Donckt's "impossibilities" to the contrary notwithstanding.

"Behold the Man Has Become as One of Us."

To illustrate his contention that man can never rise to the quality of divinity, Mr. Van Der Donckt indulges in comparisons between man and God; and, to emphasize that contrast, challenges well-known men of science to the exercise of creative powers, contrasts the frequent collisions upon our railroads with the order, regularity, and safety of the movements among the planetary systems where never a collision occurs; and then indulges in such folly as this:

> They (astronomers) can indeed predict transits and eclipses; but suppose astronomers from New Zealand, on their way to America to observe this fall's moon eclipse, meet with an accident in mid-ocean, would they at once send this wireless telegram to the United States' stargazers assembled say at Lick Observatory: "Belated by leak. Please retard eclipse two hours that we may not miss it." As well might all the telescope men in the world combined, attempt to fetch down the rings of Saturn for the construction of a royal race track, as pretend to control movements of the heavenly bodies.

The gentleman also points out how precarious are the powers of man:

> The helpless babe of yesterday may indeed rival Mozart, Haydn, and Paderewski, but tomorrow he may rise with lame hands and pierced ear-drums; and millions of worshipers of the shattered idol are powerless to restore it to the musical world.

This part of the gentleman's argument sinks far below the general high level of his Reply, and is unworthy of his intelligence. I have already pointed out, that Latter-day Saints do not teach that man in his present state and condition is a God. On the contrary, they admit man's narrowness, weakness, imperfections and limitations; and also recognize the great gulf stretching between man in his present state and that dignity of divinity to which somewhere and sometime in the eternities it is within his province and power to attain. Mr. Van Der Donckt's comparisons, therefore, between God and man, in the latter's present condition, are not in point, for the reason that the Latter-day Saints do not claim that man is now a Deity, only as he may be thought potentially one. Taking the highest type of man to start with, consider him as raised from the dead and hence immortal; give him Gods for guides, teachers, and companions, with the universe for the field of his operations, then let Mr. V. or anyone else, say what man's attainments will be one thousand millions of years hence; and that period, let it be remembered, long as it may seem to man's petty methods of computing duration, is but as a moment in the existence of an immortal being. Let Mr. Van Der Donckt institute his comparisons from that point of man's career, instead of from the present point of man's weakness and mortality, and then say if ultimately divinity seems so unattainable as now. If he shall say he is unable to institute his comparisons at the point proposed, because what man will then be is unknown, I shall agree with him; but let him acknowledge, as perforce he must, that man will be immeasurably advanced beyond what he is now; also let him admit the injustice he does our doctrine by insisting upon making his comparisons between God and man as the latter now stands, under the effects of the fall, and in his humiliation and weakness.

After indulging in the aforesaid comparisons, Mr.V. further remarks:

> I fear Mr. B. H. Roberts will be inclined to think God jealous because he gives man no show for comparison with him. This would certainly be a less blunder of the Utah man, ("I will not give my glory to another"—Isaiah 42:8) than his contention, which is a mere echo of Satan's promise in Paradise: "You shall be as Gods." (Genesis 3:5.)

To which I answer, not so; the contention of the "Utah man" is not the echo of Satan's promise, "ye shall be as Gods." On the contrary, the "Utah man's" contention is bottomed on the august and sure word of God, uttered in Eden, when he said of the man Adam—"*Behold the man is become as one of us, to know good and evil*" (Genesis 3:22)—a passage which the Reverend gentleman seems to have overlooked.

OF THE UNITY OF GOD.

There remains to be considered the Unity of God.

The Latter-day Saints believe in the unity of the creative and governing force or power of the universe as absolutely as any orthodox Christian sect in the world. One cannot help being profoundly impressed with the great truth that creation, throughout its whole extent, bears evidence of being *one* system, presents at every point *unity* of design, and *harmony* in its government. Nor am I unmindful of the force there is in the deduction usually drawn from these premises, viz., that the Creator and Governor of the universe, must necessarily be *one*. But I am also profoundly impressed by another fact that comes within the experience of man, at least to a limited extent, viz., the possibility of intelligences arriving at perfect agreement, so as to act in absolute unity. We see manifestations of this principle in human governments, and other human associations of various kinds. And this, too, is observable, viz, that the greater and more perfect the intelligence the more perfect can the unity of purpose and of effort become: so that one needs only the existence of perfect intelligences to operate together in order to secure perfect oneness, whence shall come the *one* system evident in the universe, exhibiting at every point *unity* of design, and perfect *harmony* in its government. In other words, "oneness" can be the result of perfect agreement among Many Intelligences as surely as it can be the result of the existence of One Only Intelligence. Also, the decrees and purposes of the perfectly united Many can be as absolute as the decrees and purposes of the One Only Intelligence. One is also confronted with the undeniable fact that inclines him to the latter view as the reasonable explanation of the "Oneness" that is evidently in control of the universe—*the fact that there are in existence many Intelligences, and, endowed as they are with free will, it cannot be denied that they influence, to some extent, the course of events and the conditions that obtain.* Moreover, it will be found, on careful inquiry, that the explanation of the "Oneness" controlling in the universe, on the theory that it results from the perfect agreement or unity of Many Intelligences,[A] is more in harmony with the revelations of God on the subject than the theory that there is but One Only Intelligence that enters into its government. This theory Mr. Van Der Donckt, of course, denies, and this is the issue between us that remains to be tested.

[Footnote A: John Stuart Mill, in his Essay on *Theism*, in speaking of the evident unity in nature, which suggests that nature is governed by *One Being*, comes very near stating the exact truth in an alternative statement to his first remark, viz.: "At least, if a plurality be supposed, it is necessary to assume so complete a concert of action and unity of will among them, that the difference is for most purposes immaterial between such a theory and that of the absolute unity of the Godhead" (*Essays on Religion—Theism*, p. 133).]

The Reverend gentleman affirms that the first chapter of the Bible "reveals the supreme fact that there is but One Only and Living God."

This I deny; and affirm the fact that the first chapter of the Bible reveals the existence of a plurality of Gods.

It is a matter of common knowledge that the word translated "God" in the first chapter of our English version of the Bible, in the Hebrew, is *Elohim*—plural of Eloah—and should be rendered "Gods"—so as to read "In the beginning the Gods created the heavens and the earth," etc. * * * The Gods said, "Let there be light." * * * The Gods said "Let us make man," etc., etc. So notorious is the fact that the Hebrew plural, *Elohim*, is used by Moses, that a variety of devices have been employed to make the first chapter of Genesis conform to the "One Only God" idea. Some Jews in explanation of it, and in defense of their belief in *One* Only God, hold that there are several Hebrew words which have a plural form but singular meaning—of which Elohim is one—and they quote as proof of this the word *maim*, meaning water, *shamaim*, meaning heaven, and *panim*, meaning the face or surface of a person or thing. "But," says a Christian Jewish scholar,[A] "if we examine these words, we shall find that though apparently they may have a singular meaning, yet, in reality, they have a plural or collective one; thus, for instance, '*maim*,' water, means a collection of waters, forming one collective whole; and thus again '*shamaim*,' heaven, is also, in reality as well as form, of the plural number, meaning what we call in a similar way in English, 'the heavens;' comprehending all the various regions which are included under that title."

[Footnote A: This is Rev. R. Highton, M. A., and Fellow of Queen's College, Oxford. I quote from his lecture on "God a Unity and Plurality," published in a Christian Jewish periodical called *The Voice of Israel*, February number, 1844.]

Other Jewish scholars content themselves in accounting for this inconvenient plural in the opening chapter of Genesis, by saying that in the Hebrew, *Elohim* better represents the idea of "Strong," "Mighty," than the singular form would, and for this reason it was used—a view accepted by not a few Christians. Thus, Dr. Elliott, Professor of Hebrew in Lafayette College, Easton, Pennsylvania, says: "The name *Elohim* (singular Eloah) is the generic name of God, and, being *plural* in form, is probably a plural of excellence and majesty."[A] Dr. Havernick derives the word *Elohim* from a Hebrew root now lost, *Coluit*, and thinks that the plural is used merely to indicate the abundance and super-richness contained in the divine Being. [B] Rabbi Jehuda Hallevi (twelfth century) found in the usage of the plural *Elohim* a protest against idolators, who call each personified power *Eloah* and all collectively *Elohim*. "He interpreted it as the most general name of the Deity, distinguishing him as manifested in the exhibition of his power without reference to his personality or moral qualities, or any special relations which he bears to man."[C] A number of Christian scholars attempt to account for the use of the plural *Elohim* by saying that it foreshadows the doctrine of the Christian Trinity, that is, it recognizes the existence of the three persons in one God. "It is expressive of omnipotent power; and by its use here (first chap. Genesis) in the plural form is obscurely taught at the opening of the Bible, a doctrine clearly revealed in other parts of it, viz., that though God is one, there is a plurality of persons in the Godhead—Father, Son and Spirit, who were engaged in the creative work."[D] This view was maintained at length by Rev. H. Highton, in the Christian Jewish periodical, *The Voice of Israel*, before quoted. "But Calvin, Mercer, Dresius and Ballarmine," says Dr. Hackett,[E] of the Theological Institution of Newton, Massachusetts—editor of Smith's Bible Dictionary—"have given the weight of their authority against an explanation so fanciful and arbitrary."

[Footnote A: "Vindication of Mosaic Authorship of Pentateuch," p. 65.]

[Footnote B: See "Kitto's Biblical Literature," Art. "God," Vol. 1, p. 777.]

[Footnote C: Smith's Bible Dict. (Hackett edition), Art. Jehovah, p. 1242.]

[Footnote D: "Critical and Explanatory Commentary" (Jamieson, Faussett and Brown) Gen. 1:1, 2.]

[Footnote E: Smith's Bible Dictionary (Hackett edition), Art. Jehovah, Vol. 2, p. 1242.]

Others explain the use of the plural "we" or "us," by saying that in the first chapter of Genesis Moses represents God as speaking of himself in that manner, in imitation of the custom of kings, who speak of themselves as "we," instead of in the singular, "I." In other words, it is the royal "we," or "us." This theory, however, is answered, as pointed out by Rev. H. Highton, by the fact that the use of what is called the "royal plural" is a modern, not an ancient, custom; and reference to the usage of the kings of the Bible discloses the fact that they always speak of themselves as "I" or "me," not as "we" or "us."[A]

[Footnote A: *Voice of Israel*, p. 95.]

Modern Bible criticism, usually denominated "The Higher Criticism," is to a great extent—so far as criticism of the five books of Moses is concerned—based upon the exclusive use of the plural *Elohim* in one section, and the use of *Jehovah*, singular, in another. "The Pentateuch, therefore, it is asserted, is composed of two different documents, the one Elohistic, and the other Jehovistic, consequently it cannot be the work of a single author."[A]

[Footnote A: "Vindication of Mosaic Authorship of the Pentateuch" (Elliott) p. 64.)]

With the various devices for accounting for the use of the plural form *Elohim* in the first chapter of the Bible, I have nothing to do here. They are simply pointed out as showing the wide recognition that is given to the fact of the use of the plural form *Elohim* that should be rendered in English "Gods;" and also the perplexity the use of this plural occasions among those whose principles call upon them to harmonize its use with the belief in "One Only God." Mr. Van Der Donckt admits the use of the plural *Elohim*, but undertakes to explain away the force of its use as follows:

> Whenever *Elohim* occurs in the Bible, in sense 1, (meaning the True God) it is employed with singular verbs and singular adjectives.

Relative to this, a friend[A] directs my attention to Genesis 1:26: "Let *us* make man in *our* image," etc., which in Hebrew is *Maach*—"we will make," first person plural future of the verb *Asah: betsalmaun—be* "in;" *tselem*, "image;" *Nu*, "our," possessive adjective, first person plural. So that in Genesis 1:26, we have a case where *Elohim* is used in connection with a plural verb and also a plural possessive adjective, and Mr. Van Der Donckt will not say that *Elohim* does not, in Genesis 1:26, refer to true Gods. Again in Genesis 3:22—"Man is become as one of *us*," Mr. Ramseyer suggests that here, again, the pronoun used is in the first person plural. I find this view of both these passages sustained by Rev. H. Highton in the lecture before quoted. First he says:

[Footnote A: Prof. A. Ramseyer, of the Latter-day Saints' University.]

> The Hebrew word meaning God, is itself a plural word, implying thereby, as we contend, a plurality of persons in the Godhead * * We find the plural word *Elohim*, or God, most usually, *though not always*, coupled with a singular verb or adjective. * * * but lest from the constant use of the word *Elohim* with the singular number, we should be led to suppose that God is in no sense a plurality, it has pleased him by the inspiration of his Holy Spirit, to cause that it should be sometimes used with a plural verb or adjective. I will mention some of the clearest passages in which it is so used, that you may be enabled to refer to them in the Hebrew. You will find it used in a plural verb in Genesis 20:13. "And it came to pass, when God caused me to wander from my father's house," etc.; and again in Genesis 35:7,

"And he built there an altar, and called the place *El-Bethel*: because their God appeared unto him." And with a plural adjective in Joshua 34:19, and again in Deut. 5:26 (in the original Hebrew, 5:23).

But we have not merely the plural use of the word *Elohim* to mention in this part of the argument; we have some very distinct passages, still more directly implying the plurality of persons. There is a very remarkable place of the kind in Eccle. 12:1, where it says: "Remember now thy Creator in the days of thy youth." In the original Hebrew the word is in the plural, and if translated literally, would be "Remember now thy Creators," etc. * * * In connection with this expression of Solomon about man's Creators, it is a very remarkable circumstance, that in the account of the creation of man, given by Moses in the book of Genesis, the plural is also directly used, for it is there recorded, Genesis 1, 26, "*And God said let us make*" etc., or "*we will make*," etc., so that Moses as well as Solomon very emphatically declares that the great Creator of man consists of more than one person; for whom could God have been addressing when he said, "*Let us make*," etc.? I know that in order to escape the obvious conclusion to be drawn from the passage, it has been asserted that God was here addressing and taking counsel with the angels but this explanation cannot in any degree bear the test of an accurate examination of the passage; for is there the slightest ground for supposing that the angels took any part in the creation of man, when God said, "*Let us make*"? or shall we say that man was made in the image and likeness of the angels, when God said, "*Let us make*" etc., "*in our image*?" Surely not, for Moses expressly adds, (v. 27) "*So God created man in his own image, in the image of God created he him, male and female created he them.*" But there are some other passages which we ought to examine, where God in the same way speaks of himself in the plural number. Thus in Genesis 3:22, "And the Lord God said, "Behold the *man is become as one of us*, to know good and evil; and now, lest he put forth his hand and take also of the tree of life, and eat and live forever," etc. There are no words which I know which could more distinctly assert the plurality of persons in God than these, where he says "one of us." M. Leeser, of Philadelphia, the editor of the *Occident*, which is the

American Jewish magazine, in his sermon on the Messiah, explains this passage as spoken to the angels—"one of us," meaning himself and the angels;—but never can I believe that the Great Everlasting Creator could thus put himself on a level with the created angels, and say "one of us," * * * he would either have said to the angels, "Behold, man has become as one of you," or else have said, "Behold, the man has become like me, to know good and evil."

This view of Genesis 1:26 is also maintained by Prof. W. H. Chamberlin, of Brigham Young College, Logan, Utah, in the *Era* for November, 1902. He says: That *Elohim* was used in the plural sense is shown in the twenty-sixth verse, where the *Elohim*, in referring to themselves use the plural suffix *Nu* "our," twice, and they also use the plural form of the verb *Naaseh*, "let us make." The Professor also adds the illustration of Genesis 11:7: where *Nerdhah*, "let us descend," and *Nabhlah*, "let us confuse," two verbs in the plural, proceed from the mouth of God.[A]

[Footnote A: I commend Professor Chamberlin's whole article to the reader as most worthy of his attention at this point; and personally, I wish to thank the Professor for it as a most timely contribution to the controversy. The whole article is published in Chapter v.]

In the light of these facts, the statement of Mr. V. that whenever *Elohim* occurs in the Bible, as meaning the true God, it is employed with singular verbs and singular adjectives, seems to have been made without that careful consideration which the importance of the declaration required. The facts adduced in the foregoing stand also against Mr. V.'s contention that whenever the plural "gods" occurs in Holy Writ, it applies only "to false gods and idols;" or "to representatives of God, such as angels, judges, kings." They were not false gods nor representatives of God merely, who said: "Let *us* make man in *our* image" (Genesis i:26); nor false gods, or mere representatives of God merely, who said: "The man has become as one of *us*" (Genesis 2:7); and so also with other passages in the quotation from Rev. Highton's lecture.

Here it may be as well to note the remarks of Mr. Van Der Donckt with reference to the "Mormon" Church leaders' knowledge of Hebrew. The Rev. gentleman is of the opinion that,

> Had the "Mormon" Church leaders known Hebrew, the original language of the book of Moses and nearly the whole of the Old Testament, they would not have been guilty of the outrageous blunders of the Pearl of Great Price and of the Catechism.

Mr. V. then quotes from our Catechism the account of the creation taken from the Pearl of Great Price, in which the plural "Gods" is used instead of the singular form "God." It is probable that the "Mormon" Church leaders were better acquainted with Hebrew than Mr. V. gives them credit for. A number of years ago (1870) a certain chaplain of the United States Senate presumed not a little on the ignorance of a "Mormon" Church leader—Elder Orson Pratt—respecting Hebrew, and ventured, in the notable debate held by them in the "Mormon" Tabernacle, at Salt Lake City, to parade the few Hebrew stem-words, and their derivatives, which he had conned with care before leaving Washington, with a view of making them effective in support of the marginal reading of *Leviticus* 18 and 18 in our common English version. To the chaplain's surprise, the "Mormon" apostle was able to follow him in the discussion of the original Hebrew text, and demonstrated that he had a knowledge of Hebrew which made his opponent's special preparation of a few Hebrew words and passages look very much like a cheap bid for a reputation for learning, which the chaplain's knowledge of Hebrew, at least, did not warrant. Nor is that all the story. Elder Pratt—having observed the stress which the chaplain had laid upon the marginal rendering of *Leviticus* 18:18, in a discourse delivered in Washington, D. C., before President Grant, members of his cabinet, and members of Congress—to call Dr. Newman out, to give him confidence to introduce his defense of the marginal rendering of the passage in the debate at Salt Lake City—Elder Pratt quoted the marginal reading of an unimportant passage, and thus invited the discussion of the text in the Hebrew. The Elder's bait took, the discussion largely turned, after that, upon the text in question, much to the chagrin of the Senate's chaplain; and *Leviticus* 18:18 has been somewhat historical hereabouts, and in Washington, ever since.

But how came Orson Pratt acquainted with Hebrew? The fact is, that in the winter of 1835-6 a school of languages was established by the Church, at Kirtland, which many of the leading Elders of the Church attended, Joseph Smith and Orson Pratt being among the number; and Professor Joshua Seixas, of Hudson, Ohio, was employed as teacher. The Elders were enthusiastic in their study of Hebrew, and after Prof. Seixas' term as teacher had expired, the class was continued with Joseph Smith as instructor, Orson Pratt continuing in attendance on the school. The "Mormon" Church leaders, I repeat, were better acquainted with Hebrew than Mr Van Der Donckt gives them credit for; besides, the blunders which Mr. Van Der Donckt has made in his assertions concerning the use of the plural *Elohim*, in the Old Testament, makes it rather clear that he is scarcely competent to be a judge of anybody's Hebrew. Moreover, the passage he quotes from our Catechism, where, in the account of creation, the plural "Gods" is used, is not a quotation from the Bible at all; but a translation from a record called the "Book of Abraham," which came into the hands of the Prophet Joseph Smith from the catacombs of Egypt. So that Mr. V.'s attempted criticism of what he evidently takes to be extracts of translations from parts of the Bible, is not in point at all, since they are translated extracts from a book that forms no part of the Bible. And is it not evident throughout that Mr. Van Der Donckt has rushed into the discussion without being sufficiently informed concerning the doctrines upon which he undertakes to animadvert?

Of the Father Alone, Being God.

Referring to the admission in my discourse that conceptions of God, to be true, must be in harmony with the New Testament, Mr. Van Der Donckt proceeds to quote passages from the New Testament, in support of the idea that there is but one God:

> One is good, God (Matt. 19:17). Thou shalt love the Lord thy God (Luke 10:27). My Father of whom you say that he is your God (John 8:54). Here Christ testified that the Jews believed in only one God.
>
> The Lord is a God of all knowledge (I Kings 2). ("Mormon" Catechism V. Q. 10 and 2.11).
>
> Of that day and hour no one knoweth, no not the angels of heaven, but the Father alone (Matthew 24:36).
>
> No one knoweth who the Son is but the Father (Luke 10:22).
>
> Therefore, no one is God but one, the Heavenly Father.
>
> In another form: the All-knowing alone is God. The Father alone is all-knowing. Therefore, the Father alone is God.

In the conclusion of the syllogism, "Therefore, *the Father alone is God,*" Mr. V. himself seems to have become suddenly conscious of having stumbled upon a difficulty which he ineffectually seeks to remove in a foot note. If it be true, as Mr. V. asserts it is, that *the Father alone is God*, then it must follow that the Son of God, Jesus Christ, is *not* God; that the Holy Ghost is *not* God! Yet the New Testament, in representing the Father as addressing Jesus, says—"Thy throne, O God, is forever and forever" (Heb. 1:8). Here is the positive word of the Father that Jesus, the Son, is God; for he addresses him as such. To say, then, that *the Father alone is God,* is to contradict the Father. Slightly paraphrasing the rather stern language of Mr. V., I might ask: If God the Father so emphatically declares that Jesus is God, has any one the right to contradict him by affirming that the Father alone is God? But Mr. V. insists that the Bible contradicts the Bible; in other words, that God, the author of the Bible, contradicts himself: "To say such a thing, is downright blasphemy!" But Mr. V. will say he has explained all that in his foot note. Has he? Let us see. "Therefore the Father alone is God," is the conclusion of his syllogism; and the foot note—"To the exclusion of another or separate divine being, but not to the denial of the distinct divine personalities of the Son and the Holy Ghost *in* the One Divine Being." But that is the mere assumption of my Catholic friend. When he says that *the Father alone is God*, it must be to the exclusion of every other being, or part of being, or person, and everything else, or language means nothing. Mr. V.'s foot note helps him out of his difficulty not at all.

The creed to which Mr. Van Der Donckt subscribes—the Athanasian—says: "So the Father is God, the Son is God, and the Holy Ghost is God." Now, if the quality of "all-knowing" is essential to the attributes of true Deity, then Jesus and the Holy Ghost must be all-knowing, or else not true deity.

But what of the difficulty presented by Mr. V.'s contention: "The All-knowing alone is God, the Father alone is All-knowing, therefore, the Father alone is God?" Mr. V. constructs this mighty syllogism upon a very precarious basis. It reminds one of a pyramid standing on its apex. He starts with the premise that "The Lord is a God of all knowledge:" then he discovers that there is one thing that Jesus, the Son of God does not know—the day and hour when Jesus will come to earth in his glory—"Of that day and hour no one knoweth; no, not the angels of heaven, but the Father alone (Matt 24:36)—therefore, the Father alone is God!" In consideration of facts such as are included in Mr. V.'s middle term, one is bound, in the nature of things, to take into account time, place and circumstances. In the case in question, the Twelve disciples had come to Jesus, and among other questions asked him what should be the sign of his own glorious coming to earth again. The Master told them the signs, but said of the day and hour of that coming no one knew, but his Father only. Hence, Jesus did not know, hence Jesus did not possess all knowledge, hence, according to Mr. V., Jesus was not God! But Jesus was referring to the state of matters at the particular time when he was speaking; and it does not follow that the Father would exclude his Son Jesus forever, or for any considerable time, from the knowledge of the time of the glorious advent of the Son of God to the earth. As Jesus rose to the possession of all power "in heaven and in earth" (Matt. 28:18), so also, doubtless, he rose to the possession of all knowledge in heaven and in earth; "For the Father loveth the Son, and showeth him all things that he himself doeth" (John 5:20), and, in sharing with the Son his power, and his purposes, would doubtless make known to him the day and hour of the glorious advent of Christ to the earth.

Of the Oneness of the Father, Son and Holy Ghost. Is it Physical Identity?

I next consider Mr. Van Der Donckt's argument concerning the Father, the Son and the Holy Ghost being "the same identical Divine Essence." Mr. V. bases this part of his argument on the words of Messiah—"I and my Father are one" (John 10:30); and claims that here "Christ asserts his *physical*, not merely moral, union with the Father." He holds also that in the Latin translation of the words of Jesus is better exhibited the construction he contends for: hence, I give the Latin and his remarks upon it, that we may have his contention before us at its very best. *Ego et Pater unum sumus*—I and my Father are one.

> If Christ had meant one in *mind or one morally* and not *substantially*, he would have used the masculine gender, Greek *eis, (unus)*—and not the neuter *en, (unum)*—as he did. No better interpreters of our Lord's meaning can be found than his own hearers. Had he simply declared his moral union with the Father, the Jews would not have taken up stones in protest against him making himself God, and asserting his identity with the Father. Far from retracting His statement or correcting the Jews' impression, Jesus insists that, as he is the Son of God he had far more right to declare himself God than the scripture had to call mere human judges gods, and he corroborates his affirmation of his *physical* unity with his Father by saying: "The Father is in me, and I am in the Father," which evidently signifies the same as verse 30: I and the Father are one and the same individual being, the One God.

It is amusing sometimes to observe how the learned disagree about the meaning of words—especially in the languages called dead. It must be admitted in favor of Mr. V.'s contention that the Fathers of the Council of Sardica, A. D. 347, expressly scouted the opinion that the union of the Father and Son consisted in consent and concord only, and apprehended the oneness of the Father and the Son to be a strict unity of substance;[A] still, before that time, a number of the so-called Christian Fathers, some among the most influential, too, held to a contrary opinion, as the following from Dr. Priestley's *History of the Corruptions of Christianity*, with the accompanying references to the works of the Christian Fathers themselves, will show:

[Footnote: Theodoret, Book II, Chap. 8.]

Notwithstanding the supposed derivation of the Son from the Father, and therefore their being of the same substance, most of the early Christian writers thought the text, "I and my Father are one," was to be understood of an unity or harmony of disposition only. Thus Tertullian[A] observes, that the expression is *unum*, one thing, not one person; and he explains it to mean unity, likeness, conjunction, and of the love that the Father bore to the Son. Origen says, let him consider the text, "*All that believe were of one* [unum] *heart and of one* [unum] *soul*," and then he will understand this, "*I and my Father are one*,"[B] [unum]. Novatian says: "One thing (*unum*) being in the neuter gender, signifies an agreement of society, *not an unity of person*," and he explains it by this passage in Paul: "He that planteth and he that watereth are both one" [unum][C].

[Footnote A: Against Prexas, Chap. 22, p. 513.]

[Footnote B: Against Celsum, Lib. 8, p. 386.]

[Footnote C: *Ibid*, Chap. 27, p. 99.]

Relative to Messiah's hearers being the best interpreters of our Lord's meaning in this case, I suggest that Mr. V. has limited himself too exclusively to this one passage for their interpretation of Messiah's meaning. Mr. V.'s argument is that if Jesus had only declared his moral not his physical union with God, the Jews would not have taken up stones in protest against his making himself God, and asserting his identity with the Father. Let us see. The passage quoted by Mr. V. is not the only one in which Jesus asserts his divinity. Jesus healed a man on the Sabbath. The Jews sought to slay him because he had done this thing on the Sabbath day. "But Jesus answered them, My Father worketh hitherto, and I work. Therefore the Jews sought the more to kill him, because he not only had broken the Sabbath day, but said also that God was his Father, *making himself equal with God*" (John 5:15-18). Observe that this is the same witness that Mr. V. quotes—St. John; and the offense for which they seek to kill Jesus is not because he asserts his *identity* with the Father, but because he makes himself "*equal* with God." Hence, the argument of Mr. V., based on the assumption that Jesus asserted not his moral but his physical union or identity with God; and his claim that the Jews would not have sought Messiah's life but for the reason that he claimed physical identity with the Father, falls to the ground, for the reason that we find that the Jews were eager to kill him for asserting not his *physical union* with God, but his *equality* with God.

But I shall test Mr. V.'s exegesis of the passage in question by the examination of another passage involving the same ideas, the same expressions; and this in the Latin as well as in the English. Jesus prayed for his disciples as follows:

Holy Father, keep through thine own name those whom thou hast given me, *that they may be one, as we are.* * * * * Neither pray I for these [the disciples] alone, but for them also which shall believe on me through their word; *that they all may be one:* * * * *that they may be one, even as we are one.* [A]

[Footnote A: St. John 17:11, 20, 21, 22.]

In Latin, the clauses written in *Italics* in the above, stand: *Ut sint unum, sicut et nos* (verse 11), "that they may be one, just as we." So in verse 22: *Ut sint unum, sicut et nos unum sumus*; "that they may be one in us, even as we one are." Here *unum*, "one," is used in the same manner as it is in St. John, 10:30—"Ego et Pater *unum* sumus." "I and Father one are." Mr. V. says that *unum* in the last sentence means, one thing, one essence; hence, Christ's physical union, or identity of substance, with the Father; not agreement of mind, or concord of purpose, or moral union. Very well, for the moment let us adopt his exposition, and see where it will lead us. If *unum* in the sentence, *Ego et Pater unum sumus*, means "one thing," "one substance, or essence," and denotes the physical union of the Father and Son in one substance, then it means the same in the sentence—*ut sint unum, sicut et nos*; that is, "that they [the disciples] may be one [unum] just as we are." So in the other passage before quoted where the same words occur.

Again, to Messiah's statement: "*Ego et Pater unum sumus*"—"I and my Father are one."—Mr. V. thinks his view of this passage—that it asserts the identity or physical union of the Father and the Son—is strengthened by the fact that it is followed with these remarks of Jesus: "The Father is in me, and I am in the Father." "Which evidently signifies," says Mr. V., "the same as verse 30 (John 10): I and the Father are one and the same individual being, the one God."

But the passage from the prayer of Jesus concerning the oneness of the disciples with the Father and the Son, is emphasized by well-nigh the same words in the context as those which occur in John 10:30, and upon which Mr. V. lays so much stress as sustaining his exposition of the physical union, *viz*: "The Father is in me, and I in him" (verse 38). "Which evidently signifies," Mr. V. remarks, "the same as verse 30: I and my Father are one." Good; then listen: "Holy Father, keep through thine own name those whom thou hast given me, that they may be one *as we are:* * * *as thou Father, art* *in me, and I in thee, that they may be one in us.*" There can be no doubt now but what the union between the disciples and the Father and Son is to be of the same nature as that subsisting between the Father and Son. If the Father and Son are physically one substance or essence, so, too, if the prayer of Jesus is to be realized—as surely it will be—then the disciples are to be physically united with God, in one essence or substance—not just the Twelve disciples, either, for whom Jesus immediately prayed, but those, also, in all generations who shall believe on Christ through the words of his first disciples; that is, all the faithful believers through all generations are to become physically united with God, become the same substance or essence as God himself! Is Mr. Van Der Donckt prepared to accept the inevitable conclusion of his own exposition of John 10:30? If so, then what advantage has the Christian over the Hindoo whom he has called a heathen for so many generations? The sincerest desire of the Hindoo is to be "physically united with God," even if that involve "a blowing out," or the attainment of Nirvana—annihilation—to encompass it. Of course, we had all hoped for better things from the Christian religion. We had hoped for the immortality of the individual man; for his persistence through the ages, as an individual entity, associated with God in loving converse and dearest relations of moral union; but not absorbed, or lost in absolute physical union with him. But if Mr. V.'s exposition of John 10:30 be correct, and a physical union is meant by the words—"I and my Father are one," then all Christians are to be made physically one with God under the prayer of Christ—"That they may be one, *as we are*"—i. e. as the Father and Son are one.

If, however, this doctrine of physical union should be defended up to the point of asserting the physical union of all Christians with each other and with God—and my comparison of this position with that of the heathen Hindoo resented, because that in the case of the Christian after his physical union with, or absorption into God, God would still remain, whereas, with the Hindoo nothing would remain, for his *Nirvana* is but annihilation—I could still ask, what is the difference? for the terms that describe the *Nirvana* of the Hindoo describe also the God of the Christian. "*Nirvana* is represented as something which has no antecedent cause, no qualities, no locality. It is something of which the utmost we may assert is, '*that it is.*'" [A] In all of which one may see Mr. V.'s "*That which is;*" "I Am who Am;" "Infinite Being;" God, "most *simple, or not compound*"—whose "essence is actual being or existence."

[Footnote A: Max Muller, "Chips from a German Workshop," vol. I, p. 285.]

My point is, that the text, "I and my Father are one," refers to a moral union—to a perfect union of purpose and will—not to a unity or identity of substance, or essence: and any other view than this is shown from the argument to be absurd.

But Mr. Van Der Donckt would cry out against the physical union of man with God. Both his interpretation of scripture and his philosophy—especially the latter—would require it. Man and God, in his philosophy, are not of the same nature. God is not physical, while man is. God is not material, but spiritual, that is, according to Mr. V., immaterial, while man is material. Man is finite, God infinite; nothing can be added to the infinite, therefore, man cannot be added to the infinite in physical union. "The nature of the parts would cling to the whole," and the infinity of God would be marred by the physical union of finite parts to him; hence, the oneness of Christians with Christ and God the Father is not a physical oneness. But if the union of the Christians with Christ and God is not to be physical, then neither is the union of Christ and God the Father physical, for the oneness in the one case, is to be the same as the oneness in the other—"that they all may be one; *as* thou Father, art in me, and I in thee, that they may also be one in us * * * * that they may be *one even as we are one*" (John 17:21, 22).

The doctrine of physical union between the Father and the Son, contended for by Mr. V., must be abandoned. There is no help for it, unless he is prepared to admit also the physical union of all the disciples with God—a thing most repugnant to Mr. V.'s principles. With the doctrine of physical identity gone, the "oneness" of the Father and the Son, that Mr. V. contends for, goes also, and two separate and distinct personalities, or Gods, are seen, in the Father and the Son, whose oneness consists not of physical identity, but of agreement of mind, concord of will, and unity of purpose; a oneness born of perfect knowledge, equality of power and dominion. But if a perfect oneness, as above set forth, may subsist between two persons, it may subsist with equal consistency among any number of persons capable of attaining to the same degree of intelligence and power, and thus there would appear some reason for the prayer of Christ, that all his disciples might be one, even as he and the Father are one. And thus one may account for the saying of David: "God standeth in the congregation of the mighty: he judgeth among the Gods" (Psalm 82:1); for such congregations existed in heaven before the foundations of the earth were laid; and such a congregation may yet be made up of the redeemed from our own earth, when attaining to perfect union with God and Christ.

Of The Lord Our God Being One God.

But I shall be asked how all this is to be reconciled with the scriptures quoted by Mr. V., and relied upon as the basis of his argument in this part of the discussion—"Hear, O Israel: The Lord our God is one Lord" (Deut. 6:4); and "I alone am, and there is no other God beside me" (Deut. 32:39); and, also coming to the New Testament, "There is none good but one, that is God" (Matt. 19:17).

The whole apparent difficulty is explained by Paul, who, I think, will be accepted as a remarkably good theologian. He says: "For though there be that are called Gods, whether in heaven or in earth (as there *be* Gods many and Lords many), *but to us there is but one God, the Father*" (I Cor. 8:5, 6). That is, *"pertaining to us,"* as Joseph Smith explains, *"there is but one God."* Ah, but Mr. V. has explained all that, and destroyed all the force of "Mormon" argument, based upon this Corinthian letter passage, by saying that "a man must not be a lawyer to know that the fact that not a few quacks and clowns are *called* doctors does not make them such;" and then follows this—"Neither Christ nor Paul say that they *are* or *were* Gods, but simply that they were *called* Gods!"

One wonders at this, when he takes into account the evident carefulness of Mr. V. as a writer. Jesus, whom he quotes as saying, the beings referred to as Gods are but *called* Gods, not that they *are* so, really fails to give due weight to the Psalm which Jesus quotes: *"I have said ye are Gods, and all of you are children of the Most High"* (Psalm 82:6). Of this scripture, Jesus says: "Is it not written in your law, I said, *ye are Gods,*" and he quotes with evident approval these inspired words of David, for he adds—*"the scripture cannot be broken"* (John 10:33); that is, the scripture of David saying, "ye are Gods," is true, it cannot be gainsaid. Nor is this indorsement of David's utterance weakened by the subsequent remark of Jesus, "If he *called* them Gods unto unto whom the word of God came," etc.; for, when considered in the light of all the Psalmist said, and all that Jesus said, the *"called them Gods"* by no manner of means signifies that they were *not* Gods. David said, "ye *are* Gods, and all of you are *children of the Most High"* (Psalm 82:6). The Jews accused Jesus of blasphemy, because he had said he was the son of God (John 10:36); in defense, Jesus quoted the passage from the Psalms where it is said of men, "ye are Gods; and all of you are children of the Most High"—as showing that he was but claiming for himself the relationship that in the law of the Jews was accorded to men—sons of God, children of the Most High, and hence, he was not a blasphemer. In other words, if the Psalmist could say to those he addressed, "all of you are children of the

Most High," why should he, the Christ, be considered a blasphemer because he called himself the Son of God?

Surely, also, the gentleman has overlooked Paul's very emphatic declaration in the parenthetical part of the sentence he quotes: *viz.*, "There BE Gods many and Lords many; yet to us there is but one God."

Now, consider with this explanation of Paul's the following:

"Hear, O, Israel: the Lord *our* God is one Lord."—*Moses*.

"The head of the Gods appointed *one* God for us."—Joseph Smith.[A]

[Footnote A: From discourse delivered 10th June, 1844. *Mill. Star*, vol. 24, p. 108 *et seq*.]

"He [Aaron] shall be to thee instead of a mouth, and thou shalt be to him instead of God."—*The Lord to Moses* (Exodus 4:16).

"See, I have made thee a God unto Pharaoh."—The Lord unto Moses (Exodus 7:1).

"I believe those Gods that God reveals as Gods, to be sons of God, and all can cry 'Abba, Father.'"—Joseph Smith.[A]

[Footnote A: Sixteenth of June sermon, 1844. *Mill. Star*, vol. 24, p. 140.]

It is evident from the above passages (Exodus 4:16, and Exodus 7:1) that God does appoint men to be Gods, even in this world. Why then should it be considered error to believe that from "the congregation of the Mighty," where "God judgeth among the Gods" (Psalm 82:1), there should be appointed *One* who should be *our* God? And is it strange that from henceforth, the true servants of God should stand up for the dignity and honor and exclusiveness of the power and authority of that One God over this earth against the claims, and to the exclusion of all gods and powers, that men in their vain imaginings set up against this God of heaven and earth, as did Moses, Paul and Joseph Smith? No wonder that Moses sent ringing down through the centuries that clarion sentence: "Hear, O Israel, *Our* God is one Lord;" that the Hebrew race stood as the witness of that one God, and fashioned their nomenclature accordingly; or that Paul said, "Though there be that are called Gods, whether in heaven or in earth—as *there* BE *Gods many, and Lords many*—but *to us* there is but one God;" or that Joseph Smith, in the Dispensation of the Fullness of Times, should take up the same refrain as these ancient servants of God, and say, "Pertaining to us, there is but one God;" "Those Gods whom God reveals as Gods, are sons of God, and all can cry *Abba*, Father!"

Of Our Revelations From God Being Local.

I suggest, as a further evidence, that the view here presented concerning our God, and the assertion of his oneness, that the revelations in the Bible are revelations, in the main, concerning *our* earth and the heavens pertaining to it; that these revelations do not attempt to deal with or furnish an explanation of conditions that obtain throughout the universe; that they do not attempt to give us any explicit information concerning conditions in the constellations of the Pleiades, Orion, Cassiopeia, or Ursa Major, to say nothing of those galaxies of worlds which lie beyond the vision of men, even when aided by the mightiest telescope. In other words, the revelations of the Bible are, in the main, local;[A] it is only here and there that a glimpse of things is given outside of *our* heaven and *our* earth. That being the case, the revelation of God to the Hebrew race was made in a nomenclature accordant with the facts to be expressed, hence—"Hear, O, Israel: *our* God is one Lord." This idea is emphasized in the Book of Moses, found in the Pearl of Great Price. The Lord revealed to Joseph Smith some of the writings of Moses in which the Hebrew prophet makes known the source of his knowledge concerning the creations of God, but it was concerning *our* earth and its heavens of which Moses was commanded to write:

[Footnote A: In support of this view I may here quote the Prophet Joseph Smith. "Everlasting covenant was made between three personages before the organization of this earth, and relates to their dispensation of things to men on the earth: these personages, according to Abraham's record, are called God the first, the Creator; God the second, the Redeemer; and God the third, the witness or Testator" (See Richards' and Little's Compendium, Gems, 289).]

> Worlds without number have I created, * * * but only an account of this earth, and the inhabitants thereof, give I unto you. For behold, there are many worlds that have passed away by the word of my power. And there are many that now stand, and innumerable are they unto man; but all things are numbered unto me, for they are mine, and I know them. And it came to pass that Moses spake unto the Lord, saying: Be merciful unto thy servant, O God, and tell me concerning this earth, and the inhabitants thereof, and also the heavens, and then thy servant will be content. And the Lord spake unto Moses, saying: The heavens, they are many, and cannot be numbered unto man; but they are numbered unto me, for they are mine. * * * And now, Moses, my son, I will speak unto thee concerning this earth upon which thou standest; and thou shalt write the things which I shall speak.

And again the Lord said to Moses:

> And it came to pass that the Lord spake unto Moses, saying: Behold, I will reveal unto you concerning *this* heaven, and *this* earth; write the words which I speak.

So far as the Hebrews were concerned, however, they permitted the truth of the one God idea committed to them to degenerate into mere superstition. Through race pride, and vain glory in their guardianship of the name of the one God, they hedged it about with such secrecy and superstition that, under the pretext of not using the name of God in vain, they prohibited its pronounciation except by the High Priest (and he was to pronounce it but once a year, and that on the day of Atonement, when he entered the Holy of Holies); finally they lost the true pronunciation of the name entirely. The historian of the Jews, Josephus, when writing the antiquities of his people for the information of the Gentiles, stated that it was not lawful for him, though a priest, to utter it.[A] It is a singular fact, but abundantly demonstrated in the history alike of individuals and nations, that when the adversary of men's souls fails in keeping the truth from mankind, he seeks to destroy the effect of that truth by converting it into a mere human superstition. The late Erastus Snow, an Elder in the Church of Jesus Christ of Latter-day Saints, used to present this truth by a very effective figure. Addressing himself to a congregation that had been carried into some excesses of superstitious observances, he said: "We will suppose that drawn immediately in front of you is the line of your exact duty. Satan will make every effort to hold you back from that line. When he discovers that it is impossible to hold you back, his next effort will be to push you as far beyond it as possible; and, being forced beyond the line of duty into superstitious observances, is liable to get you into as much difficulty as being held back from toeing it squarely."

[Footnote A: Smith's "Dictionary of the Bible" (Hackett Edition), vol. 2, art Jehovah. Also Antiquities of the Jews (Josephus), book 2, chap. 12.]

Such was the case with the Jews, with reference to their being made witnesses of the one God idea for our earth. When Lucifer could no longer blind their eyes by the false polytheism of the pagan world, he rushed them over the line of the truth to the other extreme—into the superstitions that have gathered about monotheism, until finally, through such teachers as Aristobulus (150 B. C.) and Philo (contemporary with Messiah), they were brought to accept many of the vagaries of the Grecian pagan philosophy, which, afterwards, as we have seen, were engrafted into the Christian theology.

Of God being One in the Generic Sense.

There is also another sense in which the "Oneness" of God may be apprehended; and yet be in harmony with the doctrines contended for in this "Rejoinder," and the discourse it defends. I have already stated the doctrines of the Church of Christ respecting the immortality of the *ego*, the intelligence of man; saying that it is self-existent, uncreated, and as eternal as God is; indeed, it is the divine in man, it is part of the Eternal; and now the time has come to say something further in reference to this matter. I find a word on the subject fitly spoken by the late Orson Pratt, in a discourse delivered in 1855, in Salt Lake City. He said:

> There is one revelation that this people are not generally acquainted with. I think it has never been published, but probably it will be in the Church History. It is given in questions and answers. The first question is, "What is the name of God in the pure language?" The answer says, "Ahman." "What is the name of the Son of God?" Answer, "Son Ahman, the greatest of all the parts of God, excepting Ahman." "What is the name of men?" "Sons Ahman," is the answer. "What is the name of angels in the pure language?" "Anglo-man." The revelation goes on to say that Sons Ahman are the greatest of all the parts of God excepting Son Ahman, and Ahman, and that Anglo-man are the greatest of all the parts of God excepting Sons Ahman, Son Ahman and Ahman, showing that the angels are a little lower than man. [A] What is the conclusion to be drawn from this? It is that these intelligent beings are all parts of God.[B]

[Footnote A: It may be thought, at the first reading of this statement, "the angels are a little lower than man," is in conflict with the scripture, "Thou madest him [man] a little lower than the angels" (Heb. 2:7). But I call attention to the marginal rendering of the passage in King James' translation, "Thou madest him *a little while inferior to* the angels." Without stopping here to consider which is the better translation of the passage, it may be said of the latter that it is in better harmony with the context of the passage as it stands here, in Hebrews, and also in Psalms, than the preferred rendering of it in the regular text; for in both places it says of man, "Thou crownedst him with glory and honor, and didst set him over the works of thy hands: thou hast put all things in subjection under his feet. For in that he put all things in subjection under him, he left nothing that is not put under him. But now we see not yet all things put under him." Moreover, we see the same thing is said of Jesus that is said of man: "We see Jesus *who was made a little lower than the angels*, for the suffering of death, crowned with glory and honor" (Heb. 2:9). Surely "made a little lower than the angels," when said of Jesus could be but for "a little while inferior to," etc.; and that only in the matter of "the suffering of death." So, too, with man; he is made "a little while inferior to the angels," after which period he would rise to the dignity of his place, when it would be seen, as said in the text with which this note deals, "the angels are a little lower than man;" that is, of course, when man shall have attained unto his exaltation and glory.]

[Footnote B: Journal of Discourses, Vol. 2, p. 342.]

This, it will be said, is a bold doctrine; and indeed it is bold. I love it for its boldness, but not so much for that, as for the reason that it is true. It is in harmony with another revelation given through Joseph Smith, wherein it is said:

> Man was also [as well as Jesus] in the beginning with God. Intelligence, or the light of truth, was not created or made, neither indeed can be. * * * For man is spirit. The elements are eternal, and spirit and element, inseparably connected, receive a fullness of joy; and when separated, man cannot receive a fullness of joy. The elements are the tabernacle of God; yea, man is the tabernacle of God, even temples (Doc. and Cov., sec. 93:29-35).

Nor is the doctrine less in harmony with the Jewish scriptures:

> For it became him, for whom are all things and by whom are all things, in bringing many sons unto glory, to make the captain of their salvation perfect through suffering. *For both he that sanctifieth and they who are sanctified are all of one; for which cause he is not ashamed to call them brethren.*

In this same chapter of Hebrews, Jesus, as well as man, is spoken of as being made "a little while inferior to the angels" (verses 7 and 9 marginal reading); and he is spoken of by the same apostle in another place as being but "the first born among many brethren" (Rom. 8:29). Also in his great discourse in Mars Hill, Paul not only declares that God "hath made of one blood all nations of men"—but he also quoted with approval the Greek poet Aratus[A], where the latter says: "For we are also his [God's] offspring;" and to this the apostle adds: "For as much, then, as we are the offspring of God [hence of the same race and nature], we ought not to think that the Godhead is like unto gold, or silver, or stone, graven by art after man's device" (Acts 17:26-30). The nature of our own being, one might add, in continuation of the apostle's reasoning, should teach those who recognize men as the offspring of God, better than to think of the Godhead as of gold, or silver, or stone, graven by art after man's device, since the nature of the offspring partakes of the nature of the parent; and our own nature teaches us that men are not as stocks and stones, though the latter be graven by art after the devices of men.

[Footnote A: He was a poet of Cilicia, of which province Tarsus, Paul's native city, was the capital. He wrote about four hundred years before Paul's time.]

Paul might also have quoted the great Hebrew poet: "God standeth in the congregation of the mighty; he judgeth among the Gods. * * * *I have said ye are Gods; and all of you are children of the Most High*" (Ps. 82:1, 6, 7); and though he adds, "But ye shall die like men, and fall like one of the princes," it does not detract from the assertion, "and all of you are children of the Most High;" for Jesus died, even as men die; but he was the Son of God, nevertheless, and he himself a Deity.

The matter is clear, then, men and Gods are of the same race; Jesus is the Son of God, and so, too, are all men the offspring of God, and Jesus but the first born of many brethren. Eternal Intelligences are begotten of God, spirits, and hence are sons of God—a dignity that never leaves them. "Beloved," said one of old, "now are we the sons of God, and it doth not yet appear what we shall be; but we know that when he [Christ] shall appear, *we shall be like him*; for we shall see him as he is" (I John 3:2).

Here, in the way of anticipating an objection, I shall pause to remark, parenthetically, that I am not unmindful of the array of evidence that may be massed to prove that it is chiefly through adoption, through obedience to the Gospel of Christ, that man in the scripture is spoken of as being a son of God. But this does not weaken the evidence for the fact for which I am contending, *viz*., that man is by nature the son of God. He becomes alienated from his Father and the Father's kingdom through sin, through the transgression of the law of God; hence the need of adoption into the heavenly kingdom, and into sonship with God. But though alienated from God through sin, man is nevertheless by nature the Son of God, and needs but the adoption that awaits him through the gospel of Jesus Christ to cry again in renewed and perfect fellowship, *Abba, Father!*

Return we now from this brief digression. Man being by the very nature of him a son of God, and a participant in the Divine Nature—he is properly a part of God; that is, when God is conceived of in the generic sense, as made up of the whole assemblage of divine Intelligences that exist in all heavens and all earths.

Of God, the Spirit of the Gods.

From the presence of the Gods goes out the influence and power men sometimes call God, or the Spirit of God; from whose presence David could not flee:

> If I ascend up into heaven, thou art there: if I make my bed in hell, behold thou art there. If I take the wings of the morning, and dwell in the uttermost parts of the sea; even there shall thy hand lead me, and thy right hand shall hold me. Yea the darkness hideth not from thee; but the light shineth as the day; the darkness and the light are both alike to thee (Ps. 139:7-12).

This Spirit is that "Something sacred and sublime," which men recognize as moving "wool-shod" behind the worlds; "weighing the stars; weighing the deeds of men."[A] This that Spirit that permeates all space; that makes all presence bright; all motion guides; the Power "unchanged through time's all-devastating flight;" that upholds and sustains all worlds. Hence it is said, in one of the most beautiful of the revelations God has given in this last dispensation:

[Footnote A: Edward Markham.]

> As also he is in the moon, and is the light of the moon, and the power thereof by which it was made, As also the light of the stars, and the power thereof by which they were made. And the earth also, and the power thereof; even the earth upon which you stand. And the light which now shineth, which giveth you light, is through him who enlighteneth your eyes, which is the same light that quickeneth your understandings; Which light proceedeth forth from the presence of God to fill the immensity of space. The light which is in all things; which giveth light to all things; which is the law by which all things are governed: even the power of God who sitteth upon his throne, who is in the bosom of eternity, who is in the midst of all things; * * * The earth rolls upon her wings, and the sun giveth his light by day, and the moon giveth her light by night, and the stars also give their light, as they roll upon their wings in their glory, in the midst of the power of God. * * * Behold, all these are kingdoms, and any man who hath seen any or the least of these, hath seen God moving in his majesty and power (Doc. and Cov., sec. 88:8-13 and 45, 47).

This, then, is God, who is not far removed from every one of us; in whom we live, and move, and have our being. This is God immanent in nature.

And as we dwell in him, so, too, dwells he in us; and, as man more expands towards divinity, more and more of the divine enters into his being, until he attains unto a fullness of light and truth; of power and glory; until he becomes perfectly one in God, and God in him. This the meaning of the Messiah's prayer, made for all those who become his disciples—"That they all may be one, *as* thou, Father, art in me, and I in thee: that they also may be one in us" (John 17:21).

To the same effect Paul also prayed:

> For this cause I bow my knees unto the Father of our Lord Jesus Christ, of whom the whole family in heaven and earth is named, that he would grant you, according to the riches of his glory, to be strengthened with might by his Spirit in the inner man; that Christ may dwell in your hearts by faith; that ye, being rooted and grounded in love, may be able to comprehend with all Saints what is the breadth, and length, and depth, and height; and to know the love of Christ which passeth knowledge, that ye may be filled with all the fullness of God (Eph. 3:14-19).

Then again he said:

> Let this mind be in you which was also in Jesus Christ: who being in the form of God, thought it not robbery to be equal with God (Philippians 2:5, 6).

It is possible for the mind of God to be in man, to will and to do, as seemeth him [God] good. The nature of the Whole clings to the Parts, and they may carry with them the light and truth and glory of the Whole. Moreover, by appointment, any One or Three of the unit Intelligences may become the embodiment and representative of all the power and glory and authority of the sum total of the Divine Intelligences; in which capacity either the One or the Three would no longer stand only in their individual characters as Gods, but they would stand also as the sign and symbol of all that is divine—and would act as and be to all intents and purposes *The One God*. And so in every inhabited world, and in every system of worlds, a God presides. Deity in his own right and person, and by virtue of the essence of him; and also by virtue of his being the sign and symbol of the Collectivity of the Divine Intelligences of the universe. Having access to all the councils of the Gods, each individual Deity becomes a partaker of the collective knowledge, wisdom, honor, power, majesty, and glory of the Body Divine—in a word, the embodiment of the Spirit of the Gods whose influence permeates the universe.

This doctrine of Deity teaches a divine government for the world that is in harmony with our modern knowledge of the universe; for, as I have remarked elsewhere in effect:[A] An infinitude of worlds and systems of worlds rising one above another in ever-increasing splendor, in limitless space and eternal duration, have, as a concomitant, an endless line of exalted men to preside over and within them, as Priests, Kings, Patriarchs, Gods! Nor is there confusion, disorder, or strife in their vast dominions; for they all govern upon the same righteous principles that characterize the government of God everywhere. The Gods have attained unto the excellence that Jesus prayed for in behalf of his apostles, and those who might believe on their word, when he said: "Holy Father, keep through thine own name those whom thou hast given me, *that they may be one as we are.*" I say the Gods have attained unto the excellence of oneness that Jesus prayed his disciples might possess, and since the Gods have attained unto it, and all govern their worlds and systems of worlds by the same spirit, and by the same principles, there is a unity in their government that makes it one even as they are one. Let worlds and systems of worlds, galaxies of systems and universes, extend as they may throughout limitless space, Joseph Smith has revealed the existence of a divine government which, while characterized by unity, is co-extensive with all these worlds and world-systems.

[Footnote A: New Witness for God, pp. 473-5.]

Concluding Reflections.

The subject enlarges as one enters into it; but I feel that here I may let the matter rest. I do not fear the effect of Mr. Van Der Donckt's criticism of our doctrine of Deity. Placed side by side with the few positive truths which God has so clearly revealed through the great prophet, seer and revelator, in these last days—Joseph Smith—yet to be recognized by the world as one of God's choicest and greatest of prophets—the vagaries of an apostate Christendom will have no attraction for the youth of Israel. It was generous in the Editors of the *Era*, to give place to the really able article of Mr. Van Der Donckt. I am glad they did so, for several reasons: *First*, because it was a courteous and generous act in itself; *second*, it stands out in marked contrast to the treatment accorded us in sectarian religious periodicals; *third*, because it must demonstrate to our youth, that we have no fear of placing our principles where they may be tested by the religious doctrines and philosophies of men; and although the elders of the Church of Christ may not be equal in learning and polemical skill with the champions of other systems, yet we have the truth, and our confidence is that it will hold its own in the conflicts that may beat upon it. We have the truth, I repeat, on this subject; that is, we have the truth so far as God has been pleased to reveal it. All truth respecting God is not yet revealed, even to the Church of Christ; but so much as he has revealed is true. Our feet in the matter have been set in the right path; we have lines of truth placed in our hands, which, if we and our children but follow patiently and with becoming humility, I am sure will lead us into that fullness of truth wherein is no incompleteness, but all is truth—God's truth, and all the truth about God.

CHAPTER IV

I.
JESUS CHRIST: THE REVELATION OF GOD. [A]

[Footnote A: A discourse delivered in the Tabernacle, Ogden, Utah, Tuesday evening, April 22, 1902, under the auspices of the Young Men's Mutual Improvement Association of the Weber Stake of Zion.]

And this is life eternal, that they might know thee, the only true God, and Jesus Christ, whom thou hast sent (St. John's Gospel 17:3).

And we know that the Son of God is come, and hath given us an understanding, that we may know him that it true, and we are in him that is true, even in his Son Jesus Christ. This is the true God, and eternal life (I John 5:20).

It will be taken for granted, I have no doubt, that the primary object in the earth-mission of the Lord Jesus Christ was to redeem mankind, to be the Savior of the world. We have the warrant of scripture for that. It is shadowed forth in the words that God spoke in Eden to the "Serpent," and having in mind the Lord Jesus:

> And I will put enmity between thee and the woman, and between thy seed and her seed; it shall bruise thy head, and thou shalt bruise his heel.[A]

[Footnote A: Gen. 3: 15.]

Turning to the New Testament, we read:

> For God so loved the world, that he gave his only begotten Son, that whosoever believeth in him should not perish, but have everlasting life. For God sent not his Son into the world to condemn the world, but that the world through him might be saved. [A]

[Footnote A: St. John 3:16, 17.]

I say to be the Savior of the world was the primary purpose of Christ's mission. But there is another purpose spoken of in scripture concerning the mission of the Lord Jesus. To one of the old prophets in Israel it was said:

"Behold, a virgin shall conceive, and bear a son; and shall 'call his name Immanuel.'"[A]—"which," says Matthew in his Gospel, "being interpreted, is God with us."[B]

[Footnote A: Isaiah 7:14.]

[Footnote B: Matt. 3:23.]

In connection with this there is one more scripture to which I desire to call your attention:

> Great is the mystery of godliness: God was manifest in the flesh, justified in the spirit, seen of angels, preached unto the Gentiles, believed on in the world, received up into glory. [A]

[Footnote A: I Tim. 3:16.]

That this passage has direct reference to the Lord Jesus Christ no one can doubt; for to none but to him does the language apply. Here let me say with reference to the Bible statement that Christ was God "manifest in the flesh," that some scholars hold that the Greek word translated "manifest," in our English Bible, should be rendered "manifested," a stronger word; so that Jesus Christ, if this rendering of the Greek be true, according to the teachings of Paul, was God "manifested" in the flesh.

With this brief scriptural introduction to the subject, and with the statement clearly before you that Jesus Christ is God, and, moreover, is God manifested in the flesh, I desire to call your attention to the ideas prevailing in the world respecting Deity at the time of Messiah's advent among men; and this to show you there certainly was a very great necessity for a revelation of God being given; for men knew him not; nor had they by searching been able to find him out. Men were without the knowledge of God, when it pleased God to reveal himself to them through his only begotten Son, Jesus, the Christ.

Beliefs in India and Egypt.

I first direct your attention to India and Egypt. In these two countries what is commonly called Pantheism prevailed. Now, I know that word represents complex rather than simple ideas to you, and needs a little explanation. Pantheism, speaking in a general way, is of two kinds: First, the Pantheism that sinks all nature into one substance, one essence, and then concludes that that one substance or essence is God. Such Pantheism as this is the purest Monism—that is, the one substance theory; and is spoken of by some of our philosophers as the purest Theism—that is, faith in one God. Indeed, Pantheism, in this aspect of it, is looked upon as a sort of exaggerated

Theism; for it regards "God" as the only substance, of which the material universe and man are but ever-changing manifestations. It is the form of Pantheism which identifies mind and matter, the finite and infinite, making them but manifestations of one universal being; but in effect it denies the personality, by which I mean the individuality, of God. This was, and, for matter of that, is now, the general belief of many millions in India. The Pantheism which expands the one substance into all the variety of objects that we see in nature, is the second kind of Pantheism referred to a moment since, and regards those various parts as God, or God expanded into nature. This leads to the grossest kind of idolatry, as it did in Egypt, at the time of which I am speaking. Under this form of Pantheism men worshiped various objects in nature; the sun, moon, stars; in fact, anything and everything that bodied forth to their minds, some quality, or power, or attribute of the Deity. This was the Pantheism of Egypt, and led to the abominable and disgusting idolatry of that land.

The Religion of China.

Turn your attention now northward from India, and take into account those great masses of our race inhabiting China; and you will find there, according to the statement of Max Muller,

> A colorless and unpoetical religion; a religion we might almost venture to call monosyllabic, consisting of the worship of a host of single spirits, representing the sky; the sun, storms and lightning, mountains and rivers; one standing by the side of the other without any mutual attraction, without any higher principle to hold them together. In addition to this we likewise meet in China with the worship of ancestral spirits, the spirits of the departed, who are supposed to retain some cognizance of human affairs, and to possess peculiar powers which they exercise for good or evil. This double worship of human and natural spirits constitutes the old and popular religion of China, and it has lived on to the present day, at least in the lower ranks of society, though there towers above it a more elevated range of half religious and half philosophical faith, a belief in two higher Powers, which, in the language of philosophy, may mean Form and Matter, in the language of ethics, Good and Evil, but which in the original language of religion and mythology are represented as Heaven and Earth.[A]

[Footnote A: Science of Religion (Muller) pp. 61, 62.]

Such was the ancient religion of China; and such, to a very large extent, is the religion of China to this day. It must be remembered that the great Chinese philosopher Confucius did not disturb this ancient religious belief. He did not, in fact, profess to be a teacher of religion at all, but was content if he could but influence men to properly observe human relations. On one occasion he was asked how the "spirits could be served," to which he made answer, "If we are not able to serve men, how can we serve the spirits?" On another occasion he said to his followers, "Respect the gods, and keep them at a distance."[A]

[Footnote A: Ibid p. 87.]

Religion in Northern Europe.

Let us now enter Northern Europe, among the Germanic tribes, and make inquiry as to what conceptions of God they held. Here you find a shadowy, undefined, and not well understood belief in the existence of an all-pervading influence, or spirit; a Supreme Being, to whom the Goths, at least, gave the name of "Alfader," meaning the Father of all; yet, strange to say, they paid him no divine honors, gave him no worship, but contented themselves in worshiping inferior deities, their old war heroes in the main, whom they had apotheosized and who, it must be acknowledged, represented the national qualities of that people at that time.

Gods of the Greeks and Romans.

Having thus briefly mentioned the faith of the people of north Europe—and I can do no more than this in each instance—I next invite your attention to the ideas about God that obtained among the highly civilized Romans. And, by the way, the Romans accepted, for the most part, the mythology and the religion of the Greeks, so that when we consider the ideas that prevailed among the Romans about God, it must be remembered that we are at the same time considering the views of God that were entertained by the Greeks—a people noted for the subtlety of their intellect, for their powers both of analysis and of synthesis: and for intuition of intellect which made them well nigh prophets, at least of an intellectual, if not of a spiritual order. The Romans for the most part were divided into the two great schools of philosophy, the Epicurean and the Stoic. Some of our young students will be telling me perhaps that I have overlooked the Academics. I do not mention them as a school of philosophy for the reason that, in my judgment, they had no philosophy; they advocated nothing; they were the agnostics of their time—that is, they were people who did not know, and like our modern agnostics, had a strong suspicion that nobody else knew. They represented merely the negative attitude of mind in their times. Still they numbered in their following some of the most considerable men of Rome, Cicero being among the number. By the way, it is through the writings of Cicero—especially through his Tusculan Disputations—that we become best acquainted with the theories of the two chief schools of philosophy I have mentioned. And it is from his writings that I shall here condense what I have to say of the creeds of these schools of philosophy, or at least that part which concerns us here—the part relating to their conceptions of Deity, and first as to the Doctrine of Epicurus.

Epicureans.

The Epicureans held that there were Gods in existence. They accepted the fact of their existence from the constant and universal opinion of mankind, independent of education, custom or law. "It must necessarily follow," they said, "that this knowledge is implanted in our minds, or, rather, innate in us." Their doctrine was: "That opinion respecting which there is a general agreement in universal nature must infallibly be true; therefore it must be allowed that there are Gods."

"Of the form of the Gods, they held that because the human body is more excellent than that of other animals, both in beauty and for convenience, therefore the Gods are in human form. All men are told by nature that none but the human form can be ascribed to the Gods; for under what other image did it ever appear to anyone either sleeping or waking?" Ye these forms of the Gods were not "body," but "something like body;" "nor do they contain blood, but something like blood." "Nor are they to be considered as bodies of any solidity, or reducible to number." "Nor is the nature or power of the Gods to be discerned by the senses, but by the mind." They held, moreover, that the universe arose from chance; that the Gods neither did nor could extend their providential care to human affairs.

The duty of worshiping the Gods was based upon the fact of their superiority to man. "The superior and excellent nature of the Gods requires a pious adoration from men, because it is possessed of immortality, and the most exalted felicity; for whatever excels has a right to veneration." Yet "all fear of the power and anger of the Gods should be banished; for we must understand that anger and affection are inconsistent with the nature of a happy and immortal being. These apprehensions being removed, no dread of the superior power remains." On the same principles that the existence of the Gods was allowed, that is, on the pre-notion and universal belief of their existence, it was held that the Gods were happy and immortal, to which the Epicurians added this doctrine: "That which is eternally happy cannot be burdened with any labor itself, nor can it impose any labor on another; nor can it be influenced by resentment or favor; because things which are liable to such feelings must be weak and frail."

It was generally held by the opponents of Epicurus that, as a matter of fact, he did not believe in the existence of the Gods at all; but dared not deny their existence for fear of the Athenian law against impiety, and because such denial would render him unpopular. But after becoming acquainted with his views as to the nature of the Gods, one is prepared to accept the criticism of his doctrines which Cicero puts in the mouth of Cotta, in his Tuscular Disputations, viz., "Epicurus has allowed a deity in words but destroyed him in fact." He rendered his Gods as intangible, as useless, as far removed from exciting adoration, or of controlling the universe, as have the orthodox Christian sects their Deity, who is said to be without body, or parts, or passions; which, if such be his nature, leaves him without quality through which he may affect humanity or the universe either for good or evil.

The Stoics.

I next take up the school of Stoics. The Stoics believed (1) that there were Gods; (2) they undertook to define their character and nature; (3) they held that the universe is governed by them, and (4) that they exercise a superintendency over human affairs.

The evidence for the existence of the Gods they saw primarily in the universe itself. "What can be so plain and evident," they argued, "when we behold the heavens, and contemplate the celestial bodies, as the existence of some supreme, divine intelligence by which these things are governed?" "Were it otherwise," they added, "Ennius would not with universal approbation have said,

> Look up to the refulgent heavens above
> which all men call unanimously Jove—
> * * * Of Gods and men the sire.

Of the nature of the Deity they held two things: First of all, that he is an animated though impersonal being; secondly, that there is nothing in all nature superior to him. "I do not see," says one well versed in their doctrines, "what can be more consistent with this idea and pre-conception than to attribute a mind and divinity to the world, the most excellent of all beings." The God of the Stoics is further described as a corporeal being, united to matter by a necessary connection; and, moreover, as subject to fate, so that he can bestow neither rewards nor punishments. That this sect held to the extinction of the soul at death, is allowed by all the learned. The Stoics drew their philosophy mainly from Socrates and Aristotle. Their cosmology was pantheistic, matter and force being the two ultimate principles, and God being the working force of the universe, giving it unity, beauty and adaptation.

The Jews.

I shall finish this brief review of the prevailing ideas about Deity at the advent of Messiah by reference to the state of belief respecting God among the Jews at this period. I have reserved the consideration of their views upon the subject until the last advisedly, chiefly for the reason that to their ancestors, in very ancient times, a knowledge of the true God was revealed. Their ancestors constituted a nation, a people, peculiarly related to God; chosen by him, it would seem, to stand as his witnesses among the nations of the earth. But at the time of the advent of Jesus Christ, the Jews were in an apostate condition, and ready to reject their God when he should come. Moreover, their leading teachers, especially in the two centuries preceding the coming of the Messiah, were taking every step that their ingenuity could devise for harmonizing the truths which God had made known to them with the more fashionable conceptions of God as entertained by one or the other of the great sects of philosophy among the Romans. The way had been prepared for the achievement of this end, in the first place, by the translation of the Hebrew Scriptures into the Greek language, which version of the Old Testament is usually called the Septuagint, or the LXX. This latter name is given to it because of a tradition that the translation was accomplished by seventy, or about seventy, elders of the Jews. The most generally accepted theory concerning it, however, is that it was a work accomplished at various times between 280 B. C. and 150 B. C. The books of Moses being first translated as early as the time of Ptolemy Philadelphus, 284-246 B. C, while the Prophets and Psalms were translated somewhat later. It is not, however, the time or manner in which the translation was accomplished that we are interested in, but the character of the translation itself; and of this, Alfred Edersheim, in his "Life and Times of Jesus, the Messiah," in the division of his work which treats of the preparation for the Gospel, says of the Septuagint:

> Putting aside clerical mistakes and misreadings, and making allowance for errors of translation, ignorance, and haste, we note certain outstanding facts as characteristic of the Greek version. It bears evident marks of its origin in Egypt, in its use of Egyptian words and references, and equally evident traces of its Jewish composition. By the side of slavish and false literalism there is great liberty, if not license, in handling the original; gross mistakes occur along with

happy renderings of very difficult passages, suggesting the aid of some able scholars. Distinct Jewish elements are undeniably there, which can only be explained by reference to Jewish tradition, although they are much fewer than some critics have supposed. This we can easily understand, since only those traditions would find a place which at the early time were not only received, but in general circulation. The distinctly Grecian elements, however, are at present of chief interest to us. *They consist of allusions to Greek mythological terms, and adaptations of Greek philosophical ideas.* However few, even one well-authenticated instance would lead us to suspect others, and in general give to the version the character of Jewish Hellenising. In the same class we reckon what constitutes the prominent characteristics of the LXX version, which, for want of better terms, we would designate as rationalistic and apologetic. Difficulties—or what seemed such—are removed by the most bold methods, and by free handling of the text; it need scarcely be said, often very unsatisfactorily. More especially, a strenuous effort is made to banish all anthropomorphisms, as inconsistent with their ideas of the Deity.[A]

[Footnote A: "Jesus, the Messiah," by Edersheim, vol. I, pp. 27-8, eighth edition.

Later the same authority points out the fact that the Septuagint version of the Hebrew scriptures became really the people's Bible to that large Jewish world through which Christianity was afterwards to address itself to mankind. "It was part of the case," he adds, "that this translation should be regarded by the Hellenists as inspired like the original. Otherwise it would have been impossible to make final appeal to the very words of the Greek; still less to find in them a mystical and allegorical meaning."[A]

[Footnote A: Ibid, p. 29.]

The foundation thus laid for a superstructure of false philosophy there was not wanting builders who were anxious to place a pagan structure upon it. About the middle of the second century B. C., one Aristobulus, a Hellenist Jew of Alexandria, sought to so explain the Hebrew scriptures as "to bring the Peripatetic philosophy out of the law of Moses, and out of the other Prophets." Following is a sample, according to Edersheim, of his allegorizing: "Thus, when we read that God stood, it meant the stable order of the world; that he created the world in six days, the orderly succession of time; the rest of the Sabbath, the preservation of what was created. And in such manner could the whole system of Aristotle be found in the Bible. But how was this to be accounted for? Of course, the Bible had not learned of Aristotle, but he and all other philosophers had learned from the Bible. Thus, according to Aristobulus, Pythagoras, Plato, and all the other sages, had really learned from Moses, and the broken rays found in their writings were united in all their glory in the Torah."[A]

[Footnote A: "Jesus, the Messiah," Edersheim, vol. 1, p. 36.]

Following Aristobulus in the same kind of philosophy was Philo, the learned Jew of Alexandria, born about the year 20 B. C. He was supposed to be a descendant of Aaron, and belonged to one of the wealthiest and most influential families among the merchants of Egypt; and he is said to have united a large share of Greek learning with Jewish enthusiasm. He followed most worthily in the footsteps of Aristobulus. According to him, the Greek sages had learned their philosophy from Moses, in whom alone was all truth to be found. "Not indeed, in the letter," says Edersheim, "but *under* the letter of Holy Scripture. If in Numbers 23:19 we read 'God is not a man,' and in Deut. 1:31 that the Lord was 'as a man,' did it not imply on the one hand the revelation of absolute truth by God, and on the other, accommodation to those who were weak? Here then, was the principle of a two-fold interpretation of the Word of God—the literal and the allegorical. * ** To begin with the former: the literal sense must be wholly set aside, when it implies anything unworthy of the Deity—anything unmeaning, impossible, or contrary to reason. Manifestly this canon, if strictly applied, would do away not only with all anthropomorphisms, but cut the knot wherever difficulties seemed insuperable. Again, Philo would find an allegorical, along with the literal, interpretation indicated in the reduplication of a word, and in seemingly superfluous words, particles, or expressions. These could, of course, only bear such a meaning on Philo's assumption of the actual inspiration of the Septuagint version."[A]

[Footnote A: When one thinks of the mischief that may arise from such perversions of scripture by the application of Philo's principles of interpretation, we do not marvel that some of the Jews regarded the translation of the Seventy "to have been as great a calamity to Israel as the making of the golden calf."]

Edersheim admits, however, that in the Talmudic canon, the interpretation where "any repetition of what had been already stated, would point to something new;" and holds that these are comparatively sober rules of exegesis. "Not so the license," he remarks, "which he [Philo] claimed, of freely altering the punctuation of sentences, and his notion that, if one from among several synonymous words was chosen in a passage, this pointed to some special meaning attaching to it. Even more extravagant was the idea that a word which occurred in the Septuagint might be interpreted according to every shade of meaning which it bore in the Greek, and that even another meaning might be given it by slightly altering the letters." Of Philo's further efforts at harmonizing the revelations of God to the Jews with the teachings of the Greeks, it will only be necessary to read the following quotation from an authority upon such subjects:

> Philo's doctrine starts from the idea that God is "being" absolutely bare of all quality. All quality in finite beings has limitation, and no limitation can be predicated of God, who is eternal, unchangeable, simple substance, free, self-sufficient. To predicate any quality of God would be to reduce him to the sphere of finite existence. Of him we can only say *that* he is, not *what* he is, and such purely negative predictions as to his being appear to Philo * * * the only way of securing his absolute elevation above the world [that is, above and outside of the material universe]. A consistent application of Philo's abstract conception of God would exclude the possibility of any active relation of God to the world, and therefore of religion; for a being absolutely without quality and movement cannot be conceived as actively concerned with the multiplicity of individual things. And so, in fact, Philo does teach that the absolute perfection, purity and loftiness of God would be violated by direct contact with imperfect, impure, and finite things. But the possibility of a connection between God and the world is reached through a distinction which forms the most important point in his theology and cosmology. The proper being of God is distinguished from the infinite multiplicity of divine ideas or forces: God himself is without quality, but he disposes of an infinite variety of divine forces, through *whose* mediation an active relation of God to the world is brought about. In the details of his teaching as to these mediating entities, Philo is guided partly by Plato and partly by the Stoics; but at the same time he makes use of the concrete religious conceptions of heathenism and Judaism. Following Plato, he first calls them "Ideas," or patterns of all things; they are thoughts of God, yet possess a real existence, and were produced before the creation of the sensible world, of which they are the keys. * * * Philo maintains that the divine forces are identical with the "demons" of the Greeks and the

"angels" of the Jews, i. e., servants and messengers of God, by means of which he communicates with the finite world. *
* * Philo regards all individual "ideas" as comprehended in one highest and most general "idea" or force—the unity of the individual idea—which he calls the "logos" or "reason" of God, and which is again regarded as operative "reason." The logos, therefore, is the highest mediator between God and man, the world, the first-born son of God, the archangel, who is the vehicle of all revelation, and the high priest who stands before God on behalf of the world. Through whom the world was created.[A]

[Footnote A: Professor E. Schurer, of University of Giessen, art. *Philo* in Encyclo. Brit.]

In all this one may see only too plainly the effort to harmonize Jewish theology with Greek philosophy—an effort to be rid of the plain anthropomorphism of the Hebrew scriptures for the incomprehensible "being" of Greek metaphysics.

Thus the Jews—the people who had been chosen to be witnesses for God to the world—appeared to have grown weary of the mission given to them. Tired were they of standing in a position where their hands seemed to be raised against all men, and all men's hands against them. They had lost the spirit that had supported their fathers, and hence were searching out these cowardly compromises by which harmony could be shown to exist between the philosophy of the Gentiles and the revelations of God to their fathers.

God Revealed to the World in the Person of Jesus Christ.

This completes the survey I intended to make of this field. Nowhere have we found a knowledge of the true and living God. Nowhere a teacher who comes with definite knowledge of this subject of all subjects—a subject so closely related to eternal life, that to know God is said in the scriptures to be life eternal; and of course, the corollary naturally follows, viz, not to know God is *not* to possess eternal life. We can form no other conclusion from the survey we have taken of the world's ideas respecting the existence and nature of God, than that forced upon us—the world stood in sore need of a revelation of God. He whom the Egyptians and Indians sought for in their Pantheism, must be made known. God, whom Confucius would have men respect, but keep at a distance, must draw near. The "Alfader" of the Goths, undefined, incomprehensible to them, must be brought out of the northern darkness into glorious light. The God-idea that prevailed among the Greek philosophers must be brought from the mists of their idle speculations and made to stand before the world, He whom the Jews were seeking to deny and forsake must be revealed again to the children of men. And lo! when the vail falls from the revelation that God gives of himself, what form is that which steps forth from the background of the world's ignorance and mystery? A MAN, as God lives! Jesus of Nazareth—the great Peasant Teacher of Judea. He is God revealed henceforth to the world. They who thought God impersonal, without form, must know him henceforth as a person in the form of man. They who have held him to be without quality, must henceforth know him as possessed of the qualities of Jesus of Nazareth. They who have regarded him as infinitely terrible, must henceforth know him also as infinitely gentle. Those who would hold him at a distance, will now permit him to draw near. This is the world's mystery revealed. This is God manifested in the flesh. This is the Son of God, who comes to reveal the Father, for he is the express image and likeness of that Father's person, and the reflection of that Father's mind. Henceforth when men shall say, Show us the Father, he shall point to himself as the complete revelation of the Father, and say, "He that hath seen me, hath seen the Father also." Henceforth, when men shall dispute about the "being" and "nature" of God, it shall be a perfect answer to uphold Jesus Christ as the complete, perfect revelation and manifestation of God, and through all the ages it shall be so; there shall be no excuse for men saying they know not God, for all may know him, from the least to the greatest, so tangible, so real a revelation has God given of himself in the person and character of Jesus Christ. He lived his life on earth—a life of sorrow and of gentleness, its pathway strewn with actions fraught with mercy, kindness, and love. A man he was, approved of God among men, by miracles, and wonders and signs which God did by him. Being delivered by the determinate counsel and foreknowledge of God, men took and by wicked hands crucified and slew him, but God raised him up, having loosed the pains of death, because it was not possible that he should be holden of it; and exalted him on high at the right hand of God, whence he shall come to judge the quick and the dead.[A]

[Footnote A: This synopsis of the Christ's life is in Acts 2.]

Mark you, in all this there is not a word about the mysterious, ineffable generation of the Son of God from the Father, together with all the mysteries that men have gathered together in their learned disquisitions about God. No question is raised as to whether Jesus was made out of nothing or begotten by ineffable generation from the substance of the Father. Whether he is consubstantial, that is, of the *same* substance with the Father, or only of a *similar* substance. Nor is there any question raised as to whether Jesus was "begotten" before or after time began. All these and a hundred other questions arose after the Christian doctrine of Deity began to come in contact with the Greek and other philosophies. Jesus accepted the existence of God as a settled fact, and proclaimed himself to be the Son of God: offending the Jews, by so doing, for they saw that he made himself equal with God;[A] and being a man, held forth himself to be God.[B] Slow indeed were they to learn the great truth plainly revealed in Jesus Christ, *that God is a perfect man.* Such was Jesus Christ, and he was God manifested in the flesh. "Was," did I say? Nay, *"is,"* I should have said; and such will he remain forever; a spirit he is, clothed with an immortal body, a resurrected body of tangible flesh and bones made eternal, and now dwelling in heaven with his Father, of whom he is the express image and likeness; as well now as when he was on earth; and hence the Father also must be a personage of flesh and bones, as tangible as the exalted man, Christ Jesus the Lord.

[Footnote A: John 5:18.]

[Footnote B: John 10:30-33.]

II.
EVIDENCE OF CHRIST'S DIVINITY FROM THE SCRIPTURE.

It is my desire on this occasion to place in the hands of the Elders of Israel such tangible proofs from the Scriptures concerning Jesus Christ being "God manifested in the flesh," that they will be able hereafter to maintain the doctrine taught upon this subject by the Church; it is my desire to cite you evidence from which our young men may maintain the doctrine that God is an exalted man. For be it known unto you, that plain and from the scriptures indisputable as this doctrine of ours is, there are those who scorn it, who call it blasphemy, and who roundly denounce the Church of Jesus Christ of Latter-day Saints for teaching it.

I call your attention then, first of all, to the fact that

Jesus Christ is Called God in the Scriptures.

The first proof I offer for this statement is from the writings of Isaiah. You remember perhaps my former quotation from Isaiah, wherein that prophet says, "Behold, a virgin shall conceive and bear a son, and shall call his name Immanuel",[A] the interpretation of which name is, according to Matthew, "God with us".[B] So that this man-child, born of a woman, and called "Immanuel," is God; and, moreover, is "God with us"—that is, with men. The same prophet also says:

[Footnote A: Isaiah 7:14.]

[Footnote B: Matt. 1:23.]

> For unto us a child is born, unto us a son is given; and the government shall be upon his shoulder; and his name shall be called Wonderful, Counselor, *The Mighty God, the Everlasting Father, the Prince of Peace.*[A]

[Footnote A: Isaiah 9:6.]

All concede that this is in plain allusion to Jesus Christ, and the scriptures here directly call Him *The Mighty God.* He is also called God in the testimony of John. Mark this language, for it is a passage around which many ideas center, and to which we shall have occasion to refer several times. In the preface to his Gospel, John says:

> In the beginning was the Word, and the Word was with God, *and the Word was God.* The same was in the beginning with God. * * * And the Word was made flesh, and dwelt among us, (and we beheld his glory, the glory as of the only begotten of the Father) full of grace and truth.

There can be no question but direct reference is here made to the Lord Jesus Christ, as being the "Word;" and the "Word," or Jesus being with the Father in the beginning, and the "Word," or Jesus Christ, also being God. The "Word," then, as used here by John, is one of the titles of Jesus in his pre-existent estate. Why called the "Word" I know not, unless it is that by a "word" we make an expression; and since Jesus Christ was to be the expression of God, the revelation of God to the children of men, he was for that reason called the "Word."[A]

[Footnote A: Since the delivery of the above discourse I note the following in a revelation to Joseph Smith: "In the beginning the Word was, for he [Christ] was the Word, even the *Messenger of Salvation.*" (Doc. and Cov. Sec. 93.) That is, it appears that Messiah was called the "Word" because He was the "Messenger"—"the Messenger of Salvation."]

Jesus Declares Himself to be God—the Son of God:

Jesus was crucified on the charge that he was an impostor—that he, being a man, said that "God was his Father, making himself equal with God" (John 5:18).

And again: "For a good work we stone thee not, but for blasphemy, and because that thou being a man, makest thyself God" (John 10:33).

Again: when accused before Pilate, who declared he could "find no fault in him," the Jews answered him, "We have a law, and by our law he ought to die, because he made himself the Son of God." Moreover, the high priest, in the course of his trial before the Sanhedrim of the Jews, directly said to

Jesus, "I adjure thee by the living God, that thou tell us whether thou be the Christ, the Son of God. Jesus said unto him, Thou hast said: nevertheless, I say unto you, Hereafter shall ye see the Son of man sitting on the right hand of power, and coming in the clouds of heaven" (Matt 27:63, 64).

And finally, when Jesus appeared to the eleven disciples after his resurrection, he said unto them, "All power is given unto me, in heaven and in earth, go ye therefore and teach all nations, baptizing them in the name of the Father, and of the Son, and of the Holy Ghost" (Matt. 28:18, 19). A clearer proclamation of his divinity could not be made than in the statement, "all power is given unto me in heaven and in earth," especially when it is followed by placing himself on equal footing with the Father and the Holy Ghost, which he does when he commands his disciples to baptize in the name of the Father, and of the Son, and of the Holy Ghost. Nothing can be added to this, except it be the words of God the Father directly addressed to Jesus, when he says, "Thy throne, O God, is for ever and ever" (Heb. 1:8).

Jesus Christ to be Worshiped, hence God.

Jesus Christ is to be worshiped by men and angels; and worship is an honor to be paid only to true Deity. The angels of heaven refuse the adoration we call worship. You remember when the Apostle John was on the isle of Patmos, and God sent a heavenly messenger to him, how the Apostle overawed by the brightness of his glory fell upon his face to worship him, and the angel said: "See thou do it not: for I am thy fellow servant, and of thy brethren the prophets, and of them which keep the sayings of this book: Worship God."[A] So you see the angels refuse divine honors. But the scriptures prove that Jesus was especially to be worshiped; hence he must be Deity:

> [Footnote A: Rev. 19:10.]
>
> For unto which of the angels said he at any time, Thou art my son, this day have I begotten thee? And again, I will be to him a Father, and he shall be to me a Son. And again, when he bringeth in the First Begotten into the world, he saith, let all the angels of God worship him.[A]

[Footnote A: Heb. 1:5, 6.]

The same doctrine is taught in the epistle to the Philippians:

> Wherefore God also hath highly exalted him, and given him a name which is above every name: That at the name of Jesus every knee should bow, of things in heaven, and things in earth, and things under the earth; and that every tongue

should confess that Jesus Christ is Lord, to the glory of God the Father.[A]

[Footnote A: Phil. 2:9, 10.]

There are other passages to the same effect, but it is perhaps unnecessary for me to turn to each of these since the ones here quoted will be sufficient to establish in your minds the fact contended for.

Jesus Christ is the Creator, hence God.

Jesus Christ is the Creator. Evidence of this is found in the testimony of John from which I have already quoted.

> In the beginning was the Word, and the Word was with God, and the Word was God. The same was in the beginning with God. All things were made by him, and without him was not any thing made that was made. In him was life; and the life was the light of men.[A]

[Footnote A: John 1:1-4.]

Again in the epistle to the Colossians:

> The Father * * * hath delivered us from the power of darkness, and hath translated us into the kingdom of heaven * * who is the image of the invisible God, the firstborn of every creature. For by him were all things created, that are in heaven, and that are in earth, visible and invisible, whether they be thrones or dominions, or principalities, or powers: all things were created by him, and for him.[A]

[Footnote A: Col. 1:12-17.]

Again in Hebrews:

God, who at sundry times and in divers manners spake in times past unto the fathers—by the prophets, hath in these last days spoken unto us by his Son, whom he hath appointed heir of all things, by whom also he made the worlds.

Now we begin to see the relation of the Father and the Son; for though the "Word" be God, though "Immanuel" is God, that is, "God with us," He does not displace God the Father, but stands in the relationship of a son to him. Under the direction of the Father, he created worlds, and in this manner is the Creator of our earth, and the heavens connected with the earth. And everywhere the scriptures command that men should worship the Creator. In fact the burden of the cry of that angel who is to restore the gospel in the hour of God's judgment is,

> Fear God, and give glory to him; for the hour of his judgment is come: and worship him that made heaven and earth and the seas and the fountains of waters.[A]

[Footnote A: Rev. 14:7.]

Jesus Christ equal with God the Father, hence God.

After the resurrection, Jesus appeared unto his disciples, and said to them, as recorded in the closing chapter of Matthew:

> All power is given unto me in heaven and in earth. Go ye, therefore, and teach all nations, baptizing them in the name of the Father, and of the Son, and of the Holy Ghost; teaching them to observe all things whatsoever I have commanded you.[A]

[Footnote A: Matt. 28:18, 19.]

Observe that the Lord Jesus Christ is placed upon a footing of equal dignity with God the Father, and with the Holy Ghost. This brings to mind the scripture of Paul, where he says, speaking of Jesus:

> Who, being in the form of God, thought it not robbery to be *equal* with God.[A]

[Footnote A: Phil. 2:6.]

So also is Christ given equal station with the Father and with the Holy Ghost in the apostolic benediction over and over again.

> May the grace of the Lord Jesus Christ, the love of God and the communion of the Holy Ghost be with you all.

In these several passages we have Jesus Christ, after his resurrection, asserting that all power had been given unto him, both in heaven and in earth; he is placed upon a footing of equal dignity with God the Father in the holy Trinity—in the Grand Triumvirate which constitutes the Presiding Council or Godhead reigning over our heavens and our earth—hence God.

I now wish to give you the proof that Jesus Christ is the express image of the Father; the express image of his person, as well as the revelation of the attributes of God. Following that language in Hebrews where Jesus is spoken of as having created worlds under the direction of the Father, it is said:

> Who being the brightness of his [the Father's] glory, *and the express image of his person,* and upholding all things by the word of his power, when he had by himself purged our sins, sat down at the right hand of the Majesty on high.[A]

[Footnote A: Heb. 3:3.]

So Paul to the Corinthians:

> The God of this world hath blinded the minds of those which believe not, lest the light of the glorious Gospel of Christ, *who is the image of God*, should shine unto them.[A]

[Footnote A: II Cor. 4:4.]

So also, in his letter to the Colossians, when speaking of Christ Paul says:

> Who is the image of the invisible God, the first born of every creature.[A]

[Footnote A: Col. 1:5.]

Being "the express image of his person," then the "image of the invisible God," Jesus becomes a revelation of the person of God to the children of men, as well as a revelation of his character and attributes. Again, you have the scriptures saying:

> For it pleased the Father that in him [Christ Jesus] should all fullness dwell. * * * For in him dwelleth all the fullness of the Godhead bodily.[A]

[Footnote A: Col. 1:19, 2:9.]

All there is, then, in God, there is in Jesus Christ. All that Jesus Christ is, God is, And Jesus Christ is an immortal man of flesh and bone and spirit, and with his Father and the Holy Spirit will reign eternally in the heavens.

III.
THE CHARACTER OF GOD REVEALED IN THE LIFE OF JESUS CHRIST.

Having proved from the scriptures that Jesus Christ is God, and the revelation of God to man, I come to another branch of my subject. I now wish to show you that Jesus Christ manifested God also in his life; and although I have been addressing you for some time, I am quite sure you yourselves would not be entirely satisfied with the treatise upon this subject, unless I pointed out how God would act under the variety of circumstances in which it is our privilege to behold him placed.

The Humility of God.

First of all, I call your attention to the deep, the profound humility of God; his great condescension in living among men, as he did, for our instruction; and from that circumstance would draw to your attention the lesson of humility his life teaches. The heights of glory to which Jesus had attained, the power and dignity of his position in the heavenly kingdom, of course, cannot be comprehended by us in our present finite condition, and with our limited knowledge of things. Great and exalted as we might think him to be, you may depend upon it he was exalted infinitely higher than that. Then when you think of one living and moving in the courts of heaven and mingling in the councils of the Gods, consenting to come down to this earth and pass through the conditions that Jesus passed through, do you not marvel at his humility? To be born under such circumstances as would enable wicked man to cast reflection upon his very birth![A] To be born, too, in a stable, and to be cradled in a manger! To grow up a peasant, with a peasant's labor to perform, and a peasant's fare to subsist upon from childhood to manhood—do you not marvel at this great humility, at this great condescension of God? And by his humility, are not men taught humility, as they are taught it by no other circumstance whatsoever!

[Footnote A: St. John 8:41.]

The Obedience of God.

Of his youth, we know but little; but the little we know reveals a shining quality, either for God or man to possess. You must remember, in all our consideration of the life of Messiah, one truth, which comes to us from the scriptures in an incidental way, viz., that "In his humiliation his judgment was taken from him."[A] As the veil is drawn over our minds when our pre-existent spirits come into this world, and we forget the Father and mother of the spirit world, and the positions we occupied there, so, too, with Jesus; in his humiliation his judgment was taken from him; he knew not at first whence he came, nor the dignity of his station in heaven. It was only by degrees that he felt the Spirit working within him and gradually unfolding the sublime idea that he was peculiarly and pre-eminently the Son of God in very deed. When at Jerusalem, about twelve years of age, he began to be conscious of the suggestions of the Spirit within him, and hence allowed the caravan with which he had come from distant Galilee to Judea to start upon the return journey without him, much to the perplexity and sorrow of his supposed father, Joseph, and his mother Mary. They missing him, returned and found him in the temple disputing with the doctors and lawyers. They reprimanded him, as they would reprimand any boy guilty of similar conduct; but when they reproved him, he answered, "Wist ye not that I must be about my Father's business." He began to understand his mission. The spirit promptings were at work in his soul. And while ultimately the spirit was given without measure unto him,[B] it was not so at first, for "He received not of the fullness at the first, but received grace for grace."[C]

The child Jesus "grew, and waxed strong in spirit, filled with wisdom: and the grace of God was upon him. * * * And Jesus increased in wisdom and stature, and in favor with God and man."[D] But notwithstanding Jesus, at twelve years of age, and earlier, began to experience the operations of the Spirit calling his soul to his mission, still we are told that he returned with his parents to Galilee, "and was subject unto them." He who had given the law, "Honor thy father and thy mother," in this act exemplified the honor that he entertained for that law, in his practice of it.

[Footnote A: Acts 8:33.]

[Footnote B: St. John 3:34.]

[Footnote C: Doc. and Cov., Sec. 93:12, 13]

[Footnote D: Luke 2:40, 52.]

We next see him coming to the banks of Jordan, where a prophet of God is baptizing—one of those strange, eccentric men, who lived for the most part in the wilderness, whose food was locusts and wild honey, and whose clothing was the skins of wild animals; and yet through all this eccentricity, through all this oddness of character, shone the divine powers of God in this messenger, and multitudes of people gathered to his preaching by the Jordan, where he baptized them for the remission of their sins. By and by, Jesus comes and demands baptism at this man's hands; and as he enters the water, the prophet stays him, and says, "I have need to be baptized of thee, and comest thou to me?" Already, doubtless, shining, through this "expression of God,"—this Jesus of Nazareth,—the servant of the Lord, in attune, through the spirit of inspiration, with the very God who was approaching him, felt the divinity of his presence, and would fain acknowledge his own inferiority. What was the reply? "Suffer it to be so now: for thus it becometh us to fulfill all righteousness." He who had said that men must be baptized for the remission of sins, though himself sinless, would honor that law by obedience unto it. Thus we learn that God can not only give law, but he can obey law. Indeed, only those who know how to obey law are qualified to make it.

The Patience of God Under Temptation.

Next we shall see how God, in the person of Jesus Christ, manages himself under temptation. After his baptism, he was driven of the spirit into the wilderness, where he fasted forty days and forty nights. There under the quiet stars, and in the desert, he was consecrating his life to the service of God the Father, and gathering to himself those spiritual forces, and calling up those divine powers, that should carry him through the three years of storm and tempest that must be his in the fulfillment of his mission. When he had reached his greatest point of weakness, when "an hungered," and fainting from his long fast, whom do you suppose came into his presence to tempt him? No other than his arch-enemy; the one with whom he contended in the councils of God before the foundations of this earth were laid, when the great plan of life and salvation was being discussed—Lucifer, in the full pride of his strength and glory came tempting him. I say Lucifer came in the fullness of his strength and glory; for I take it that at this time he had well-nigh reached the pinnacle of his power. We have seen that he had blinded all the races of men respecting God. Truly, he held the nations of the world and their glory within his own hands: and the knowledge of the true God was not had among men. Proudly, therefore, he steps to the side of the weakened God, to propound certain questions to him. In substance, he said, "You have had whisperings of the Spirit that you are Deity, that you are the Son of God. If so, exercise your creative power, turn these stones into bread, and satisfy your hunger. Come, since you are a God, you must needs have creative powers; try it upon these stones and hunger no more." God, in the presence of his arch-enemy, still retained his humility, and answered out of the scriptures: "It is written, Man shall not live by bread alone."

After that, Lucifer takes the Christ to the pinnacle of the temple, and tries him upon another side—a side upon which good men are particularly vulnerable, the side of their vanity, that prompts them to believe they are the special favorites of heaven, and that God had given his angels charge concerning them. Christ's tempter said, "If thou be the Son of God, cast thyself down: for it is written, he shall give his angels charge concerning thee: and in their hands they shall bear thee up, lest at any time thou dash thy foot against a stone." Again the Son of God answers in humility, and still out of the scriptures: "It is written also, Thou shalt not tempt the Lord thy God." Because God has given you certain promises, you apostles, and prophets, and men of God; because you, by your righteousness, perchance have made yourselves of the elect of God, it is not becoming that you should be putting God constantly upon trial. "Thou shalt not tempt the Lord thy God." Walk your pathway in the light of common sense, and be not puffed up with vanity because there is something special in your relationship with God.

Lucifer next approaches Jesus upon the side most vulnerable of all, in quick and mighty spirits—on the side of ambition. I take it that there have been but few strong men who have not felt the desire to rule, to govern; and not always selfishly, either, or for personal ends, but sometimes out of an honest thought that they can do somewhat of good to humanity. Even good men may love power, and may aspire to the righteous exercise of it. It was upon this side that Lucifer sought to break in upon the virtue of Jesus.

He unveils the kingdoms of the world; which he holds in his thraldom; he reveals their glory, and the might and majesty to which men may attain, if only they can grasp the sceptre of some great empire. Now, says he, "All these things will I give thee, if thou wilt fall down and worship me." He who has answered in tones so humble up to this point; and has endured the taunts and questionings of his great enemy with becoming modesty and humility, now, evidently, feels stirring within him some of those master powers that may shake the world and send the stars out of their courses, "Get thee hence, Satan," said he, "for it is written, Thou shalt worship the Lord thy God, and him only shalt thou serve." The spirit of the Son of God was aroused, it was time for Lucifer's departure, and so he left Jesus, and angels came and ministered unto him. So God deports himself under trial and temptation. How splendid the lesson for man!

The Compassion and Impartiality of God.

Jesus was possessed of infinite compassion. The incidents that I shall relate to you, in support of this statement, are in quotations that are free, and yet, I think, justified by the spirit of the several occasions. After all, it is the spirit that giveth life; the letter killeth; so let us look at these things in the spirit of them. You see him one day with some of his disciples approaching the little village of Nain, "his raiment dusty and his sandals worn." As they draw near, the gate is opened and a funeral procession marches out. The mother of the young man whose body is being borne by his neighbors to the final resting place, walks feebly and weeping beside the bier, desolate in her loneliness. As Jesus saw that poor woman in the midst of her sorrow, his heart—I pray you think of it, for we are speaking of God when we speak of Jesus Christ, the Creator of heaven and earth—the heart of God, is moved with compassion towards this woman. He stops the bier, takes the dead by the hand, and says, "Young man, I say unto you, Arise." And he arose. Jesus Christ gave this woman back her son. It was an act of beautiful compassion, one of many, which illustrates how tender and sympathetic is the heart of our God!

Nor was his ministry confined exclusively to the poor, to the widows, to the lonely. He despised not rulers, nor the rich, because they were rich; but was willing, if only they could put themselves in a position to receive the manifestations of his compassion—he was willing to minister unto them. This is proved in the case of Jairus, one of the rulers of the Jews, and a man of great wealth. You will remember that he came running to the Master with his sorrow—his daughter was lying dangerously ill at home; and such was his faith that if the Master would but speak the word, she would be healed. While yet he spake, one of his servants came running, saying, "Thy daughter is dead: trouble not the Master." But Jesus heeded not the word of the servant. He had heard Jairus' cry of faith, and responsive to that faith-cry, he made his way to the home of the ruler, put out those who were unbelieving, and taking the maid by the hand, gave her back to the gladness of life, into the arms of the joyous father. The faith of that rich man was as great as the faith of any we meet with in all the ministry of the Lord. So, wealth is not necessarily a hindrance to faith. God is as close to the faithful rich as to the faithful poor, and as ready to grant them his mercy, according to their faith. I sometimes think we make a mistake when we would flout those who are rich and put them outside the pale of God's mercy and goodness because of what may be nothing but a prejudice—which in reality may be our envy—of the rich.

While on the way to the ruler's house, another incident happened that is very remarkable. A woman in the throng, a long time afflicted with a grievous ailment, said in her heart as she saw him pass, "If I may but touch his garment, I shall be whole." Accordingly she crowded her way forward, dropped upon her knee, clutched the garment, and received the divine power from him which cleansed her body and healed her completely. Jesus, observing that something had happened to him, turned to the apostles and said, "Who touched me?" They replied, "Master, the multitude throng thee and press thee, and sayest thou, Who touched me?" as if that was not to be expected in such a crowd, Ah! said Jesus, but "I perceive that virtue is gone out of me." What was it? Simply that through this poor woman's faith—who supposed herself so far removed from God that she dare—not come into his presence and ask for the blessing she desired, but undertook to obtain it by indirect means—through her faith and touching the garment of the Lord, the healing virtues passed from God to her in such a tangible manner that he felt their departure, just as some of you elders, when administering to one who was full of faith have felt your spiritual strength and life go out from you leaving you weak and almost helpless, but giving healthful life to the afflicted. I speak to men who have experience in these things, and I know that scores of you could bear witness to the truth of this phenomenon. If our lives can but touch the life of God, such is his nature that we shall partake of the virtues that go out from him.

What shall I say of lepers that crowded into Messiah's presence, and who, notwithstanding the loathsomeness of their disease, found sympathy and help from contact with him? What of the blind, the lame, the halt? Why, let us not speak of them; for though it is a great thing that their bodies should be healed, and they should go through the community singing the praises of him who had restored them, there are better things to speak of—the healing of men's souls, the purifying of their spirits.

God's Treatment of Sinners.

Let us ask, rather, how did Jesus Christ—God—deal with sinners? I take one incident that has always appealed very strongly to me, and illustrates the spirit in which Christ deals with sinners; for this God of ours is peculiarly the friend of sinners, not because of their sins, however, but in spite of them; and because of his compassion upon those so unfortunate as to be under the bondage of sin. The over-righteous Pharisees of Christ's time would not for the world come in contact with sinful men, lest they themselves should be polluted. They gathered the robes of their sanctity about them, and considered themselves in such close relation with God that they could afford to despise his poor, unfortunate, sinful children, instead of holding out the hand that would bring them from the kingdom of darkness into the brightness and glory of the kingdom of God. But not so with Jesus Christ. When he was accused by this class of men of mingling with publicans and sinners, his answer to them was, "They that are whole need not a physician; but they that are sick. I came not to call the righteous, but sinners to repentance." As if he had said, you who are righteous and have no need of healing for sin, stand by yourselves; my mission is not to you, but to those who have need of God's help. Such was the spirit of his answer. The incident to which I refer as illustrative of his compassion for sinners, is this: The Jews were always on the alert to entrap the Messiah's feet and bring him into contradiction with the law of Moses. The law of Moses, as first given to Israel, was that if any should be found in adultery they should be stoned to death; but the Rabbis, by nice discriminations of words, practically had rendered that law a dead letter, by reason of which the adulterers in Israel escaped the punishment that God had decreed against them. Therefore, they thought if they could take a person who unquestionably had been guilty of this crime and bring him or her into the presence of Jesus, they would either bring him in conflict with the law of Moses, or with the tradition of the elders, and in either case would have sufficient cause to denounce him before the people. So they found a woman, caught in the act; they dragged her through the streets, and cast her at his feet. "Master," said they, "this woman was taken in adultery, in the very act. Now Moses in the law commanded us, that such should be stoned: but what sayest thou?" He replied, "He that is without sin among you, let him first cast a stone at her." One by one they slunk away, until the woman was left alone with Jesus. When Jesus looked around, and saw none but the woman, he said to her, "Woman, where are thine accusers? hath no man condemned thee?" "No man, Lord," she said. Then Jesus said: "Neither do I condemn thee: go and sin no more." That is how God deals with sinners. It is written that God cannot look upon sin with the least degree of allowance, and that is true, he cannot; but how about the sinner? Why, he may look upon the sinner with infinite compassion. While sin must always be hateful, yet will he help and love the sinner, if he will but go his way and sin no more. Such is our human weakness, and so nearly the level upon which we all move, that there is none of us but will plead mightily for mercy; and, thank God, we shall not plead in vain; for, while our Judge cannot look upon sin with any degree of allowance, his heart goes out in compassion and love to men and he will help them to overcome sin, to fight a good fight, to keep the faith, and at last enable them to win the crown in the kingdom of our God.

God's Spirit of Toleration.

Jesus, moreover, was tolerant. You will recall the circumstance of his having to go through Samaria, and you remember that the Samaritans hated the Jews, and Jesus was a Jew. Some of his disciples went into a village of Samaria, through which Jesus would have to pass, and sought to make arrangements for the Master to stay over night; but the Samaritans closed their doors against him. They had heard of him; he was a Jew; and in the narrowness of their minds they would not admit the hated Jew into their homes. This very much angered the disciple John, who loved Jesus dearly. He was one of the "sons of thunder," and possessed of a spirit that could love; and being strong in love, as is often the case—I was going to say as is always the case—he was likewise strong in hating. He was the type of man that does both heartily. Hence, he went to the Master and asked him if he might not call down fire from heaven upon those Samaritans for thus rejecting the Master. Jesus replied: "Ye know not what spirit ye are of. The Son of Man came to save, not to destroy." A broadness, a liberality truly glorious.

Jesus was properly broad minded—liberal. On one occasion some of the disciples found one casting out devils in the name of Jesus, and they forbade him, because he followed not the Master. When they came into the presence of Jesus, they reported this case and told what they had done. Jesus said, "Forbid him not: for there is no man which shall do a miracle in my name, that can lightly speak evil of me." Then he gave us the other half of that truth, "He that is not for me is against me," by saying, "For he that is not against us is for us." Thus he corrected the narrow-mindedness of his own apostles.

The Severity of God.

But notwithstanding all his mercy, his tolerance, his patience and gentleness, there were times when he, who was so infinitely merciful could also be infinitely just; he who was so infinitely compassionate could be infinitely severe. I give you an instance of it. He had struggled long and hard with those hypocrites, the Scribes and Pharisees; and finally the voice of justice and reproof, as it is to be found in God, speaks forth through Jesus Christ, and this is what he said:

> Woe unto you, scribes and Pharisees, hypocrites! for ye shut up the kingdom of heaven against men: for ye neither go in yourselves, neither suffer ye them that are entering to go in. Woe unto you, scribes and Pharisees, hypocrites! for ye devour widows' houses, and for a pretense make long prayers: therefore ye shall receive the greater damnation.

That is not so gentle, is it? Listen again:

> Woe unto you, scribes and Pharisees, hypocrites! for ye compass sea and land to make one proselyte, and when he is made, ye make him twofold more the child of hell than yourselves. Woe unto you, ye blind guides, which say, Whosoever shall swear by the temple, it is nothing; but whosoever shall swear by the gold of the temple, he is a debtor! Ye fools and blind: for whether is greater, the gold, or the temple that sanctifieth the gold? And, Whosoever, shall swear by the altar, it is nothing; but whosoever sweareth by the gift that is upon it, he is guilty. Ye fools and blind: for whether is greater, the gift, or the altar that sanctifieth the gift? * * * Ye blind guides, which strain at a gnat, and swallow a camel. Woe unto you, scribes and Pharisees! for ye make clean the outside of the cup and of the platter, but within they are full of extortion and excess. Thou blind Pharisee, cleanse first that which is within the cup and platter, that the outside of them may be clean also. Woe unto you, scribes and Pharisees, hypocrites! for ye are like unto whited sepulchres, which indeed appear beautiful outward, but are within full of dead men's bones, and of all uncleanness. Even so ye also outwardly appear righteous unto men, but within ye are full of hypocrisy and iniquity. Woe unto you, scribes and Pharisees, hypocrites! because ye build the tombs of the prophets, and garnish the sepulchres of the righteous, and say, If we had been in the days of our fathers, we would not have been partakers with them in the blood of the prophets. Wherefore ye be witnesses unto yourselves, that ye are the children of them which killed the prophets. Fill ye up then the measure of your fathers. Ye serpents, ye generation of vipers, how can ye escape the damnation of hell?

And this from that gentle, compassionate man! The voice of God in its severity speaks through these tones, and bids us understand that it must be a terrible thing to fall under the displeasure of God. Think of the infinite difference between that sweet compassion which he has for the penitent sinner, and this severe but just arraignment of those who persist in their sins! A warning to all men to beware of the justice of God, when once it shall be aroused!

God Completely Revealed Through Christ.

My friends, this Jesus Christ is God manifested in the flesh, proved to be so from the scripture; the character of God is revealed in the wonderful life that Jesus, the Son of God, lived on earth; in it we see God in action; and from it we see the gentleness, the compassion, and also the justice and severity of God. Jesus Christ is God; and he is also man; but I take no stock in those sectarian refinements which try to tell us about the humanity of Jesus being separate from the divinity of Jesus. He himself made no such distinctions. He was divine, spirit and body, and spirit and body was exalted to the throne of his Father, and sits there now with all the powers of the Godhead residing in him bodily, an immortal, glorified, exalted man! The express image and likeness God of the Father; for as the Son is, so is the Father. Yet when we announce to the world that we believe God to be an exalted man, we are told that we are blasphemers. But as long as the throne of Jesus Christ stands sure, so long as his spirit remains in his immortal body of flesh and bones, glorified and everlasting, shall keep his place by the side of the Father, so long will the doctrine that God is an exalted man hold its place against the idle sophistries of the learned world. The doctrine is true. It cannot be enthroned. A truth is a solemn thing. Not the mockery of ages, not the lampooning of the schoolmen, not the derision of the multitude, not the blasphemy of the world, can affect it; it will always remain true. And this doctrine, announced by Joseph Smith to the world, that God is an exalted man, that Jesus Christ is the revelation of God to the world, and that he is just like his Father, and that those who are his brethren may become as he is, when they have walked in his footsteps—that is a doctrine that will stand sure and fast as the throne of God itself. For Jesus Christ was God manifested in the flesh. He was the revelation of God to the world. He was and is and ever will remain an exalted man. He is, and always will remain, God.

CHAPTER V

A COLLECTION OF PASSAGES FROM "MORMON" WORKS, SETTING FORTH "MORMON" VIEWS OF DEITY.

In this chapter I present a collection of "Mormon" utterances on the subject of Deity, of man, and of his relationship to God. They are selected from discourses and other writings of the Prophet Joseph Smith, from the Book of Mormon, the revelations in the Doctrine and Covenants, the Pearl of Great Price, some of the earlier Church publications, and last of all, I give, by permission, a recent discourse by President Joseph F. Smith. These utterances are arranged in an order, and with the view of establishing the fact that from the beginning of what the world calls "Mormonism," the views contended for in the body of this work, have been the doctrine of the Church.

The Father and the Son are Represented as Distinct Persons, and also as Being in the Form of Men, in the First Vision of the Prophet of the New Dispensation.

It is well known that while the Prophet Joseph Smith was a lad, but fourteen years of age, he became much exercised on the subject of religion, and very much perplexed in consequence of the division and strife existing among the religious sects, by which he was surrounded. And now his own account as to how he sought wisdom and obtained a very important revelation, in which he learned very important truths, both concerning God and the state of the religious world:

> In the midst of this war of words and tumult of opinions, I often said to myself: What is to be done? Who of all these parties are right; or, are they all wrong together? If any one of them be right, which is it, and how shall I know it? While I was laboring under the extreme difficulties caused by the contests of these parties of religionists, I was one day reading the Epistle of James, first chapter and fifth verse, which reads:

If any of you lack wisdom, let him ask of God, that giveth to all men liberally, and upbraideth not; and it shall be given him.

Never did any passage of scripture come with more power to the heart of man than this did at this time to mine. It seemed to enter with great force into every feeling of my heart. I reflected on it again and again, knowing that if any person needed wisdom from God, I did; for how to act I did not know, and unless I could get more wisdom than I then had, I would never know; for the teachers of religion of the different sects understood the same passages of scripture so differently as to destroy all confidence in settling the question by an appeal to the Bible.

At length I came to the conclusion that I must either remain in darkness and confusion, or else I must do as James directs, that is, ask of God. I at length came to the determination to ask of God, concluding that if he gave wisdom to them that lacked wisdom, and would give liberally, and not upbraid, I might venture.

So, in accordance with this, my determination to ask of God, I retired to the woods to make the attempt. It was on the morning of a beautiful clear day, early in the spring of eighteen hundred and twenty. It was the first time in my life that I had made such an attempt, for amidst all my anxieties, I had never as yet made the attempt to pray vocally.

After I had retired to the place where I had previously designed to go, having looked around me, and finding myself alone, I kneeled down and began to offer up the desires of my heart to God. I had scarcely done so when immediately I was seized upon by some power which entirely overcame me, and had such an astonishing influence over me, as to bind my tongue so that I could not speak. Thick darkness gathered around me, and it seemed to me for a time as if I were doomed to sudden destruction.

But, exerting all my powers to call upon God to deliver me out of the power of this enemy which had seized upon me; and at the very moment when I was ready to sink into despair and abandon myself to destruction—not to an imaginary ruin, but to the power of some actual being from the unseen world, who had such marvelous power as I had never before felt in any being—just at this moment of great alarm, I saw a pillar of light exactly over my head, above the brightness of the sun, which descended gradually until it fell upon me. It no sooner appeared than I felt myself delivered from the enemy which held me bound.

When the light rested upon me I saw two personages, whose brightness and glory defy all description, standing above me in the air. One of them spake unto me, calling me by name, and said, pointing to the other: "This is my beloved Son, hear Him!"

My object in going to enquire of the Lord, was to know, which, of all the sects, was right; that I might know which to join. No sooner, therefore, did I get possession of myself, so as to be able to speak, than I asked the personages who stood above me in the light, which of all the sects, was right—and which I should join.

I was answered that I must join none of them, for they were all wrong, and the personage who addressed me said that all their creeds were an abomination in his sight; that those professors were all corrupt; that they draw near to me with their lips, but their hearts are far from me; they teach for doctrines the commandments of men, having a form of godliness, but denying the power thereof.

He again forbade me to join with any of them; and many other things did he say unto me, which I cannot write at this time.[A]

[Footnote A: Pearl of Great Price, pp. 83-85. Also History of Church Vol. I, pp. 4-6.]

Of the importance of this vision, and the effects growing out of it, I have elsewhere said:

First, it is a flat contradiction to the sectarian assumption that revelation had ceased; that God had no further communication to make to man.

Second, it reveals the errors into which men had fallen, concerning the personages of the Godhead. It makes it manifest that God is not an incorporeal being without form, or body, or parts; on the contrary he appeared to the Prophet in the form of a man, as he did to the ancient prophets. Thus, after centuries of controversy, the simple truth of the Scriptures, which teach that man was created in the likeness of God—hence God must be the same in form as man—was re-affirmed.

Third, it corrected the error of the theologians respecting the oneness of the persons of the Father and the Son. Instead of being one person, as the theologians teach, they are distinct in their personality; and there is a plurality of Gods, for the Father and the Son are two individuals, as much so as any father and son on earth; and the oneness of the Godhead referred to in the scriptures, must have reference to unity of purpose and of will; the mind of one being the mind of the other, and so as to will and other attributes. In other words, the oneness of the Godhead is a moral and spiritual union, not a physical one.

The announcement of these truths, coupled with that other truth proclaimed by the Son of God, *viz*: that none of the sects and churches of Christendom were acknowledged as the church or kingdom of God, furnish the elements for a religious revolution that will affect the very foundations of modern Christian theology. In a moment, all the rubbish concerning theology, which had accumulated through all the centuries since the gospel and authority to administer its ordinances had been taken from the earth, was grandly swept aside—the living rocks of truth were made bare upon which the Church of Christ was to be founded—a New Dispensation of the gospel was about to be committed to the earth—God had raised up a witness for himself among the children of men.[A]

[Footnote A: New Witnesses for God, vol. I, pp. 173-4.]

THE DOCTRINE OF THE GODHEAD ACCORDING TO THE BOOK OF MORMON.

The Book of Mormon is not a formal treatise on the subject of theology. It is in the main an abridgment of ancient Nephite and Jaredite records, and recounts the hand-dealings of God with these ancient peoples. The existence of God it takes for granted, and, of course, since its revelations are local, that is, they pertain to this earth and its inhabitants only, it has reference to our Godhead alone. It makes reference, therefore, only to our God, and speaks of him in the singular number—as being one. But notwithstanding this, the three persons of the Godhead are frequently spoken of as being separate and distinct personalities, as the following passages will illustrate. A Nephite prophet, reasoning upon the subject of the resurrection and the restoration that will be brought about in connection therewith, says:

> But all things shall be restored to their perfect frame, as they are now, or in the body, and shall be brought and be arraigned before the bar of Christ the Son, and God the Father, and the Holy Spirit, which is one eternal God, to be

judged according to their works, whether they be good or whether they be evil.[A]

[Footnote A: Alma, 11:44.]

Again, the Savior when instructing the Nephites in the manner of baptizing, said:

> And now behold, these are the words which ye shall say, calling them [those to be baptized] by name; saying: Having authority given me of Jesus Christ, I baptize you in the name of the Father, and of the Son, and of the Holy Ghost. Amen. * * * And after this manner shall ye baptize in my name, for behold, verily I say unto you; that the Father, and the Son, and the Holy Ghost are one; and I am in the Father, and the Father in me, and the Father and I are one. * * * * And this is my doctrine, and it is the doctrine which the Father hath given unto me; and I bear record of the Father, and the Father beareth record of me, and the Holy Ghost beareth record of the Father and me. * * * * This is my doctrine, and I bear record of it from the Father; and whoso believeth in me, believeth in the Father also, and unto him will the Father bear record of me; for he will visit him with fire, and with the Holy Ghost.[A]

[Footnote A: III Nephi, 11:24-27; 32, 35.]

Also the Prophet Mormon, speaking of the work of Christ, says:

> And he hath brought to pass the redemption of the world, whereby he that is found guiltless before him at the judgment day, hath it given unto him to dwell in the presence of God in his kingdom, to sing ceaseless praises with the choirs above, unto the Father and unto the Son, and unto the Holy Ghost, which are one God.[A]

[Footnote A: Mormon, 7:7.]

Seeing, then, that reference is so frequently made to the members of the Godhead as separate and distinct persons, it is clear that the Book of Mormon is in harmony with the views contended for in the body of this work, as to the plurality of Gods, and the doctrine receives increased emphasis from other passages of the work. The Prophet Alma, for instance, says:

> He [God] gave commandments unto men, they having first transgressed the first commandments as to things which were temporal, *and becoming as Gods,* knowing good from evil, etc.[A]

[Footnote A: Alma, 12:31.]

Then again, the Savior when instructing the Nephite apostles, said to them:

> Ye shall be judges of this people, according to the judgment which I shall give unto you, which shall be just; therefore, what manner of men ought ye to be? Verily I say unto you, *even as I am.* * * * * And ye shall sit down in the Kingdom of my Father; yea, your joy shall be full, even as the Father hath given me fullness of joy; *and ye shall be even as I am, and I am even as the Father; and the Father and I are one.*[A]

[Footnote A: III Nephi, 27:27; 28:10.]

If the disciples became as Christ, and Christ, we are assured, is as the Father is, then these words of Jesus contemplate that these men will become as God now is, and hence Gods, and hence a plurality of Gods.

With reference to the form of God, the Book of Mormon has two very important and very emphatic passages on the subject. The first Nephi, in a great vision given to him of the future, was attended by a spirit who gave him explanations, as the several parts of his vision passed before him. And now Nephi's account:

> And it came to pass that the Spirit said unto me, Look! and I looked, and beheld a tree; * * * * and the beauty thereof was far beyond, yea, exceeding all beauty, and the whiteness thereof did exceed the whiteness of the driven snow. And it came to pass after I had seen the tree, I said unto the Spirit: I behold thou hast shown unto me the tree which is precious above all. And he said unto me: What desirest thou? And I said unto him: To know the interpretation thereof; *for I spake unto him as a man speaketh; for I beheld that he was in the form of a man; yet, nevertheless, I knew that it was the Spirit of the Lord; and he spake unto me as a man speaketh with another.*[A]

[Footnote A: I Nephi, 11:8-11.]

The second passage alluded to is found in the book of Ether. The Prophet Moriancumr, the brother of Jared, when about to depart with his colony in barges across the great deep, had prepared certain stones which he prayed the Lord to make luminous, that they might have light in the barges while on their journey. He had approached the Lord with great faith, and expressed full confidence in the power of God to do the thing for which he prayed; and now the Book of Mormon statement of the matter:

And it came to pass that when the brother of Jared had said these words, behold the Lord stretched forth his hand and touched the stones, one by one with his finger; and the vail was taken from off the eyes of the brother of Jared, and he saw the finger of the Lord; and it was as the finger of a man, like unto flesh and blood; and the brother of Jared fell down before the Lord, for he was struck with fear. * * * * And the Lord said unto him, arise, why hast thou fallen? And he said unto the Lord, I saw the finger of the Lord, and I feared lest he should smite me; for I knew not that the Lord had flesh and blood. And the Lord said unto him, Because of thy faith thou hast seen that I shall take upon me flesh and blood; and never has man come before me with such exceeding faith as thou hast; for were it not so, you could not have seen my finger. * * * * And when he had said these words, behold, the Lord shewed himself unto, him, and said, Because thou knowest these things, you are redeemed from the fall; therefore you are brought back into my presence; therefore I shew myself unto you. Behold, I am he who was prepared from the foundation of the world to redeem my people. Behold, I am Christ. I am the Father and the Son.[A] In me shall all mankind have light, and that eternally, even they who shall believe on my name; and they shall become my sons and my daughters. And never have I shewed myself unto, man whom I have created, for never has man believed in me as thou hast. Seest thou that thou art created after mine own image? Yea, even all men were created in the beginning, after mine own image. Behold, this body, which you now behold, is the body of my spirit; and man have I created after the body of my spirit; and even as I appear unto thee to be in the spirit, will I appear unto my people in the flesh.[B]

[Footnote A: This expression made several times in the Book of Mormon, should not confuse the reader. Jesus is spoken of in this passage as both Father and Son for the reason that he received of the fullness of the Father; that is, a fullness of his glory, his power, and dominion, hence Jesus represented God in his completeness—"in him dwelleth all the fullness of the Godhead bodily" (Col. 2:9); hence Deity complete, hence both Father and Son. In another sense also is Jesus the "very eternal Father of heaven and earth:" he is the immediate creator of them: and to the extent that a creator may be regarded as a father, Jesus may be regarded as the very eternal

Father of heaven and earth. He is called the Son because he tabernacled in the flesh, and, in his earthly career, received not a fullness of the Godhead at first. See Doctrine and Covenants, Sec. 93. Also Mosiah 15:1-4, and the remarks of President Joseph F. Smith in this chapter.]

[Footnote B: Ether 3:6-16.]

From this it will be seen that the Book of Mormon is in harmony with the Bible's plain anthropomorphism; as also the one is in harmony with the other in affirming the necessary plurality of Gods.

THE DOCTRINES OF THE GODHEAD AND MAN ACCORDING TO THE BOOK OF ABRAHAM.

The book of Abraham came into the hands of the Prophet Joseph Smith in the form of Egyptian papyrus, in the summer of 1835. The following winter in his history the Prophet frequently speaks of working upon the translation of this ancient record. The translation was not completed and published, however, until March, 1842, at Nauvoo, when it appeared in the *Times and Seasons*, numbers 9 and 10, Vol. III. In his writings and teachings the Prophet frequently refers to this ancient record with every mark of approval. In the first publication of the work the introductory heading declared it to be "the Book of Abraham, written by his own hand upon papyrus." It will be understood, then, that its doctrines are those of the great prophet-patriarch, Abraham. The book gives an account of the call of Abraham from Ur of the Chaldees and his sojourn and adventures in Egypt. The extracts from it here given deal with the revelations of God to the patriarch concerning the planetary system, pre-existence and nature of man, and the creation of the earth by the Gods—for Abraham throughout his account of creation uses the plural, "the Gods said let there be light;" "the Gods said let us make man in our image," etc., etc., hence it is clear that the doctrine of the plurality of Gods was plainly taught through this sacred scripture in the days of Joseph Smith, for he translated it, and it was published by him in the *Times and Seasons* while he was the editor of that journal. And now a few extracts from the book itself:

> And I, Abraham, had the Urim and Thummim, which the Lord my God had given unto me, in Ur of the Chaldees; and I saw the stars, that they were very great, and that one of them was nearest unto the throne of God; and there were many great ones which were near unto it; and the Lord said unto me: These are the governing ones; and the name of the great one is Kolob, because it is near unto me, for I am the Lord thy God: and I have set this one to govern all those which belong

to the same order as that upon which thou standest. And the Lord said unto me, by the Urim and Thummim, that Kolob was after the manner of the Lord, according to its times and seasons in the revolutions thereof; that one revolution was a day unto the Lord, after his manner of reckoning, it being one thousand years according to the time appointed unto that whereon thou standest. This is the reckoning of the Lord's time, according to the reckoning of Kolob. * * * *

And the Lord said unto me: Now, Abraham, these two facts exist, behold thine eyes see it; it is given unto thee to know the times of reckoning, and the set time, yea, the set time of the earth upon which thou standest, and the set time of the greater light which is set to rule the day, and the set time of the lesser light which is set to rule the night. Now the set time of the lesser light is a longer time as to its reckoning than the reckoning of the time of the earth upon which thou standest. And where these two facts exist, there shall be another fact above them, that is, there shall be another planet whose reckoning of time shall be longer still; and thus there shall be the reckoning of the time of one planet above another, until thou come nigh unto Kolob, which Kolob is after the reckoning of the Lord's time, which Kolob is set nigh unto the throne of God, to govern all those planets which belong to the same order as that upon which thou standest. And it is given unto thee to know the set time of all the stars that are set to give light, until thou come near unto the throne of God. Thus I, Abraham, talked with the Lord face to face, as one man talketh with another; and he told me of the works which his hands had made: and he said unto me: My son, my son, (and his hand was stretched out,) behold I will show you all these. And he put his hand upon mine eyes, and I saw those things which his hand had made, which were many; and they multiplied before mine eyes, and I could not see the end thereof.
* * * *

And it was in the night time when the Lord spake these words unto me: I will multiply thee, and thy seed after thee, like unto these; and if thou canst count the number of sands, so shall be the number of thy seeds. And the Lord said unto me: Abraham, I show these things unto thee before ye go into Egypt, that ye may declare all these words. If two things exist, and there be one above the other, there shall be greater things above them; therefore Kolob is the greatest of all the Kokaubeam (stars) that thou hast seen, because it is nearest unto me. Now, if there be two things, one above the other, and the moon be above the earth, then it may be that a planet or star may exist above it; * * * as, also, if there be two spirits, and one shall be more intelligent than the other, yet these two spirits, notwithstanding one is more intelligent than the other, have no beginning; they existed before, they shall have no end, they shall exist after, for they are gnolaum, or eternal. And the Lord said unto me: These two facts do exist, that there are two spirits, one being more intelligent than the other; there shall be another more intelligent than they; I am the Lord thy God, I am more intelligent than them all. * * * *

I dwell in the midst of them all; I now, therefore, have come down unto thee to deliver unto thee the works which my hands have made, wherein my wisdom excelleth them all, for I rule in the heavens above, and in the earth beneath, in all wisdom and prudence, over all the intelligences thine eyes have seen from the beginning; I came down in the beginning in the midst of all the intelligences thou hast seen.

Now the Lord had shown unto me, Abraham, the intelligences that were organized before the world was; and among all these there were many of the noble and great ones; and God saw these souls that they were good, and he stood in the midst of them, and he said: These I will make my rulers; for he stood among those that were spirits, and he saw that they were good; and he said unto me: Abraham, thou art one of them; thou wast chosen before thou wast born. And there stood one among them that was like unto God, and he said unto those who were with him: We will go down, for there is space there, and we will take of these materials, and we will make an earth whereupon these may dwell; and we will prove them herewith, to see if they will do all things whatsoever the Lord their God shall command them; and they who keep their first estate shall be added upon; and they who keep not their first estate shall not have glory in the same kingdom with those who keep their first estate; and they who keep their second estate shall have glory added upon their heads for ever and ever. And the Lord said: Whom shall I send? And one answered like unto the Son of Man: Here am I, send me. And another answered and said: Here am I, send me. And the Lord said: I will send the first. And the second was angry, and kept not his first estate; and, at that day, many followed after him. And then the Lord said: Let us go down. And they went down at the beginning, and they, that is, the Gods, organized and formed the heavens and the earth. And the earth, after it was formed, was empty and desolate, because they had not formed anything but the earth; and darkness reigned upon the face of the deep, and the Spirit of the Gods was brooding upon the face of the waters. And they (the Gods) said: Let there be light; and there was light. And they (the Gods) comprehended the light, for it was bright; and they divided the light, or caused it to be divided, from the darkness. And the Gods called the light Day, and the darkness they called Night, And it came to pass that from the evening until morning they called night; and from the morning until the evening they called day; and this was the first, or the beginning, of that which they called day and night. And the Gods also said: Let there be an expanse in the midst of the waters, and it shall divide the waters from the waters. And the Gods ordained the expanse, so that it divided the waters which were under the expanse from the waters which were above the expanse; and it was so, even as they ordained. (Pearl of Great Price, pp. 60-67.)

And thus the account of creation proceeds throughout the seven periods thereof, and it is always the Gods did this or that until the whole work of creation was prepared for man.

THE GODHEAD ACCORDING TO THE DOCTRINE AND COVENANTS.

The book of Doctrine and Covenants in the main is a collection of revelations given through the Prophet Joseph Smith. It is not a formal treatise upon theology. This collection of revelations assumes the existence of God, and only incidentally treats of His being and attributes. And since the revelations pertain to our earth, and its heavens, and our God, the singular number is used in speaking of God; and yet in these revelations the persons of the Godhead are spoken of as being distinct from one another in the sense of being separate and distinct individuals, as the following passages illustrate:

There is a God in heaven, who is infinite and eternal, from everlasting to everlasting, the same unchangeable God, the framer of heaven and earth, and all things which are in them; and that he created man, male and female, after his own image and his own likeness, created he them and gave unto them commandments that they should love and serve him, the only living and true God, and that he should be the only being whom they should worship. But by the transgression of these holy laws, man became sensual and devilish, and became fallen man. Wherefore the Almighty God gave his Only Begotten Son, as it is written in those scriptures which have been given of him. He suffered temptations but gave no heed unto them; he was crucified, died, and rose again the third day; and ascended into heaven, to sit down on the right hand of the Father, to reign with almighty power according to the will of the Father, that as many as would believe and be baptized in his holy name, and endure in faith to the end, should be saved; not only those who believed after he came in the meridian of time, in the flesh, but all those from the beginning, even as many as were before he came, who believed in the words of the holy prophets, who spake as they were inspired by the gift of the Holy Ghost, who truly testified of him in all things, should have eternal life, as well as those who should come after, who should believe in the gifts and callings of God by the Holy Ghost, which beareth record of the Father, and of the Son; which Father, Son, and Holy Ghost are one God, infinite and eternal, without end. Amen.[A]

[Footnote A: Doc. and Cov. Sec. 20:17-28.]

So also in section ninety-three the distinction between Father and Son and Holy Spirit is clearly made; and man declared to be of the same race with God. Indeed one may say that the supposed gulf of separation is swept away; that on the one hand the divinity of man is proclaimed, and on the other, the humanity of God. That is, there is identity of race between Gods and men; though man is now in a fallen state, working upward towards God, through the plan of redemption in Christ Jesus:

> Every soul who forsaketh his sins and cometh unto me, and calleth on my name, and obeyeth my voice, and keepeth my commandments, shall see my face and know that I am, and that I am the true light that lighteth every man that cometh into the world; and that I am in the Father, and the Father in

me, and the Father and I are one: the Father because he gave me of his fullness, and the Son because I was in the world and made flesh my tabernacle, and dwelt among the sons of men. I was in the world and received of my Father, and the works of him were plainly manifest; and John saw and bore record of the fullness of my glory, and the fullness of John's record is hereafter to be revealed: and he bore record, saying, I saw his glory that he was in the beginning before the world was; therefore in the beginning the Word was, for he was the Word, even the messenger of salvation the light and the Redeemer of the world; the Spirit of truth, who came into the world, because the world was made by him, and in him was the life of men and the light of men. The worlds were made by him; men were made by him: all things were made by him, and through him, and of him. And I, John, bear record that I beheld his glory, as the glory of the Only Begotten of the Father, full of grace and truth, even the Spirit of truth, which came and dwelt in the flesh, and dwelt among us. And I, John, saw that he received not of the fullness at the first, but received grace for grace: and he received not of the fullness at first, but continued from grace to grace, until he received a fullness; and thus he was called the Son of God, because he received not of the fullness at the first. And I, John, bear record, and lo, the heavens were opened, and the Holy Ghost descended upon him in the form of a dove, and sat upon him, and there came a voice out of heaven saying, This is my beloved Son. And I, John, bear record that he received a fullness of the glory of the Father; and he received all power, both in heaven and on earth, and the glory of the Father was with him, for he dwelt in him. * * * And I give unto you these sayings that ye may understand and know how to worship, and know what you worship, that you may come unto the Father in my name, and in due time receive of his fullness. * * * And now, verily I say unto you, I was in the beginning with the Father, and am the first-born. * * * Ye were also in the beginning with the Father; that which is Spirit, even the Spirit of truth. * * * Man was also in the beginning with God. Intelligence, or the light of truth, was not created or made, neither indeed can be. All truth is independent in that sphere in which God has placed it, to act for itself, as all intelligence also, otherwise there is no existence. Behold, here, is the agency of man, and here is the condemnation of man, because that which was from the beginning is plainly manifest unto them, and they receive not the light. And every man whose spirit receiveth not the light is under condemnation, for man is spirit. The elements are eternal, and spirit and element, inseparably connected, receive a fullness of joy; and when separated, man cannot receive a fullness of joy. The elements are the tabernacle of God; yea man is the tabernacle of God, even temples; and whatsoever temple is defiled, God shall destroy that temple. [A]

[Footnote A: Doc. and Cov. Sec. 93:1-35.]

Again:

The Father has a body of flesh and bones as tangible as man's; the Son also: but the Holy Ghost has not a body of flesh and bones, but is a personage of Spirit. Were it not so, the Holy Ghost could not dwell in us.[A]

[Footnote A: Ibid Sec. 130:22.]

Since then there is in these revelations, a recognition of the distinction between the persons of the Godhead, it is clear that the doctrine of a plurality of Gods is recognized. It is also incidentally recognized in other passages of the Doctrine and Covenants. In section seventy-six, where a description is given of the blessedness of those who believe and obey the gospel, it is said:

They are they who are the church of the first born. They are they into whose hands the Father has given all things. They are they who are Priests and Kings, who have received of his fullness, and of his glory, and are Priests of the Most High, after the order of Melchizedek, which was after the order of Enoch, which was after the order of the Only Begotten Son; wherefore, as it is written, *they are Gods, even the sons of God*—wherefore all things are theirs; whether life or death, or things present, or things to come, all are theirs and they are Christ's and Christ is God's.[A]

[Footnote A: Doc. and Cov. Sec. 76:54-59.]

The revelation in which the above passage appears was first published in the *Evening and Morning Star*, July, 1832. Again, in a prayer and prophecy written by Joseph Smith while in Liberty prison, March, 1839, in the course of describing the power and glory and blessedness to be revealed in the dispensation of the Fullness of Times, the prophet declares that all things shall be made known—

According to that which was ordained in the midst of *the Council of the Eternal God of all other Gods*, before this world was.[A]

[Footnote A: Doc. and Cov. Sec. 121:32.]

Again, in speaking of those who fall short of complete obedience to the fullness of the Gospel of Jesus Christ, and describing their limitations the Prophet says:

> From henceforth they are not Gods, but are angels of God, forever and ever.[A]

[Footnote A: Doc. and Cov. Sec. 132:17.]

On the other hand he declares that all those who obey the fullness of the gospel—

> Shall pass by the angels, *and the Gods*, * * * to their exaltation and glory in all things. * * * *Then shall they be Gods*, because they have no end; therefore shall they be from everlasting to everlasting, because they continue; then shall they be above all, because all things are subject unto them. *Then shall they be Gods*, because they have all power, and the angels are subject unto them.[A]

[Footnote A: Doc. and Cov. Sec. 132:19, 20.]

Thus the revelations of God to the Church from the earliest times, and now collected in the Doctrine and Covenants, teach that men and Gods are identical in race, and that there is a plurality of Gods.

THE "MORMON" DOCTRINE OF DEITY AS SET FORTH IN THE DISCOURSES OF THE PROPHET JOSEPH SMITH AND EARLY CHURCH PUBLICATIONS.

From the King Follett Sermon, April 7, 1844. [A]

[Footnote A: *Millenial Star*, vol. xxiii, p. 245 *et seq.*]

> It is necessary for us to have an understanding of God himself in the beginning.
>
> * * * *
>
> There are but a very few beings in the world who understand rightly the character of God. The great majority of mankind do not comprehend anything, either that which is past, or that which is to come, as respects their relationship to God.

* * * *

If men do not comprehend the character of God, they do not comprehend themselves.

* * * *

What sort of a being was God in the beginning? Open your ears and hear, all ye ends of the earth. * * * God himself was once as we are now, and is an exalted Man, and sits enthroned in yonder heavens! That is the great secret. If the vail was rent today, and the great God who holds this world in its orbit; and who upholds all worlds and all things by his power, was to make himself visible—I say, if you were to see him today, you would see him like a man in form—like yourselves, in all the person, image, and very form as a man; for Adam was created in the very fashion, image, and likeness of God, and received instructions from, and walked, talked, and conversed with him, as one man talks and communes with another.

* * * *

It is necessary we should understand the character and being of God, and how he came to be so; for I am going to tell you how God came to be God. We have imagined and supposed that God was God from all eternity. I will refute that idea, and will take away the vail, so that you may see. * * * It is the first principle of the gospel to know for a certainty the character of God, and to know that we may converse with him as one man converses with another, and that he was once a man like us; yea, that God himself, the Father of us all, dwelt on an earth, the same as Jesus Christ himself did.

* * * *

The scriptures inform us that Jesus said, "As the Father hath power in himself, even so hath the Son power"—to do what? Why, what the Father did. The answer is obvious—in a manner to lay down his body and take it up again. Jesus, what are you going to do? To lay down my life, as my Father did, and take it up again. Do you believe it? If you do not believe it, you do not believe the Bible.[A]

* * * *

[Footnote A: The argument here made by the Prophet is very much strengthened by the following passage: "The Son can do nothing of himself, but what he seeth the Father do; for what things soever he [the Father] doeth, these also the Son doeth likewise" (St. John 5:19).

Here, then, is eternal life: to know the only wise and true God; and you have got to learn how to be Gods yourselves, and to be kings and priests to God, the same as all Gods have done before you—namely, by going from one small degree to another, and from a small capacity to a great one; from grace to grace, from exaltation to exaltation, until you attain to the resurrection of the dead, and are able to dwell in everlasting burnings, and to sit in glory, as do those who sit enthroned in everlasting power.

* * * *

How consoling to the mourners when they are called to part with a husband, wife, father, mother, child or dear relative, to know that although the earthly tabernacle is laid down and dissolved, they shall rise again to dwell in everlasting burnings, in immortal glory, not to sorrow, suffer, or die any more; but they shall be heirs of God and joint heirs with Jesus Christ. What is it? [i. e., to be joint heirs with Jesus Christ]. To inherit the same power, the same glory, and the same exaltation, until you arrive at the station of a God and ascend the throne of eternal power, the same as those who have gone before. What did Jesus do? Why, I do the things I saw my Father do when worlds came rolling into existence. My Father worked out his kingdom with fear and trembling, and I must do the same; and when I get my kingdom, I shall present it to my Father, so that he may obtain kingdom upon kingdom, and it will exalt him in glory. He will then take a higher exaltation, and I will take his place, and thereby become exalted myself. So that Jesus treads in the tracks of his Father, and inherits what God did before; and God is thus glorified and exalted in the salvation and exaltation of all his children. It is plain beyond disputation, and you thus learn some of the first principles of the gospel, about which so much has been said.

* * * *

When you climb up a ladder, you must begin at the bottom, and ascend step by step, until you arrive at the top; and so it is with the principles of the gospel—you must begin with the first, and go on until you learn all the principles of exaltation. *But it will be a great while after you have passed through the vail before you will have learned them. It is not all to be comprehended in this world: it will be a great work to learn our salvation and exaltation, even beyond the grave.*

* * * *

I shall comment on the very first Hebrew word in the Bible; I will make a comment on the very first sentence of the history of the creation in the Bible. *Berosheit*: I want to analyze the word. *Baith*—in, by, through, etc. *Rosh*—the head. *Sheit*—grammatical termination. When the inspired man wrote it, he did not put the bath there. A Jew, without any authority, added the word: he thought it too bad to begin to talk about the *head*! It read at first, "The head one of the Gods brought forth the Gods." That is the true meaning of the words. *Baurau* signifies to bring forth. If you do not believe it, you do not believe the learned man of God. * * * Thus the head God brought forth the Gods in the grand council. * * * The head God called together the Gods, and sat in grand council to bring forth the world. The grand Councilors sat at the head in yonder heavens, and contemplated the creation of the worlds which were created at that time. * * * In the beginning, the head of the Gods called a council of the Gods, and they came together and concocted a plan to create the world and people it.

* * * *

From the Discourse of June 16, 1844. [A]

[Footnote A: *Mill. Star* Vol. 24, p. 108, *et seq.*

The Prophet's text was: "And hath made us kings and priests unto God *and his Father*: to him be glory and dominion forever and ever, Amen." (Revelation of St. John 1:6.)

It is altogether correct in the translation. Now, you know that of late some malicious and corrupt men have sprung up and apostatized from the Church of Jesus Christ of Latter-day Saints, and they declare that the Prophet believes in a plurality of Gods; and, lo and behold! we have discovered a very great secret, they cry—"The Prophet says there are many Gods, and this proves that he has fallen."

* * * *

I will preach on the plurality of Gods. I have selected this text for the express purpose. I wish to declare I have always, and in all congregations when I have preached on the subject of the Deity, it has been the plurality of Gods. It has been preached by the Elders fifteen years. I have always declared God to be a distinct personage, Jesus Christ a separate and distinct personage from God the Father, and that the Holy Ghost was a distinct personage and a spirit; and these three constitute three distinct personages and three Gods. If this is in accordance with the New Testament, lo and behold! we have three Gods anyhow, and they are plural; and who can contradict it? The text says—"And hath made us kings and priests unto God *and his Father.*" The Apostles have discovered that there were Gods above, for Paul says God was the Father of our Lord Jesus Christ. My object was to preach the Scriptures, and preach the doctrine they contain, there being a God above the Father of our Lord Jesus Christ I am bold to declare. I have taught all the strong doctrines publicly, and always teach stronger doctrines in public than in private. John was one of the men, and the Apostles declare they were made kings and priests unto God the Father of our Lord Jesus Christ. It reads just so in the Revelations. Hence, the doctrine of a plurality of Gods is as prominent in the Bible as any other doctrine. It is all over the face of the Bible. It stands beyond the power of controversy. "A wayfaring man, though a fool, need not err therein."

* * * *

Paul says there are Gods many, and Lords many, * * but to us there is but one God—that is, *pertaining* to us; and he is in all and through all. But if Joseph Smith says there are Gods many, and Lords many, they cry:—"Away with him! Crucify him, crucify him!" * * * Paul, if Joseph Smith is a blasphemer, you are. I say there are Gods many, and Lords many, but to us only one; and we are to be in subjection to that one. * * * Some say I do not interpret the Scriptures the same as they do. They say it means the heathen's gods. Paul says there are Gods many, and Lords many; and that makes a plurality of Gods, in spite of the whims of all men. You know, and I testify, that Paul had no allusion to the heathen gods. I have it from God. * * * I have a witness of the Holy

Ghost, and a testimony that Paul had no allusion to the heathen gods in the text.

I will show from the Hebrew Bible that I am correct, and the first word shows [the existence of] a plurality of Gods. * * * *Berosheit baurau Eloheim ait aushamayeen vehau auraits*, rendered by King James' translators, "In the beginning God created the heavens and the earth." I want to analyze the word *Berosheit*: *Rosh*, the head; *Sheit*, a grammatical termination. The *Baith* was not originally put there when the inspired man wrote it, but it has been since added by a Jew. *Baurau* signifies to bring forth; *Eloheim* is from the word, *Eloi*, God, in the singular number; and by adding the word *heim*, it renders it Gods. It read first—"In the beginning the head of the Gods brought forth the Gods," or, as others have translated it—"The head of the Gods called the Gods together."

* * * *

The head God organized the heavens and the earth. * * * In the beginning the heads of the Gods organized the heavens and the earth. * * * * If we pursue the Hebrew text further it reads *Berosheit baurau Eloheim ait aushamayeen vehau auraits.*-"The head one of the Gods said, Let us make man in our own image." I once asked a learned Jew if the Hebrew language compels us to render all words ending in heim in the plural, why not render the first, Eloheim, plural? He replied, That is the rule with few exceptions; but in this case it would ruin the Bible. He acknowledged I was right.

* * * *

In the very beginning the Bible shows there is a plurality of Gods beyond the power of refutation. * * * The word *Eloheim* ought to be in the plural all the way through—Gods. The head of the Gods appointed one God for us; and when you take a [this] view of the subject, it sets one free to see all the beauty, holiness, and perfection of all the Gods.

Many men say there is one God; the Father, the Son, and the Holy Ghost are only one God! I say that is a strange God, three in one, and one in three! It is a curious organization. "Father, I pray not for the world; but I pray for them which thou hast given me." * * * * I want to read the text to you myself—"Holy Father, keep through thine own name those whom thou hast given me, that they may be one, as we are." I am agreed with the Father and the Father is agreed with me, and we are agreed as one. The Greek shows that it should be *agreed*.

"Father, I pray for them which thou hast given me out of the world, and not for these alone, but for them also which shall believe on me through their word, that they may all be agreed, as thou, Father, art agreed with me, and I with thee, that they also may be agreed with us," and all come to dwell in unity, and in all the glory and everlasting burnings of the Gods; and then we shall see as we are seen, and be as our God, and he is as his Father.

* * * *

I want to reason a little on this subject. I learned it by translating the [Egyptian] papyrus which is now in my house. I learned a testimony concerning Abraham, and he reasoned concerning the God of heaven. "In order to do that," said he, "suppose we have two facts: that supposes another fact may exist—two men on the earth, one wiser than the other, would logically show that another who is wiser than the wisest may exist. Intelligences exist one above another, so that there is no end to them." If Abraham reasoned thus—If Jesus Christ was the Son of God, and John discovered that God, the Father of Jesus Christ, had a Father, you may suppose that *he* had a Father also. Where was there ever a son without a father? And where was there ever a father without first being a son? Whenever did a tree or anything spring into existence without a progenitor? And everything comes in this way: Paul says that which is earthly is in the likeness of that which is heavenly. Hence, if Jesus had a Father, can we not believe that he [that Father] had a Father also? I despise the idea of being scared to death at such doctrine, for the Bible is full of it. * * * Jesus said that the Father wrought precisely in the same way as his Father had done before him. As the Father had done before, he laid down his life, and took it up the same as his Father had done before [him].

* * * *

They found fault with Jesus Christ because he said he was the Son of God, and made himself equal with God. * * * What did Jesus say, "Is it not written in your law, I said, Ye are Gods? If he called them Gods, unto whom the word of God came, and the Scriptures cannot be broken, say ye of him whom the Father has sanctified and sent into the world, Thou blasphemest, because I said I am the Son of God?" It was through him that they drank of the spiritual rock. * * * * Jesus, if they were called Gods unto whom the word of God came, why should it be thought blasphemy that I should say I am the Son of God?

* * * *

They who obtain a glorious resurrection from the dead are exalted far above principalities, powers, thrones, dominions, and angels, and are expressly declared to be heirs of God and joint heirs with Jesus Christ, all having eternal power. The Scriptures are a mixture of very strange doctrines to the Christian world, who are blindly led by the blind. I will refer to another Scripture. "Now," says God, when he visited Moses in the bush, * * * "Thou shalt be a God unto the children of Israel." God said: "Thou shalt be a God unto Aaron, and he shall be thy spokesman." I believe those Gods that God reveals as Gods, to be sons of God, and all can cry Abba, Father! Sons of God who exalt themselves to be Gods, even from before the foundation of the world, and are the only Gods I have a reverence for. John said he was a king. "And from Jesus Christ, who is the faithful witness, and the first begotten of the dead, and the Prince of the kings of the earth. Unto him that loved us, and washed us from our sins in his own blood, and hath made us kings and priests unto God and his Father; to him be glory and dominion forever and ever. Amen." O thou God who art King of kings and Lord of lords, the sectarian world, by their actions, declare— "We cannot believe thee."

USE OF THE WORD ELOHIM. [A]

BY PROFESSOR W. H. CHAMBERLIN, OF THE BRIGHAM YOUNG COLLEGE, LOGAN, UTAH.

[Footnote A: During the progress of the discussion between the Rev. C. Van Der Donckt and myself, as published in the *Improvement Era*, Professor William H. Chamberlin of the Brigham Young College, Logan, Utah, contributed the following brief though valuable paper on the use of the word "Elohim" in the Bible, which by his kind consent I am permitted to publish here.]

Two words, *El*, of which *Elim* was the plural form, and *Eloah*, of which *Elohim* was the plural, were applied generally to Deity by the Hebrew people. All these forms are found in the other Semitic languages, and are, therefore, very ancient in origin.

Under severest discipline the people of Israel were educated in the school of monotheism, in order that God's nature might be revealed to man, and in order that unity might be introduced into the moral life of man. Under this discipline, the people of Israel must have learned to apply the plural form Elohim, which their fathers had used of Deity, in speaking of the one God whom they had been taught to serve.

The Hebrew language would allow them to do this, for a few nouns, when used by them in the plural, seemed to magnify the original idea. In such cases the plural form was treated grammatically as singular. An example may be found in Job 40:15, where the plural form behemoth is used to intensify the image of the animal there being described, as is shown by context. In the same verse, the behemoth is referred to by the singular pronoun he.

But the use of *Elohim*, in this sense, by the later writers of Israel, is not necessarily opposed to the view that in the earliest documents or writings which the Hebrews possessed, it was applied to a plurality of Gods.

The objection to this view has been made that, with the plural form *Elohim*, in Gen. 1, the singular verb is used. Such a use of a singular predicate with a plural subject is, however, common in Hebrew of *Harper's Hebrew Syntax* we find the following rule covering the case, viz: "When the predicate precedes the subject it may agree with the subject in number or it may assume the *primary form*, viz.: third masculine singular, whatever be the number of the following subject." So the plural form *Elohim* after a singular verb, the construction found in Gen. i, and elsewhere, is no proof that it is singular in any sense. Similar constructions are found with other words in Gen. i:14, where the singular of the verb *haya*, be, is followed by the plural noun *meoroth*, lights; in Gen. 41:50, where the singular verb *yullodh*, was born, is followed by the plural noun *sheney banim*, two sons; in Job 42:15, where the singular verb *nimtsa*, was found, is followed by the plural noun *nashim*, women. Many similar examples might be given to illustrate the rule.

That *Elohim* was used in the plural sense in Gen. 1, is shown in the 26th verse, where the *Elohim* in referring to themselves use the plural suffix, *nu*, our, twice; and they also use the plural form of the verb *naaseh*, let us make. Also in Gen. 11:7, where *nerdhah*, let us descend, and *nabhlah*, let us confuse, two verbs in the plural form, proceed from the mouth of God, In Gen 3:5. the plural construct participle, *yodhe*, knowers of, modifies the noun, *Elohim*, which therefore is also plural. It is just possible that this participle is predicated of the subject you, but the participle would then follow the finite verb, giving a very unusual construction for the early Hebrew writers. One such construction is, however, found in Gen. 4:17, "he became (one) building a city."

The thought of the possibility of God's having with him great associates was alive even to the time of Isaiah, as is shown in Isaiah 6:8, where Jehovah said, "Whom shall I send, and who will go for *us*?" Jehovah was a personal name applied to the Being who guided Israel, and afterwards lived on the earth as Jesus Christ. (III Nephi, 15:5, Doc. and Cov. sec. 110.) Probably few of the Jews were ever able to distinguish Jehovah from *Elohim*, as it was latterly used, i. e., in the singular sense, and so when late writers wrote down the portion of Genesis where the name of Jehovah began to be used, they placed next to it, for the same purpose for which we now place the marginal reading, the word *Elohim*. So we have in Gen. 2:4; 3:24, and in some other places, the expression *Jehovah Elohim*, translated the Lord God. The words were put together late in Israel's history when *Elohim* had come to be used in the singular; *Jehovah Elohim* meant Jehovah, i. e., God. Later the explanatory use of the word *Elohim* was forgotten, and the two words combined to apply to God. (See page 219 of *Brown's Hebrew Lexicon*, the most authoritative lexicon in English, for the above explanation.)

The use of the singular noun *Eloah* is almost confined to poetry. It is used in Psalm 18 and in Deut. 32. There is ground for saying that the Savior on the cross in crying out to his Father, used the singular form *Eloah*. In combining *Eloah* with the suffix *i*, meaning my, and expressing the result in Greek the h would be dropped, for there is no letter h in the Greek alphabet. A, which was merely introduced to assist the Hebrew to pronounce the h, would also be dropped. The result would give us *Eloi*, the form given in the basic gospel, in Mark 15:34. (See also Judges 5:5, of the Septuagint).

In the year 1830, we find Joseph Smith, in the face of the tradition of the whole world, daring to render the word *Elohim* in Gen i, *et seq*., in the plural. It is one great evidence of the divinity of the Church of Jesus Christ restored in these last days that its prophet said many things, in the day in which he lived, that a progressive people are beginning to appreciate as true; and so we find learned men sympathizing with the daring position taken above. With reference to Gen. 1:26, and similar passages, we find as one explanation in the lexicon mentioned above, a lexicon based on the work of Gesenius, the great German Hebrew scholar, that God was in consultation with angels. Now, since the term "angel," a term used loosely by the scholars, is made there to mean and refer to superhuman beings sufficiently advanced in intelligence to be included in a consultation with God, we have our prophet's explanation exactly. In conclusion I shall quote the words of the great Biblical scholar, the Rev. A. B. Davidson of Edinburgh, in explanation of the same: "The use of 'us' by the divine speaker (Gen. 1:26, 3:22, 11:17) is strange, but is perhaps due to his consciousness of being surrounded by other beings of a loftier order than men (Is. 5:8)." (See *Hasting's Dictionary of the Bible*, page 205.)

OMNIPRESENCE OF GOD. [A]

BY ELDER WILLIAM HENRY WHITTALL.

[Footnote A: Millennial Star Vol. xxiii No. 19, p. 292.]

In comparing the ideas of others with our own upon any subject, with a view of coming to a clear understanding and just conclusion on the points discussed, it is both important and necessary that a clear definition of terms be given and received. Most of the disputes which arise in all classes of society, religious and secular, would be avoided to a great extent, if the disputants clearly understood and attended to each other's terms, and clearly defined their own.

Words are frequently used in such different sense—sometimes primary, and sometimes secondary—sometimes literal, and sometimes figurative, that a misconception is often likely to arise, which might be easily prevented, were a plain definition of terms given at the outset. Opposite parties are too apt to place their own constructions on each other's expressions.

"*Omnipresence*" as all will admit means *presence everywhere*.

Now, strictly speaking, *matter*, in its most extensive and comprehensive sense, is the only thing that can be said to be literally *everywhere*. There are various kinds and degrees of matter; but matter as a whole, and in a general sense, is the only thing that we can conceive of as being everywhere present, and nowhere absent.

One reservation, however, must here be made, for the sake of scientific accuracy,—namely, that wherever matter exists and moves, there is of necessity a corresponding or proportionate extent of space wherein to move.

There is no such thing, however, in all the creations of God, as what is called *empty* space.

But this fact does not in the least affect our argument; for the motion of matter is merely the displacement of one thing by another—one particle occupying the space which had been previously occupied by another. Thus, if I thrust my hand into a mass of sand, I do not penetrate the grains of sand, (although I do penetrate the sand as a mass,) the hand merely going between, or making its way by displacing the grains with which it comes in contact. No particle of matter can occupy the same identical space as another at the same time; consequently, no *portion* of matter can in an exclusive and strictly literal sense be omnipresent.

The nearest approach to a literal omnipresence, that we can conceive of, is that of the particles of one kind and degree of matter *commingling* with those of another.

The following may serve as a simple illustration: In a homely cup of tea, we find the particles of the tea itself intimately mingling with those of the water; those of the sugar mingling with those of the other two elements; and then, again, there are the particles of caloric or heat everywhere present throughout the whole. Yet no one particle of either water, (itself a compound of gases), or tea, or sugar, or cream, can occupy the same space as any other particle. This simple illustration, however homely and commonplace, may serve as an example, on a small scale, of the nearest idea that can be formed of a literal omnipresence, or presence everywhere. The plainer the simile, the better for ease and clearness of thought.

We have now to define what we mean by the term "God."

This word, like many others, is frequently used to represent different ideas. We sometimes employ it in reference to Deity as a person. One of the old prophets saw God sitting on a throne. Of course, then, according to this personal sense of the word, God could not have been everywhere present; for he was on a throne. We often read of God as sitting down, standing up, walking about, &c. Now, a person, when sitting down, does not occupy the same space as when standing up. He always occupies the same amount of space, but no more, whatever posture he may place himself in, or however much he may change his relative positions by moving hither and thither.

Hence it is utterly impossible for God to be *personally* omnipresent.

But we sometimes speak of God in reference to his attributes of love, wisdom, goodness, influence, power, authority, &c.

The next question, then, is, Can he be said to be omnipresent in these respects?

Yes, undoubtedly so; but not *literally*.

As these are all abstract terms, it is evident that they cannot be used in a strictly literal sense. Love, power, goodness, wisdom, &c., are not things which occupy space. We cannot measure knowledge by the yard, wisdom by the pint, influence by the inch, or power by the gallon. We cannot speak of authority as occupying so many square or cubic feet of space, or describe the height, depth, length, or width of intelligence or faith. These are all abstract terms; and in describing the extent of any attribute of God or man, we are bound to speak figuratively. We thus speak of "infinite power," of "boundless love," of "illimitable wisdom," of "unbounded influence," of "unlimited authority," of "infinite goodness," &c. If we examine such expressions closely, we cannot but see that they are used in a relative and figurative sense, and not in a strictly literal one. We cannot find room for all these things *everywhere*. If one thing occupied all space literally, we certainly could not locate half a dozen everywhere! The absurdity of the thing only proves the fallacy of the idea of literal ubiquity in reference to any attribute, the terms, expressive of which cannot be literalized.

But again: We often speak of God in reference to his agents. For example, the Apostle Paul says, "No man taketh this honor unto himself, but he that is called of God, as was Aaron." Moses, who called and ordained Aaron, was God's agent. All the servants of the Lord are called by his agents acting in his name and by his authority. When a man is called and ordained to certain functions of the Priesthood, we say that God called him, and that he is a servant of God. Thus, in a relative sense, God may be and is said to be present where he is personally absent, just as her Majesty the Queen may be said to be present throughout all her dominions by her official and representative agents. She is not literally, but virtually or officially, representatively or vicariously present wherever her regal authority is swayed. It is not actually she who is present, but her agents or authorities, who act in her name in her various principalities and colonies.

Again: We often use the term "God" in reference to his *Spirit*, whereby he is said to be omnipresent.

But we also frequently use the term "Spirit" in more sense than one. Sometimes we speak of the Holy Spirit or Holy Ghost as a person. The Father, the Son, and the Spirit are three distinct persons,—the first two being personages of tabernacle, and the last a personage of spirit. In this sense the Spirit can be no more spatially extended, and no more omnipresent, than the Father or the Son. If, indeed, either of the three could be personally and substantially present everywhere—that is, filling all space, it would puzzle the astutest intellect to conceive where the other two could be located!

The spirit of God, then, or the Holy Ghost, as a personage, cannot be *literally* omnipresent, although we may (as we often do) speak of him as being present here and there by his influence, authority, and power.

But we also frequently speak of the Spirit of God as a divine substance or influence, of power diffused throughout the spiritual and physical universe, giving vitality, activity, and force to the various things around us, according to certain spiritual and natural laws.

It is, indeed, the inherent life and soul of all things—the inner and eternal principle of life and being. Whether we speak of "Nature" or of the "God of nature," we mean the same thing, unless, by way of distinction, we connect with the latter expression the idea of personality. In the former sense, God is *everywhere*.

President Young, upon this subject, says—"It is the Deity within us that causes increase. * * * He is in every person upon the face of the earth. The elements that every individual is made of and lives in possess the Godhead * * The Deity within us is the great principle that causes us to increase and to grow in grace and truth."

It will thus be evident that God is, by his Spirit, in this sense, *omnipresent*. Indeed, we arrive at the conclusion that God (although local in personality) may be said, in various ways and in different senses of the word, to be everywhere present. President Young says—"He is omnipotent, and fills immensity by his agents, by his influence, by his Spirit, and by his ministers." So that, go wheresoever we may, God is there, in some way or other. If we ascend to the heavens above, he is there; if we make the grave our bed, he is there; if we fly to any part of the earth or sea, he is there, and his providence will protect the just.

CHAPTER VI

THE PROPHET JOSEPH SMITH'S VIEWS IN RELATION TO MAN AND THE PRIESTHOOD.

As in the "Mormon" doctrine of Deity discussed in these pages, man is an important factor, and as his relations to God, and the possibilities that are open to him in the never-ending future are a part of the discussion between the Reverend Mr. Van Der Donckt and myself, the following remarks of the Prophet respecting man and his relations to God, and the relationship of certain leading men to each other, in the several dispensations of the Gospel which have been given, cannot fail to be an interesting and instructive contribution to this chapter. The remarks under division I are taken from a discourse by the Prophet delivered in June, 1839, in answer to some inquiries concerning Priesthood. The Prophet's remarks under division I appear in the *Millennial Star*, vol. xvii, pages 310, 311. Those in division II are from an article on Priesthood prepared by the Prophet, and read by Robert B. Thompson at the general conference of the Church held at Nauvoo, October 5, 1840, and are to be found in the *Millennial Star*, vol xviii, pages 164, 165:

I.

The Priesthood was first given to Adam; he obtained the First Presidency, and held the keys of it from generation to generation. He obtained it in the creation, before the worlds were formed, as in Genesis 1:20, 26, 28. He had dominion given him over every living creature. He is Michael, the Archangel, spoken of in the Scriptures. Then to Noah, who is Gabriel; he stands next in authority to Adam in the Priesthood; he was called of God to this office, and was the Father of all living in his day, and to him was given the dominion. These men held keys first on earth, and then in heaven.

The Priesthood is an everlasting principle, and existed with God from eternity, and will to eternity, without beginning of days or end of years. The keys have to be brought from heaven whenever the Gospel is sent. When they are revealed from heaven it is by Adam's authority. Daniel 7 speaks of the Ancient of Days; he means the oldest man, our Father Adam, Michael; he will call his children together and hold a council with them to prepare them for the coming of the Son of Man. He (Adam) is the father of the human family and presides over the spirits of all men, and all that have had the keys must stand before him in this grand council. This may take place before some of us leave this stage of action. The Son of Man stands before him, and there is given Him glory and dominion. Adam delivers up his stewardship to Christ, that which was delivered to him as holding the keys of the universe, but retains his standing as head of the human family.

The spirit of man is not a created being; it existed from eternity, and will exist to eternity. Anything created cannot be eternal; and earth, water, etc., had their existence in an elementary state, from eternity. Our Savior speaks of children and says, their angels always stand before my Father. The Father called all spirits before him at the creation of man, and organized them. He (Adam) is the head, and was told to multiply. The keys were first given to him, and by him to others. He will have to give an account of his stewardship and they to him.

The Priesthood is everlasting. The Savior, Moses, and Elias, gave the keys to Peter, James, and John, on the mount, when He was transfigured before them. The Priesthood is everlasting—without beginning of days or end of years; without father, mother, etc. If there is no change of ordinance, there is no change of Priesthood. Wherever the ordinances of the Gospel are administered, there is the Priesthood.

How have we come at the Priesthood in the last days? It came down, in regular succession. Peter, James, and John had it given to them, and they gave it to others. Christ is the great High Priest: Adam next. Paul speaks of the Church coming to an innumerable company of angels—to God, the Judge of all—the spirits of just men made perfect; to Jesus, the Mediator of the new covenant, etc. (Heb. 3:23).

I saw Adam in the valley of Adam-ondi-Ahman. He called together his children and blessed them with a patriarchal blessing. The Lord appeared in their midst, and he (Adam) blessed them all, and foretold what should befall them to the latest generation. (See Doc. and Cov., sec. cvii: 53, 56.)

This is why Abraham blessed his posterity; he wanted to bring them into the presence of God. They looked for a city, etc. Moses sought to bring the children of Israel into the presence of God, through the power of the Priesthood, but he could not. In the first ages of the world they tried to establish the same thing; and there were Eliases raised up who tried to restore these very glories, but did not obtain them, but they prophesied of a day when this glory would be revealed. Paul spoke of the Dispensation of the Fullness of Times, when God would gather together all things in one, etc.; and those men to whom these keys have been given, will have to be there, and they without us cannot be made perfect.

These men are in heaven, but their children are on earth. Their bowels yearn over us. God sends down men for this reason (Matt. 13:41). And the Son of Man shall send forth his angels, etc. All these authoritative characters will come down and join hand in hand in bringing about this work.

II.

In order to investigate the subject of the Priesthood, so important to this as well as every succeeding generation, I shall proceed to trace the subject, as far as I possibly can, from the Old and New Testaments.

There are two Priesthoods spoken of in the Scripture, viz., the Melchizedek and the Aaronic or Levitical. Although there are two Priesthoods, yet the Melchisedek Priesthood comprehends the Aaronic or Levitical Priesthood, and is the grand head, and holds the highest authority which pertains to the Priesthood, and the keys of the Kingdom of God in all ages of the world to the latest posterity on the earth, and is the channel through which all knowledge, doctrine, the plan of salvation, and every important matter is revealed from heaven.

Its institution was prior to the "foundations of this earth, or the morning stars sang together, or the sons of God shouted for joy," and is the highest and holiest Priesthood, and is after the order of the Son of God, and all other Priesthoods are only parts, ramifications, powers, and blessings belonging to the same, and are held, controlled, and directed by it. It is the channel through which the Almighty commenced revealing his glory at the beginning of the creation of this earth, and through which he has continued to reveal himself to the children of men to the present time, and through which he will make known his purposes to the end of time.

Commencing with Adam, who was the first man, who is spoken of in Daniel as being the "Ancient of Days," or, in other words, the first and oldest of all, the great grand progenitor, of whom it is said in another place he is Michael, because he was the first and father of all, not only by progeny, but the first to hold the spiritual blessings, to whom was made known the plan of ordinances for the salvation of his posterity unto the end, and to whom Christ was first revealed, and through whom Christ has been revealed from heaven, and will continue to be revealed from henceforth. Adam holds the keys of the Dispensation of the Fullness of Times, i. e. the dispensation of all the times, have been and will be revealed through him from the beginning to Christ, and from Christ to the end of all the dispensations that are to be revealed: Ephesians, 1st chap., 9th and 10th verses—"Having made known unto us the mystery of his will, according to his good pleasure which he hath purposed in himself: that in the dispensation of the fullness of times he might gather together in one all things in Christ, both which are in heaven and which are on earth, even in him."

Now the purpose in himself in the winding-up scene of the last dispensation is that all things pertaining to that dispensation should be conducted precisely in accordance with the preceding dispensations.

And again: God purposed in himself, that there should not be eternal fullness until every dispensation should be fulfilled and gathered together in one, and that all things whatsoever that should be gathered together in one in those dispensations unto the same fullness and eternal glory, should be in Christ Jesus; therefore he set the ordinances to be the same for ever, and set Adam to watch over them, to reveal them from heaven to man, or to send angels to reveal them: Hebrews 1:14—"Are they not all ministering spirits, sent forth to minister to those who shall be heirs of salvation?"

These angels are under the direction of Michael or Adam, who acts under the direction of the Lord. From the above quotation we learn that Paul perfectly understood the purposes of God in relation to his connection with man, and that glorious and perfect order which he established in himself, whereby he sent forth power, revelations, and glory.

God will not acknowledge that which he has not called, ordained, and chosen. In the beginning God called Adam by his own voice. See Genesis 3rd chap., 9th and 10th verses—"And the Lord called unto Adam, and said unto him, Where art thou? And he said, I heard thy voice in the garden, and I was afraid because I was naked, and hid myself." Adam received commandments and instruction from God; this was the order from the beginning.

That he received revelations, commandments and ordinances at the beginning is beyond the power of controversy; else, how did they begin to offer sacrifices to God in an acceptable manner? And if they offered sacrifices they must be authorized by ordination. We read in Gen. 4th chap., 4th v., that Abel brought of the firstlings of the flock and the fat thereof, and the Lord had respect to Abel and to his offering. And again: Hebrews 11:4—"By faith Abel offered unto God a more excellent sacrifice than Cain, by which he obtained witness that he was righteous, God testifying of his gifts; and by it he being dead, yet speaketh." How doth he yet speak? Why, he magnified the Priesthood which was conferred upon him, and died a righteous man, and therefore has become an angel of God by receiving his body from the dead, holding still the keys of his dispensation; and was sent down from heaven unto Paul to minister consoling words, and to commit unto him a knowledge of the mysteries of Godliness.

And if this was not the case, I would ask, how did Paul know so much about Abel, and why should he talk about his speaking after he was dead? Hence, that he spoke after he was dead must be by being sent down out of heaven to administer.

This, then, is the nature of the Priesthood; every man holding the presidency of his dispensation, and one man holding the presidency of them all, even Adam; and Adam receiving his presidency and authority from the Lord, but cannot receive a fullness until Christ shall present the Kingdom to the Father, which shall be at the end of the last dispensation.

OF ADAM AND HIS RELATION TO THE INHABITANTS OF THE EARTH.

(From the Doctrine and Covenants.)

In March, 1832, the Lord gave a revelation to the Church commanding them to effect an organization for the betterment of their material condition, that the poor might be better cared for, and all the Saints be more equal in the possession of earthly things, and then adds:

> That you may come up to the crown prepared for you, and be made rulers over many kingdoms, saith the Lord God, the Holy One of Zion, who hath established the foundations of Adam-ondi-Ahman; who hath appointed Michael your prince, and established his feet, and set him upon high, and given unto him the keys of salvation under the counsel and direction of the Holy One, who is without beginning of days or end of life. Verily, verily, I say unto you, ye are little children, and ye have not as yet understood how great blessings the Father hath in his own hands and prepared for you; and ye cannot bear all things now; nevertheless, be of good cheer, for I will lead you along; the kingdom is yours, and the blessings thereof are yours, and the riches of eternity are yours (Doc. and Gov., sec. 78:15-18).

Who the "Michael" here spoken of is, who is "appointed" our "prince," and unto whom the "keys of salvation are given under the counsel and direction of the Holy One," is made very plain afterwards in a revelation given March 28, 1835, from which I quote the following:

> Three years previous to the death of Adam, he called Seth, Enos, Cainan, Mahalaleel, Jared, Enoch, and Methuselah, who were all high priests, with the residue of his posterity who were righteous, into the valley of Adam-ondi-Ahman, and there bestowed upon them his last blessing. And the

Lord appeared unto them, and they rose up and blessed Adam, and called him Michael, the Prince, the Archangel. And the Lord administered comfort unto Adam, and said unto him, I have set thee to be at the head—a multitude of nations shall come of thee, and thou art a prince over them for ever. And Adam stood up in the midst of the congregation, and notwithstanding he was bowed down with age, being full of the Holy Ghost, predicted whatsoever should befall his posterity unto the latest generation. These things were all written in the Book of Enoch, and are to be testified of in due time (Doc. and Cov., sec. 107:53-57).

From this it will appear that the Prophet Joseph Smith understood that Adam would stand at the head of his posterity in this earth; that he would be their Prince and hold the keys of salvation "under the counsel and direction of the Holy One, who is without beginning of days or end of life." Doubtless it was this which led the Prophet to say-after referring to the fact that the Lord said to Moses, "Thou shalt be a god unto the children of Israel," and again, "Thou shalt be a god unto Aaron, and he shall be thy spokesman"—it was these considerations, I repeat, which led the Prophet to say, "I believe those Gods that God reveals as Gods to be sons of God, and all can cry, 'Abba, Father!' sons of God, who exalted themselves to be Gods even before the foundation of the world, and are the only Gods I have a reverence for" (Discourse of June 16, 1844, *Millennial Star*, vol. xxiv, p. 140).

THE LIVING GOD. [A]

(From the Times and Seasons.)

[Footnote A: The article under this title, is an editorial in the "Times and Seasons," published at Nauvoo, Feb. 15, 1845, presumably written by the late President John Taylor, who, at the time it was written, was both editor and proprietor of the "Times and Seasons."]

There is no subject among men, that engrosses so much time and attention, and, at the same time, is so little understood, as the being, knowledge, substance, attributes, and disposition of the living God. In the first place, Christians and believers in Christianity, with a few exceptions, believe in one God; or, perhaps we should say, in their own language, that the Father, Son, and Holy Ghost, *are one God*. But to be obedient unto the truth, we will not thus transgress upon reason, sense and revelation. It will then be necessary to treat the subject of the "Living God," in contradiction to a *dead God*, or, one that has "no body, parts or passions," and, perhaps it may be well enough to say at the outset, that "Mormonism" embraces a plurality of Gods, as the apostle said, there were "Gods many and Lords many." In doing which, we shall not deny the scripture that has been set apart for this world, and allow one God, even Jesus Christ, the very eternal Father of this earth; and, if Paul tells the truth—"by him the worlds were made."

It was probably alluded to by Moses, when the children of Israel were working out their salvation, with fear and trembling, in the wilderness, at the time that he spake these words: (Deut. 5:23-26.) "And it came to pass when ye heard the voice out of the midst of the darkness (for the mountain did burn with fire,) that ye came near unto me, even all the heads of your tribes, and your elders. And ye said: Behold, the Lord our God hath showed us his glory, and greatness, and we have heard his voice out of the midst of the fire; we have seen this day that God doth talk with man, and he liveth. Now, therefore, why should we die? For this great fire will consume us. If we hear the voice of the Lord our God any more, then we shall die. For who is there of all flesh, that had heard the voice of the living God speaking out of the midst of the fire, as we have, and lived?"

* * * *

The first line of Genesis, purely translated from the original, excluding the first *Baith* (which was added by the Jews,) would read:—*Rosheit* (the head) *baurau*, (brought forth,) *Eloheim* (the Gods) *ate* (with) *hah-shau-mahyiem* (the heavens) *veh-ate*, (and with) *hauaurates*, (the earth.) In simple English, the Head brought forth the Gods, with the heavens and with the earth. The "Head" must have meant the "living God," or Head God; Christ is our head. The term "Eloheim," plural of Elohah, or ale, is used alike in the first chapter of Genesis, for the creation, and the quotation of Satan. In the second chapter, and fourth verse, we have this remarkable history: *"These are the generations of the heavens and of the earth, when they were brought forth; in the day that the Lord of the Gods made earth and heavens."* The Hebrew reads so.

Truly Jesus Christ created the worlds, and is Lord of Lords, and, as the Psalmist said: "Judges among the Gods." Then Moses might have said with propriety, he is the "living God," and, Christ, speaking of the flesh could say: I am the Son of man; and, Peter, enlightened by the Holy Ghost: Thou art the Son of the Living God, meaning our Father in heaven, who is the Father of all spirits, and who, with Jesus Christ, his first begotten son and the Holy Ghost, are one in power, one in dominion, and one in glory, constituting the first presidency of this system, and this eternity. But they are as much three distinct persons as the sun, moon, and earth are three different bodies.

Again, the "twelve kingdoms," which are under the above mentioned presidency of the Father, Son, and Holy Ghost, are governed by the same rules, and destined to the same honor (Book Doc. & Cov. p. 135, sec. 13). For "Behold, I will liken these kingdoms unto a man having a field, and he sent forth his servants into the field, to dig in the field; and he said unto the first, go ye and labor in the field, and in the first hour I will come unto you, and ye shall behold the joy of my countenance; and he said unto the second, go ye also into the field, and in the second hour I will visit you with the joy of my countenance; and also unto the third, saying, I will visit you: and unto the fourth, and so on unto the twelfth."

Without going into the full investigation of the history and excellency of God, the Father of our Lord Jesus Christ, in this article, let us reflect that Jesus Christ, as Lord of Lords, and King of Kings, must have a noble race in the heavens, or upon the earth, or else he can never be as great in power, dominion, might, and authority, as the scriptures declare. But hear; the mystery is solved. John says (Rev. 14:1,) "And I looked, and lo, a Lamb stood on the mount Zion, and with him an hundred forty and four thousand, having his Father's name written in their foreheads."

Their Father's name, bless me! that is GOD! Well done for Mormonism; *one hundred and forty-four thousand Gods,* among the tribes of Israel, and, two living Gods and the Holy Ghost, for this world! Such knowledge is too wonderful for men, unless they possess the spirit of Gods. It unravels the little mysteries, which, like a fog, hides the serene atmosphere of heaven, and looks from world to world; from system to system; from universe to universe, and from eternity to eternity, where, in each and all, there is a presidency of Gods, and Gods many, and Lords many; and, from time to time, or from eternity to eternity, Jesus Christ shall bring in another world, regulated and saved as this will be, when he delivers it up to the Father; and God becomes *all in all.* "And," as John the Revelator says (22:3, 4): "there shall be no more curse: but the throne of God and of the Lamb shall be in it; and his servants shall serve him, and they shall see his face; and his name shall be in their foreheads."

"His name in their foreheads," undoubtedly means *"God"* on the front of their crowns; for, when all things are created new, in the celestial kingdom, the servants of God, the innumerable multitude are crowned, and, are perfect men and women in the Lord, one in glory, one in knowledge, and one in image; they are like Christ, and he is like God; then, O, then, they are all "Living Gods," having passed from death unto life, and possess the power of eternal lives!

MATERIALITY. [A]

(From the "Prophet.")

[Footnote A: This article on the nature of God, man, and angels appears in the editorial columns of the "Prophet" for May 24, 1845. The "Prophet" was published in New York and Boston, and at the time of the appearance of this article Elder Parley P. Pratt was the editor, and hence it was doubtless written by him.]

God, the Father, is material.

Jesus Christ is material.

Angels are material.

Spirits are material.

Men are material.

The universe is material.

Space is full of materiality.

Nothing exists which is not material.

The elementary principles of the material universe are eternal; they never originated from nonentity, and they never can be annihilated.

Immateriality is but another name for nonentity — it is the negative of all things, and beings — of all existence.

There is not one particle of proof to be advanced to establish its existence. It has no way to manifest itself to any intelligence in heaven or on earth. Neither God, angels nor men, could positively conceive of such a substance, being or thing. It possesses no property or power by which to make itself manifest, to any intelligent being in the universe, reason and analogy never scan it, or even conceive of it. Revelation never reveals it, nor do any of our senses witness its existence. It cannot be seen, heard, tasted, or smelled, even by the strongest organs, or of the most acute sensibilities. It is neither liquid or solid, soft or hard, — it can neither extend nor contract. In short, it can exert no influence whatever — it can neither act, nor be acted upon. And even if it does exist, it is of no possible use. It possesses no one desirable property, faculty or use, yet, strange to say, "Immateriality" is the modern Christian's God, his anticipated heaven, his immortal self — his all.

O sectarianism! O atheism!! O annihilation!!! Who can perceive the nice shades of difference between the one and the other? They seem alike all but in name. The atheist has no God.

The sectarian has a God without body or parts. Who can define the difference? for our part we do not perceive a difference of a single hair; they both claim to be the negative of all things which exist—and both are equally powerless and unknown.

The atheist has no after life, or conscious existence beyond the grave.

The sectarian has one, but it is immaterial like his God; and without body or parts. Here again both are negative, and both are at the same point. Their faith and hope amount to the same, only they are expressed by different terms.

Again, the atheist has no heaven in eternity.

The sectarian has one, but it is immaterial in all its proprieties, and is therefore the negative of all riches in substance. Here again they are equal, and arrive at the same point.

As we do not envy them the possession of all they claim, we will now leave them in the quiet and undisturbed enjoyment of the same and proceed to examine the portion still left for the "poor Mormons" to enjoy.

What is God? He is a material intelligence, possessing both body and parts. He is in the form of man, and is in fact of the same species; and is a model, or standard of perfection to which man is destined to attain: he being the great Father, and head of the whole family.

He can go, come, converse, reason, eat, drink, love, hate, rejoice, possess and enjoy. He can also travel space with all the ease and intelligence necessary, for moving from planet to planet, and from system to system.

This being cannot occupy two distinct places at once. Therefore, he cannot be (in person) everywhere present. For evidence and illustration of this God, and his personal powers, and attributes, we refer to the scriptures of the Old and New Testament which speak substantially of his body, parts, passions, powers, and of his conversing, walking, eating, drinking, etc.; for instance, his taking dinner with Abraham.

What is Jesus Christ? He is the son of God, and is every way like his father, being "the brightness of his father's glory, and the express image of his person." He is material intelligence, with body, parts and passions; possessing immortal flesh and immortal bones. He can and does eat, drink, converse, reason, love, move, go, come, and in short, perform all things even as the Father—possessing the same power and attributes. And he, too, can travel space, and go from world to world, and from system to system, precisely like the Father; but cannot occupy two places at once.

What are angels? They are intelligences of the human species. Many of them are offsprings of Adam and Eve. That is they are men, who have, like Enoch or Elijah, been translated; or, like Jesus Christ, been raised from the dead; consequently they possess a material body of flesh and bones, can eat, drink, walk, converse, reason, love, fight, wrestle, sing, or play on musical instruments. They can go or come on foreign missions, in heaven, earth, or hell; and they can travel space, and visit the different worlds, with all the ease and alacrity with which God and Christ do the same, being possessed of similar organizations, powers and attributes in a degree.

What are spirits? They are material intelligences, possessing body and parts in the likeness of the temporal body; but not composed of flesh and bones, but of some substance less tangible to our gross senses in our present life; but tangible to those in the same element as themselves. In short they are men in embrio—intelligences waiting to come into the natural world and take upon them flesh and bones, that through birth, death, and the resurrection they may also be perfected in the material organization. Such was Jesus Christ, and such were we before we came into this world, and such we will be again, in the intervening space between death and the resurrection.

What are men? They are offspring of God, the Father, and brothers of Jesus Christ. They were once intelligent spirits in the presence of God, and were with him before the earth was formed. They are now in disguise as it were, in order to pass through the several changes, and the experience necessary to constitute them perfect beings.

They are capable of receiving intelligence and exaltation to such a degree, as to be raised from the dead with a body like that of Jesus Christ's, and to possess immortal flesh and bones, in which they will eat, drink, converse, reason, love, walk, sing, play on musical instruments, go on missions from planet to planet, or from system to system: being Gods, or sons of God, endowed with the same powers, attributes, and capacities that their heavenly Father and Jesus Christ possess.

What are all these beings taken together, or summed up under one head? They are one great family, all of the same species, all related to each other, all bound together by kindred ties, interests sympathies, and affections. In short they are all Gods; or rather, men are the offspring or children of the Gods, and destined to advance by degrees, and to make their way by a progressive series of changes, till they become like their Father in heaven, and like Jesus Christ their elder brother.

Thus perfected, the whole family will possess the material universe, that is, the earth, and all other planets, and worlds, as "an inheritance incorruptible undefiled and that fadeth not away." They will also continue to organize, people, redeem, and perfect other systems which are now in the womb of chaos, and thus go on increasing their several dominions, till the weakest child of God which now exists upon the earth will possess more dominion, more property, more subjects, and more power and glory than is possessed by Jesus Christ or by his Father; while at the same time Jesus Christ and his Father, will have their dominion, kingdoms, and subjects increased in proportion.

Such are the riches, glories, blessings, honors, thrones, dominions, principalities, and powers, held out by the system of materialism.

Such the wealth, the dignity, the nobility, the titles and honors to which "Mormons" aspire. Such the promises of him whose word can never fail.

With these hopes and prospects before us, we say to the Christian world, who hold to immateriality, that they are welcome to their God—their life—their heaven, and their all.

They claim nothing but that which we throw away, and we claim nothing but that which they throw away. Therefore, there is no ground for quarrel, or contention between us.

CHAPTER VII

DISCOURSES ON DEITY AND MAN.[A]

[Footnote A: In these discourses, it will be observed that in speaking of man reference is made only to the pre-existence of his spirit, and his being "begotten" a spirit by the heavenly Father; no reference is made to the eternal intelligence of man, the "ego" that was not created or made, "neither indeed can be," as set forth. The brethren in these discourses are not dealing with that phase of the subject; their purpose is met by referring merely to the pre-existence of the spirits of men.

This remark also opens a way for a word which really should have been spoken when explaining our views in relation to the immortality of man, . I mean the distinction that exists between "generation" and "creation;" between a being "begotten," and a thing "created," or "made." And here, somewhat to my surprise, I may quote with approval one of the very eminent "Christian Fathers." "Let it be repeated," he remarks, "that a created thing is external to the nature of the being who creates; but a generation is the proper offspring of the nature" [of him who begets it]. And this Athanasius, the "Christian Father" referred to, puts forth in explaining how the Son of God is consubstantial, i. e., of the same substance, or essence, with the Father, And he remarks further, by way of illustration: "It were madness to say that a house is co-essential or con-substantial with the builder: or a ship with the shipwright; but it is proper to say, that every son is co-essential or consubstantial with his father." (The foregoing extracts from Athanasius are quoted by Shedd, History Christian Doctrine, Vol. I, p. 322.)

I call attention to this distinction that when in our literature we say "God created the spirits of men," it is understood that they were "begotten," We mean "generation," not "creation." Intelligences, which are eternal, uncreated, self-existing beings, are begotten spirits, and these afterwards begotten men. When intelligences are "begotten" spirits they are of the nature of him who begets them—sons of God, and con-substantial with their Father.]

I.
PRESIDENT BRIGHAM YOUNG. [A]

To Know God is Eternal Life.

[Footnote A: This discourse was delivered in the Tabernacle, Salt Lake City, February 8, 1857. *Journal of Discourses*, Vol. IV, pp. 215 *et seq.*]

It is one of the first principles of the doctrine of salvation to become acquainted with our Father and our God. The Scriptures teach that this is eternal life, to "know thee, the only true God, and Jesus Christ whom thou hast sent;" this is as much as to say that no man can enjoy or be prepared for eternal life without that knowledge.

You hear a great deal of preaching upon this subject; and when people repent of their sins, they will get together, and pray and exhort each other, and try to get the spirit of revelation, try to have God their Father revealed to them, that they may know him and become acquainted with him.

There are some plain, simple facts that I wish to tell you, and I have but one desire in this, which is, that you should have understanding to receive them, to treasure them up in your hearts, to contemplate upon these facts, for they are simple facts, based upon natural principles; there is no mystery about them when once understood.

I want to tell you, each and every one of you, that you are well acquainted with God our heavenly Father, or the great Eloheim. You are all well acquainted with him, for there is not a soul of you but what has lived in his house and dwelt with him year after year; and yet you are seeking to become acquainted with him, when the fact is, you have merely forgotten what you did know. I told you a little last Sabbath about forgetting things.

There is not a person here today but what is a son or a daughter of that Being. In the spirit world their spirits were first begotten and brought forth, and they lived there with their parents for ages before they came here. This, perhaps, is hard for many to believe, but it is the greatest nonsense in the world not to believe it. If you do not believe it, cease to call him "Father;" and when you pray, pray to some other character.

It would be inconsistent in you to disbelieve what I think you know, and then to go home and ask the Father to do so and so for you. The Scriptures which we believe have taught us from the beginning to call him our Father, and we have been taught to pray to him as our Father, in the name of our eldest brother whom we call Jesus Christ, the Savior of the world; and that Savior, while here on earth, was so explicit on this point, that he taught his disciples to call no man on earth father, for we have one which is in heaven. He is the Savior, because it is his right to redeem the remainder of the family pertaining to the flesh on this earth; if any of you do not believe this, tell us how and what we should believe. If I am not telling you the truth, please to tell me the truth on this subject, and let me know more than I do know. If it is hard for you to believe, if you wish to be Latter-day Saints, admit the fact, as I state it, and do not contend against it. Try to believe it, because you will never become acquainted with our Father, never enjoy the blessings of his Spirit, never be prepared to enter into his presence, until you most assuredly believe it; therefore you had better try to believe this great mystery about God.

I do not marvel that the world is clad in mystery, to them he is an unknown God; they cannot tell where he dwells nor how he lives, nor what kind of a being he is in appearance or character. They want to become acquainted with his character and attributes, but they know nothing of them. This is in consequence of the apostasy that is now in the world. They have departed from the knowledge of God, transgressed his laws, changed his ordinances, and broken the everlasting covenant, so that the whole earth is defiled under the inhabitants thereof. Consequently it is no mystery to us that the world knoweth not God, but it would be a mystery to me, with what I now know, to say that we cannot know anything of him. We are his children.

To bring the truth of this matter close before you, I will instance your fathers who made the first permanent settlement in New England. There are a good many in this congregation whose fathers landed upon Plymouth Rock in the year 1620. Those fathers began to spread abroad; they had children, those children had children, and their children had children, and here are we their children. I am one of them, and many of this congregation belong to that class. Now ask yourselves this simple question upon natural principles, has the species altered? Were not the people who landed at Plymouth Rock the same species with us? Were they not organized as we are? Were not their countenances similar to ours? Did they not converse, have knowledge, read books? Were there not mechanics among them, and did they not understand agriculture, etc., as we do? Yes, every person admits this.

Now follow our fathers further back and take those who first came to the island of Great Britain, were they the same species of beings as those who came to America? Yes, all acknowledge this; this is upon natural principles. Thus you may continue and trace the human family back to Adam and Eve, and ask, "are we of the same species with Adam and Eve?" Yes, every person acknowledges this; this comes within the scope of our understanding.

But when we arrive at that point, a vail is dropt, and our knowledge is cut off. Were it not so, you could trace back your history to the Father of our spirits in the eternal world. He is a being of the same species as ourselves: he lives as we do, except the difference that we are earthly, and he is heavenly. He has been earthly, and is of precisely the same species of being that we are. Whether Adam is the personage that we should consider our heavenly Father, or not, is considerable of a mystery to a good many. I do not care for one moment how that is; it is no matter whether we are to consider him our God, or whether his Father, or his Grandfather, for in either case we are of one species—of one family—and Jesus Christ is also of our species.

You may hear the divines of the day extol the character of the Savior, undertake to exhibit his true character before the people, and give an account of his origin.

Now to the facts in the case; all the difference between Jesus Christ and any other man that ever lived on the earth, from the days of Adam until now, is simply this, the Father, after he had once been in the flesh, and lived as we live, obtained his exaltation, attained to thrones, gained the ascendancy over principalities and powers, and had the knowledge and power to create—to bring forth and organize the elements upon natural principles. This he did after his ascension, or his glory, or his eternity, and was actually classed with the Gods, with the beings who create, with those who have kept the celestial law while in the flesh, and again obtained their bodies. Then he was prepared to commence the work of creation, as the Scriptures teach. It is all here in the Bible; I am not telling you a word but what is contained in that book.

Things were first created spiritually; the Father actually begat the spirits, and they were brought forth and lived with him. Then he commenced the work of creating earthly tabernacles, precisely as he had been created in this flesh himself, by partaking of the coarse material that was organized and composed this earth, until his system was charged with it, consequently the tabernacles of his children were organized from the coarse materials of this earth.

When the time came that his first-born, the Savior, should come into the world and take a tabernacle, the Father came himself and favored that spirit with a tabernacle instead of letting any other man do it. The Savior was begotten by the Father of his spirit, by the same Being who is the Father of our spirits, and that is all the organic difference between Jesus Christ and you and me. And the difference there is between our Father and us consists in that he has gained his exaltation, and has obtained eternal lives. The principle of eternal lives is an eternal existence, eternal duration, eternal exaltation. Endless are his kingdoms, endless his thrones and his dominions, and endless are His posterity; they never will cease to multiply from this time henceforth and forever.

To you who are prepared to enter into the presence of the Father and the Son, what I am now telling will eventually be no more strange than are the feelings of a person who returns to his father's house, brethren, and sisters, and enjoys the society of his old associates, after an absence of several years upon some distant island. Upon returning he would be happy to see his father, his relatives and friends. So also if we keep the celestial law when our spirits go to God who gave them, we shall find that we are acquainted there and distinctly realize that we know all about that world.

Tell me that you do not know anything about God! I will tell you one thing, it would better become you to lay your hands upon your mouths and them in the dust, and cry, "unclean, unclean."

Whether you receive these things or not, I tell you them in simplicity. I lay them before you like a child, because they are perfectly simple. If you see and understand these things, it will be by the Spirit of God; you will receive them by no other spirit. No matter whether they are told to you like the thunderings of the Almighty, or by simple conversation; if you enjoy the Spirit of the Lord, it will tell you whether they are right or not.

I am acquainted with my Father. I am as confident that I understand in part, see in part, and know and am acquainted with him in part, as I am that I was acquainted with my earthly father who died in Quincy, Illinois, after we were driven from Missouri. My recollection is better with regard to my earthly father than it is in regard to my heavenly Father; but as to knowing of what species he is, and how he is organized, and with regard to his existence, I understand it in part as well as I understand the organization and existence of my earthly father. That is my opinion about it, and my opinion to me is just as good as yours is to you; and if you are of the same opinion you will be satisfied as I am.

I know my heavenly Father and Jesus Christ whom he has sent, and this is eternal life. And if we will do as we have been told this morning, if you will enter into the spirit of your calling, into the principle of securing to yourselves eternal lives, eternal existence, eternal exaltation, it will be well with you.

II.
ELDER ORSON PRATT. [A]

Salvation Tangible—Personality and Character of God—Jesus our Elder Brother—Transformation of the Earth—Its Final Destiny.

[Footnote A: This discourse was delivered in the Tabernacle, Salt Lake City, Nov. 12, 1876.]

As a people the Latter-day Saints have passed through many scenes trying and afflicting to their natures, and they have endured them because of the anxiety of their hearts to obtain salvation. People who are sincere will manifest their sincerity in undergoing great tribulation, if necessary, for the sake of being saved. This mortal life is of small consideration, compared with eternal salvation in the kingdom of the Father. There is nothing pertaining to the things of this present life that is worthy of being named, in contrast with the riches of eternal life. Jesus, in speaking upon this subject when he was on the earth, asks this question: "For what is man profited, if he gain the whole world, and lose his own soul? Or what shall a man give in exchange for his soul?" There is nothing so precious, nothing of so great importance, as that of securing in this life, the salvation of our souls in the world to come. Far better is it if we can gain salvation by passing through various scenes of affliction and persecution in this world, than to give way to its pleasures and vanities, which can only be enjoyed for a season, and afterwards lose that eternal reward which God has in store for the righteous.

It is true we look upon our future reward in quite a different light from the religious world generally. We look for something tangible, something we can form some degree of rational conception of, having a resemblance in some measure to the present life. But how very imaginary are the ideas of the religious world! I do not now refer to the heathen world, but to the enlightened Christian nations, the two hundred million of Christians now existing on the earth. If you ask these people about the future state of man, some will give you one idea and some another, all more or less, perhaps, differing from each other, but in the main they all agree, namely, that it is a state entirely spiritual, that is, unconnected with anything tangible like this present life, an existence which cannot be conceived of by mortals.

You may think I am misrepresenting our Christian friends. I will therefore say that for many years now I have been engaged, more or less, in the study of religion, and have therefore read quite extensively the ideas of the religious world. I have not accepted the ideas of a few individuals belonging to the various sects, but I have appealed to their standard writings, their articles of faith, which are adopted by the various religious bodies and known as their creeds. For instance, in the articles of faith of a great many of the religious sects, an idea like this is set forth—that there is a Being who is entirely spiritual, called God, and that Being is described as consisting of three persons, and these three persons are without body, without parts, without passions. Such is the God that is worshiped by the Methodists—a people whom I highly respect, and whose meetings I attended in my early youth more than those of any other religious denomination. The three persons that compose this one God are the Father, the Son, and the Holy Ghost, all of whom are said to be without bodies or passions; and in connection with this, one of the cardinal doctrines of their faith, they tell us that one of this holy Trinity, namely Jesus, was crucified, dead and buried, and that on the third day he arose again from the dead and ascended into heaven.

When I was a boy, attending the Methodist meetings, as many now do who are of maturer years, I accepted sincerity for truth. But when I grew to manhood my attention was called to this article of faith; I tried in all earnestness to comprehend it, but could not and cannot to this day. It is one of those incomprehensible things which cannot be grasped by the human mind. You, my hearers, try now with me for a few moments to comprehend, if you can, a being consisting of three persons, and these three persons without any body, parts or passions. I had been taught, when studying the exact sciences, that everything that existed was composed of parts, that there could not exist anything as a whole unless it existed as parts. I could not, therefore, understand how it was that one of these three persons could be crucified if he had no body; how it was possible, and be consistent with reason, for him to lay down his body—something he never possessed—and arise again from the tomb, taking up that same body. This is indeed a mystery.

Now it so happens that the Scriptures do not teach anything so absurd, so irreconcilable and so contrary to our senses. This is a man-made doctrine, the creation of uninspired men. The Methodists did not originate this doctrine—it existed and was widely believed in before the days of the good man, John Wesley.

The Latter-day Saints believe that there is a true and living God, that this true and living God consists of three separate, distinct persons, which have bodies, parts and passions, which belief is in direct opposition to this man-made doctrine. We believe that God, the Eternal Father, who reigns in yonder heavens, is a distinct personage from Jesus Christ, as much so as an earthly father is distinct in his existence from his son. That is something I can comprehend, which I conceive to be the doctrine of revelation. We read about Jesus having been seen after he arose from the dead. Stephen the Martyr, just before he was stoned to death, testified to the Jewish people that were standing before him at the time, saying, "Behold, I see the heavens opened, and the Son of Man standing on the right hand of God." Here, then, the Father and Jesus, two distinct personages, were seen, and both had bodies. We find numerous other authorities bearing out this same idea, I do not intend to dwell upon this subject, because the greater portion of this congregation understand the scriptural view of this subject; hence it is not necessary to speak lengthily on it. We may, however, say a few things with regard to the passions of these personages.

It is declared, as part of the belief of the Methodists, that God is without passions. Love is one of the great passions of God. Love is everywhere declared a passion, one of the noblest passions of the human heart. This principle of love is one of the attributes of God. "God is love," says the Apostle John, "and he that dwelleth in love dwelleth in God, and God in him." If, then, this is one of the great attributes of Jehovah, if he is filled with love and compassion towards the children of men, if his son Jesus Christ, so loved the world that he gave his life to redeem mankind from the effects of the fall, then, certainly, God the Eternal Father must be in possession of this passion. Again, he possesses the attribute of justice, which is sometimes called anger, but the real name of this attribute is justice. "He executeth justice," says the Psalmist; also, "Justice and judgment are the habitation of thy throne." Justice is one of the noble characteristics of our heavenly Father; hence another of his passions (attributes).

We have it recorded too in this sacred Bible, that God was seen by ancient men of God. Jacob testifies as follows: "For I have seen God face to face." I know that there are other passages of Scripture, which would seem to militate against this declaration. For instance there is one passage which reads, "No man hath seen God at any time." This is in direct contradiction to the testimony of Jacob. The way I reconcile this is that no *natural* man can see the face of God the Father and live, it would overpower him; but one quickened by the Spirit, as old father Jacob was, could look upon God and converse with him face to face, as he says he did, he must have seen a personage, a being, in his general outlines like unto himself; man, as Moses informs us, having been created in the image of God.

We might refer to many other passages of Scripture, bearing on this subject. The Prophet Isaiah saw God; he saw not only the Lord, but a great congregation in connection with him, so that his train filled the Temple. He is always represented by those who have seen him as a personage in the form of man.

Having cited a very few evidences, let us inquire into the character and being of God, the Eternal Father. We are the offspring of the Lord, but the rest of animated nature is not; we are just as much the sons and daughters of God as the children in this congregation are the sons and daughters of their parents. We are begotten by him. When? Before we were born in the flesh; this limited state of existence is not our origin, it is merely the origin of the tabernacle in which we dwell. The mind we are possessed of, the being that is capable of thinking and reflecting, that is capable of acting according to the motives presented to it, that being which is immortal, which dwells within us, which is capable of reasoning from cause to effect, and which can comprehend, in some measure, the laws of its Creator, as well as trace them out as exhibited in universal nature, that being, which we call the Mind, existed before the tabernacle.

But says one, "that does not look reasonable." Why not? Do you not believe that the spirit will endure forever? O, yes. You may ask, what becomes of the spirit, separated from the body of flesh and bones, when this body lies in the grave? Has it life and intelligence and power to think and reflect? Let us hear what was said by those who sat under the altar, who were slain for the word of God, and for the testimony which they held, as seen and heard by John while on Patmos: "And they cried with a loud voice, saying, How long, O Lord, holy and true, dost thou not judge and avenge our blood on them that dwell on the earth?" The Lord tells them that they should "rest yet for a little season." These faithful servants of God are anxiously awaiting the time when the Lord will avenge their blood. Why? Because that will be the time when their bodies will be redeemed, they look forward with great anxiety to the time when they shall be again identified with the fleshly tabernacle with which they were known and distinguished while on the earth-hence this prayer.

Here we find another and further existence for the spirits of men who exist in heaven, who are capable of thinking, of using language, of understanding the future, and of anticipating that which was to come. Now, if they could exist after they leave this tabernacle, while the tabernacle lies mouldering in the dust, why not exist before the tabernacle had any existence? Was it not just as easy for an existence to be given to spiritual personages before they took possession of bodies as it is for them to exist after the body decays? Yes, and these are our views, founded upon new revelation; not the views of uninspired men, but founded upon direct revelation from God.

Where did we exist before we came here? With God. Where does he exist? In the place John denominated heaven. What do we understand heaven to be? Not the place described by our Christian friends, beyond the bounds of time and space, for there is no such place, there never was, nor ever will be; but I mean a tangible world, a heaven that is perfect, a heaven with materials that have been organized and put together, sanctified and glorified as the residence and world where God resides. Born there? Yes, we were born there. Even our great Redeemer whose death and sufferings we are this afternoon celebrating, was born up in yonder world before he was born of the Virgin Mary. Have you not read, in the New Testament, that Jesus Christ was the first-born of every creature? From this reading it would seem that he was the oldest of the whole human family, that is, so far as his birth in the spirit world is concerned. How long ago since that birth took place is not revealed; it might have been unnumbered millions of years, for aught we know. But we do know that he was born and was the oldest of the family of spirits. Have you not also read in the New Testament that he is called our elder brother? Does this refer to the birth of the body of flesh and bones? By no means, for there were hundreds of millions who were born upon our earth before the body of flesh and bones was born whom we call Jesus. How is it, then, that he is your elder brother? We must go back to the previous birth, before the foundation of this earth; we have to go back to past ages, to the period when he was begotten of the Father among the great family of spirits. He became, by his birthright, the great Creator. God, through him, created not only this little world, this speck of creation, but by him the worlds were made and created. How many we know not, for it has not been revealed. Suffice it to say, a great many worlds were created by him. Why by him? Because he had the birth right, he being the oldest of his father's family, and this birthright entitles him, not only to create worlds, but to become the Redeemer of those worlds, not only the Redeemer of the inhabitants of this our earth, but of all the others whom he created by the will and power of his Father.

But says one, "By that expression one would infer that other worlds had fallen as well as our own, having doubtless been placed in a state of temptation, and if so it would be fair to presume that there was a Garden of Eden to each of these worlds, containing all kinds of fruit, among which was the Tree of Knowledge of good and evil, and that they became fallen precisely in the same manner as ours did, and consequently they would need a Redeemer; and, therefore, the people of these worlds would be redeemed and saved according to their diligence and faithfulness in keeping the commandments of God?" Have you not read in the first chapter of Genesis of two persons appearing on this earth before man was made, when one who was God, said to the other, "Let us make man in our image, after our likeness?" Does not that bespeak a pre-existence of another personage besides the Almighty? And have you not read too in the same chapter that "God created man in his own image; male and female created he them?" When? It is said to have been on the sixth period, or, according to King James' translation, "on the sixth day." Do you mean to say we were all in existence on the sixth day? Yes. But on the seventh day, we are told in the following chapter, "there was not a man to till the ground." Is it not very singular that all should have an existence on the sixth day, and on the following day there was not a man in existence to till the ground? Why not? Because man was not yet placed in this temporal creation, but he had an existence then in heaven, where we were begotten. You and I were present when this world was created and made—you and I then understood the nature of its creation, and I have no doubt that we rejoiced and sang about it. Indeed, the Lord put a very curious question to the Patriarch Job, *apropos* of this. He said to him, "Where wast thou when I laid the foundation of the earth? Where wast thou when the morning stars sang together, and all the sons of God shouted for joy?"

Supposing Job to be living now, and this same question put to him, and supposing, too, that, instead of answering it himself, he were to seek to the learned Christian world for enlightenment on the subject, what do you think would be the nature of the answer he would receive? It would be, in effect, "Why Job, when the Lord laid the foundation of the earth, you had no existence, for you were not born." Why did not Job so answer the Lord? It was because he understood something about man's previous estate. He was wise in making no reply to the Lord, for doubtless he felt himself unable to do so. But we find that Moses understood the subject, for at the time the children of Israel transgressed he and his brother Aaron fell upon their faces before the Lord, and Moses pleading with great power and faith in behalf of the children of Israel, used these words, "O God, the God of the spirits of all flesh," etc. He understood that God was the Father of our spirits, and he addressed him as such. I think too that the apostles in ancient days must have had an idea of the pre-existence of man, judging from a certain question which they put to the Savior. It is said that "as Jesus passed by, he saw a man which was blind from his birth. And his disciples asked him, saying, Master, who did sin, this man, or his parents, that he was born blind?"

Let us now consider this question in connection with present modern ideas, and we shall at once perceive how utterly foolish it will appear. To state the question fairly in other words we might say, Master, was this man born blind because he had sinned? The very nature of this question would indicate to those even who do not believe in the principle, that this blind man had an existence before he was born into this world, and that he was capable, too, of committing sin. To show yet more clearly that the principle of man's pre-existence is founded on Biblical authority, I will quote you part of the Savior's prayer to the Father, just prior to his crucifixion—"And now, O Father glorify thou me with thine own self, with the glory which I had with thee before the world was." Here we find Jesus actually referring to the time he dwelt with his Father before he took upon himself a body of flesh and bones. He also says, "For I came down from heaven, not to do mine own will, but the will of him that sent me." He came down from the presence and abode of his Father. On another occasion while addressing the Jews, he says, "Verily, verily, I say unto you, before Abraham was, I am." He was, in fine, the *first*-born of every creature, and consequently the eldest of our Father's family.

If, therefore, it be now admitted that our Elder Brother had a previous existence with the Father, why should it be thought unreasonable that the rest of the family should have a pre-existence as well as the First Born? He was born according to man in the flesh, and why not his younger brethren have a similar birth with him in the spirit?

But now this carries us back still further, and invites us to ascertain a little in relation to his Father. A great many have supposed that God the Eternal Father, whom we worship in connection with his Son, Jesus Christ, was always a self-existing, eternal being from all eternity, that he had no beginning as a personage. But in order to illustrate this, let us inquire, What is our destiny? If we are now the sons and daughters of God, what will be our future destiny? The Apostle Paul, in speaking of man as a resurrected being, says: "Who (Jesus) shall change our vile body, that it might be fashioned like unto his glorious body" (Phil. 3:21), which harmonizes with what John says, "It doth not yet appear what we shall be, but we know that when he shall appear we shall be like him" (I John 3:2). Our bodies will be glorified in the same manner as his body is; then we shall be truly in his image and likeness, for as he is immortal, having a body of flesh and bone, so we will be immortal, possessing bodies of flesh and bones. Will we ever become gods? Let me refer you to the answer of the Savior to the Jews when accused of blasphemy because he called himself the Son of God. Says he, "Is it not written in your law, I said, Ye are Gods? If ye called them gods, unto whom the word of God came, and the Scriptures cannot be broken." This clearly proves to all Bible believers that in this world, in our imperfect state, being the children of God, we are destined, if we keep his commandments, to grow in intelligence until we finally become like God our Father. By living according to every word which proceeds from the mouth of God, we shall attain to his likeness, the same as our children grow up and become like their parents; and, as children through diligence attain to the wisdom and knowledge of their parents, so may we attain to the knowledge of our Heavenly parents' and if they be obedient to this commandment they will not only be called the sons of God, but be gods.

In the first verse of the 14th chapter of Revelation, we are told that John saw one hundred and forty-four thousand persons standing with the Lamb upon Mount Zion, and they had a peculiar name written in their foreheads— even their Father's name, him whom we call, in our language, God. Then there will be written upon the foreheads of these hundred and forty-four thousand this insignia, the Father's name, and they will be gods; and they will associate with him as do tho Father and his Only Begotten, that is, his only son begotten in the flesh.

From this we can draw the conclusion that God our Eternal Father, who is a spiritual being, has a body of flesh and bones, the same as his children will have after the resurrection.

Says one, to carry it out still further, "if we become gods and are glorified like unto him, our bodies fashioned like unto his most glorious body, may not he have passed through a mortal ordeal as we mortals are now doing?" Why not? If it is necessary for us to gain experience through the things that are presented before us in this life, why not those beings who are already exalted and become gods, obtain their experience in the same way? We would find, were we to carry this subject from world to world, from our world to another, even to the endless ages of eternity, that there never was a time but what there was a Father and Son. In other words when you entertain that which is endless, you exclude the idea of first being, a first world; the moment you admit of a first, you limit the idea of endless.

* * *

Says one, "this is incomprehensible." It may be so in some respects. We can admit, though, that duration is endless, for it is impossible for man to conceive of a limit to it. If duration is endless there can never be a first minute, a first hour, or first period; endless duration in the past is made up of a continuation of endless successive moments—it had no beginning. Precisely so with regard to this endless succession of personages; there never will be a time when fathers, and sons, and worlds will not exist; neither was there ever a period through all the past ages of duration, but what there was a world, and a Father and Son, a redemption and exaltation to the fullness and power of the Godhead. This is what Jesus prayed for, and he did not limit his prayer to his Apostles, but he said, "Neither pray I for these alone, but for them also which shall believe on me through their word; that they all may be one, as thou, Father, art in me, and I in thee, that they also may be one in us."

But, says one, "Does not that oneness mean one person?" No; Jesus meant that those who believed in him through his servants, might be able to come up to that fullness and glory and power and exaltation which he inherited, even to the fullness of the celestial glory, to be crowned with God the Eternal Father, and with his Only Begotten, to be made equal, as it were, with them, in power and dominion; agreeing with some modern revelations God has given through the Prophet Joseph Smith. He said all they that receive this Priesthood, that is, those who receive the testimony of the servants of God, they receive me; and whosoever receives my Father, receives my Father's kingdom; whereupon all that my Father hath shall be given to him. This is a glorious promise, to be joint heirs with the Son of God in the inheritance of all things, even the fullness and glory of the celestial world, their bodies eventually to become glorified, spiritual bodies of flesh and bones, the same as God the Father.

Before the earth was rolled into existence we were his sons and daughters. Those of his children who prove themselves during this probation worthy of exaltation in his presence, will beget other children, and, precisely according to the same principle, they too will become fathers of spirits, as he is the Father of our spirits; and thus the works of God are one eternal round—creation, glorification, and exaltation in the celestial kingdom.

How many transformations this earth had before it received its present form of creation, I do not know. Geologists pretend to say that this earth must have existed many millions of years, and this assertion is generally made by men who do not believe in God or the Bible, to disprove the history of the creation of the world, as given by the Prophet Moses. We will go further than geologists dare to go, and say that the materials of which the earth is composed are eternal, they will never have an end.

What is meant by creation? Merely organization. In six days we are told, God created this world, also every living thing that then existed. Did he create any of these things out of nothing? Did the materials then originate? No; there is no Scripture to be found within the lids of the Old and New

Testament, or Book of Mormon, or Doctrine and Covenants, or in any of the revelations of God, ancient or modern, that even intimates such a thing, for such was not the case; but go to the creeds of men and you will find these things taught. I was taught them in my youth; they were instilled into my young mind, and, of course, I believed them. But as I matured in years and thought, especially after I began to study the Hebrew language, I learned that the material of which this earth was made always did exist, and that it was only an organization or formation which took place, during the time spoken of by Moses.

How many transformations this earth passed through before the one spoken of by Moses, I do not know, neither do I particularly care. If it had gone through millions on millions of transformations, it is nothing to us. We are willing, for the sake of argument, to admit that the materials themselves are as old as geologists dare to say they are; but then, that does not destroy the idea of a God, that does not destroy the idea of a great Creator, who, according to certain fixed and unalterable laws, brought these materials, from time to time, into a certain organization, and then by his power completed the worlds that were thus made, by placing thereon intelligent and animated beings, capable of thinking and having an existence; and then again, for various reasons, he destroys their earthly existence, until finally he exalts them from their former condition, and makes them celestial in their nature.

This is the destiny of this globe of ours; it will eventually attain a state of organization that will no more be destroyed. When? After God has fulfilled and accomplished his purposes, after it has rested from wickedness one thousand years, during which time Satan will not have power to tempt the children of men, during which time the faithful will reign, as kings and priests on the earth in their resurrected bodies, when, too, the kingdom and the greatness of the kingdom under the whole heaven will be in possession of the Saints of the Most High; not only in the possession of those who are mortal Saints, but also in the possession of those who are immortal Saints, appearing as they will in their resurrected bodies, rising up as rulers, as kings, and priests, upon the face of our globe.

A government administered by such men will be one that can be depended on; in that respect it will be very different from the political nations of mortal man. Then there will not be the contention we now have, for all things pertaining to the government of God's kingdom will be conducted in order and on the eternal principles of righteousness.

The Twelve Apostles who were called by Jesus, and who ministered in his name while they tarried on the earth, will sit upon twelve thrones hereafter, and judge the twelve tribes of Israel. There will be nothing intangible or etherial about these thrones, they will be just as real as any kingly throne of the earth. And the Twelve Apostles will rule over the twelve tribes of Israel for the space of a thousand years, having, as they will have, their celestial bodies, and they will eat and drink at the table of the Lord. He will be here also, he will be King of kings, before whom all must bow, all must acknowledge his power—and that will be for the space of a thousand years.

By and by, when the time comes for this earth to die—for there has been a great deal of wickedness here—Satan will be loosed to go forth again to deceive, for there will still be some of the Saints mortal, who will be subject to temptation, and even Satan will not only try to deceive the mortal Saints, but he will gather together his armies around the camp of the Saints.

Then another time comes, when a great white throne will appear, and he who sits thereon will be glorious in his majesty and power, from before whose face the earth will flee away and no place be found for it. Will he annihilate it? No, not a particle of the earth will be annihilated, not a particle of the earth was ever originated, consequently not a particle of it will go out of existence, but it will flee away to its original element in the same manner as the human body would were it burned at the stake. The elements would be diffused among original matter, so with the elements of our earth when it undergoes its change. John was not satisfied with only seeing the earth pass away, but he saw still further even until he beheld a new heaven and a new earth, for, said he, the first heaven and the first earth were passed away and there was no more sea. Again, he testifies further, saying, "And I, John, saw the holy city, new Jerusalem, coming down from God, out of heaven, prepared as a bride adorned for her husband. And I heard a great voice out of heaven saying, Behold the tabernacle of God is with men, and he will dwell with them, and they shall be his people, and God himself shall be with them, and be their God, And God shall wipe away all tears from their eyes; and there shall be no more death, neither sorrow, nor crying, neither shall there be any more pain; for the former things are passed away. And he that sat upon the throne said, Behold, I make all things new."

This creation, when made new, will be inhabited by immortal beings, who will no more be subject to death, consequently there will be no more pain or sorrow, nothing to mar their peace or to prevent them from entering into the fullness of happiness and joy.

This, I say, is the destiny of this earth, and the Lord has told us that the time is nigh at hand. In other words, this is the last dispensation and we are preparing for the work of the Millennium. When the thousand years are passed, the earth will be made new—it will then become a heaven, the habitation of the Former and Latter-day Saints, as well as all they who prove themselves faithful who will be born during the Millennium. How long will they inhabit it? Forever.

When I was a boy, nineteen years old, I first saw Joseph Smith; I attended a conference of the Church of Jesus Christ of Latter-day Saints, on the 2nd of January, 1831. At that conference the people desired him to inquire of the Lord for them—they were anxious to know his mind and will. They were at that time comparatively few in number, not being more than two hundred. Joseph Smith sat down at a table, and received a great revelation, which is now contained in this Book of Doctrine and Covenants. Part of it, in relation to a land of promise, reads as follows:

> And I will give it unto you for the land of your inheritance, if you seek it with all your hearts: and this shall be my covenant with you, ye shall have it for the land of your inheritance, and for the inheritance of your children for ever, while the earth shall stand, and ye shall possess it again in eternity, no more to pass away.[A]

[Footnote A: Doc. and Cov. Sec. 38; 19-20.]

When I sat and heard that revelation,—it was uttered by the Prophet Joseph, and written by his scribe,—I thought to myself, that is a very curious doctrine, for I had not then learned that this earth was to become our future home and heaven, and I did not think Joseph Smith knew it. But it seemed so curious to me to bring myself to believe that the Lord was going to give us part of this earth, to possess it, and our children after us, while time should last, and to retain it through all eternity, never more to pass away. This was so different from anything I had been taught—I was utterly confounded—to think that my Father in heaven would come and live here on this earth! But when I came to read the Bible on this subject and found how numerous the passages were promising that the Saints should inherit the earth forever, I was perfectly astonished that I had never thought of it before. "Blessed are the meek," says the Savior, "for they shall inherit the earth."[A] The meek have been driven into the dens and mountains of the earth, having had to hide themselves up from their persecutors while the wicked, the proud, and the haughty have inherited the earth. Yet here is a promise that the meek shall inherit this earth, which all of course would readily admit has never had its fulfillment. Then again I was still more confirmed in the truth of this doctrine, when finding other corroborative passages. David, for instance, in the 37th Psalm, says, "The wicked shall be cut off. The righteous shall inherit the land, and dwell thereon for ever." I go back to the Books of Moses and there ascertain that the earth is promised to the Saints for ever. I came to the Acts of the Apostles, wherein the martyr Stephen, in answering the charge of blasphemy, tells of Abraham, how he came to leave his own country, and how the Lord had promised him a land for an inheritance, which "he would give to him for a possession, and to his seed after him," and yet he never possessed any of it, "no, not so much as to set his foot on," and this same promise was confirmed to Isaac and Jacob. And when I read in the Revelations of John about the new song that he heard them sing in heaven about their coming back to the earth (Rev. 5: 9, 10), I was fully confirmed that the new revelation was from God. One portion of the song which John heard the angels sing, was, "For thou wast slain, and hast redeemed us to God by thy blood out of every kindred, and tongue and people, and nation; and hast made us unto our God kings and priests; and we shall reign on the earth."

[Footnote A: Matt. 5:5.]

How very plain it is when we once learn about our future heaven. We do not have to pray, according to the Methodists, for the Lord to take us to a land beyond time and space, the Saints' secure abode. How inconsistent to look for a heaven beyond space! The heaven of the Saints is something we can look forward to in the confident hope of realizing our inheritances and enjoying them forever, when the earth becomes sanctified and made new. And there, as here, we will spread forth, and multiply our children. How long? For eternity. What, resurrected Saints have children? Yes, the same as our God, who is the Father of our spirits; so you, if you are faithful to the end, will become fathers to your sons and daughters, who will be as innumerable as the sands upon the sea shore; they will be your children, and you will be their heavenly fathers, the same as our heavenly Father is Father to us, and they will belong to your kingdoms through all the vast ages of eternity, the same as we will belong to our father's kingdom.

He that receiveth my father, says the Savior, receiveth my Father's kingdom, wherefore all that my father hath shall be given to him. It is a kind of joint stock inheritance, we are to become joint heirs with Jesus Christ to all the inheritances and to all the worlds that are made. We shall have the power of locomotion; and like Jesus, after his resurrection, we shall be able to mount up and pass from one world to another. We shall not be confined to our native earth. There are many worlds inhabited by people who are glorified, for heaven is not one place, but many, heaven is not one world but many. "In my Father's house are many mansions." In other words—In my Father's house there are many worlds, which in their turn will be made glorified heavens, the inheritance of the redeemed from all the worlds, who, having been prepared through similar experience to our own, will inhabit them; and each one in its turn will be exalted through the revelations and laws of the Most High God, and they will continue to multiply their offspring through all eternity, and new worlds will be made for their progeny. Amen.

CHAPTER VIII

"I KNOW THAT MY REDEEMER LIVES." [A]

President Joseph F. Smith on the "Mormon" Doctrine of Deity.

[Footnote A: This discourse was delivered in the Tabernacle, Salt Lake City, March 16, 1902, and by the kind permission of President Smith I am allowed to reproduce it here.]

My beloved brethren and sisters, while listening to the singing of the last hymn, my mind reverted to a revelation contained in the Book of Doctrine and Covenants, and I feel impressed to read a portion of it, and then make a few remarks concerning it, if I am led to do so. This revelation was given through the Prophet Joseph Smith, at Kirtland, in May, 1833:

> Verily, thus saith the Lord, it shall come to pass that every soul who forsaketh his sins and cometh unto me, and calleth on my name, and obeyeth my voice, and keepeth my commandments, shall see my face and know that I am.

You will remember that the hymn which was sung by the choir begins thus:

> I know that my Redeemer lives,
> What comfort this sweet sentence gives!
> He lives, he lives, who once was dead;
> He lives, my ever-living Head.

It occurs to me that in the words I have just read from the revelation there is a key given to us, as the people of God, by which we may know how to obtain the knowledge which is spoken of by the poet in this hymn— "I know that my Redeemer lives." The conditions are stated by which we may secure this knowledge. Furthermore, every soul who observeth these conditions shall not only know that he is, but he shall know also—

> That I am the true light that lighteth every man that cometh into the world;
>
> And that I am in the Father, and the Father in me, and the Father and I are one.

This is not speaking of the greater light which is especially bestowed upon those who are born again; for not every man that cometh into the world is born again and entitled to receive the greater light by the gift of the Holy Ghost. Perhaps it may be well for me to make a few remarks in relation to this distinction between the light of Christ that lighteth every man that cometh into the world, and that light which comes after repentance and baptism for the remission of sins.

It is by the power of God that all things are made that have been made. It is by the power of Christ that all things are governed and kept in place that are governed and kept in place in the universe. It is the power which proceeds from the presence of the Son of God throughout all the works of his hands, that giveth light, energy, understanding, knowledge, and a degree of intelligence to all the children of men, strictly in accordance with the words in the Book of Job, "There is a spirit in man; and the inspiration of the Almighty giveth them understanding." It is this inspiration from God, proceeding throughout all his creations that enlighteneth the children of men; and it is nothing more nor less than the spirit of Christ, that enlighteneth the mind, that quickeneth the understanding, and that prompteth the children of men to do that which is good and to eschew that which is evil; which quickens the conscience of man and gives him intelligence to judge between good and evil, light and darkness, right and wrong. We are indebted to God for this intelligence that we possess. It is by the spirit which lighteth every man that cometh into the world that our minds are quickened and our spirits enlightened with understanding and intelligence. And all men are entitled to this. It is not reserved for the obedient alone; but it is given unto all the children of men that are born into the world.

Gift of the Holy Ghost.

But the gift of the Holy Ghost, which bears record of the Father and the Son, which takes of the things of the Father and shows them unto men, which testifies of Jesus Christ, and of the ever-living God, the Father of Jesus Christ, and which bears witness of the truth—this Spirit, this intelligence is not given unto all men until they repent of their sins and come into a state of worthiness before the Lord. Then they receive it by the laying on of the hands of those who are authorized of God to bestow His blessings upon the heads of the children of men. The Spirit spoken of in that which I have read is that Spirit which will not cease to strive with the children of men until they are brought to the possession of the greater light and intelligence. Though a man may commit all manner of sin and blasphemy, if he has not received the testimony of the Holy Ghost he may be forgiven by repenting of his sins, humbling himself before the Lord, and obeying in sincerity the commandments of God. As it is stated here, "Every soul who forsaketh his sins and cometh unto me, and calleth on my name, and obeyeth my voice, and keepeth my commandments, shall see my face and know that I am." He shall be forgiven, and receive of the greater light; he will enter into a solemn covenant with God, into a compact with the Almighty, through the Only Begotten Son, whereby he becomes a son of God, and heir of God, and a joint heir with Jesus Christ. Then, if he shall sin against the light and knowledge he has received, the light that was within him shall become darkness, and oh, how great will be that darkness! Then, and not till then, will this Spirit of Christ that lighteth every man that cometh into the world cease to strive with him, and he shall be left to his own destruction.

This is in accordance with the doctrine of Christ as it is revealed in the New Testament; it is in accordance with the word of God as it has been revealed in the latter-day through the Prophet Joseph Smith. God will not condemn any man to utter destruction, neither shall any man be thrust down to hell irredeemably, until he has been brought to the possession of the greater light that comes through repentance and obedience to the laws and commandments of God; but if, after he has received light and knowledge, he shall sin against that light and will not repent, then, indeed, he becomes a lost soul, a son of perdition!

The question is often asked, Is there any difference between the Spirit of the Lord and the Holy Ghost? The terms are frequently used synonymously. We often say the Spirit of God when we mean the Holy Ghost; we likewise say the Holy Ghost when we mean the Spirit of God. The Holy Ghost is a personage in the Godhead, and is not that which lighteth every man that comes into the world. It is the Spirit of God which proceeds through Christ to the world, that enlightens every man that comes into the world, and that strives with the children of men, and will continue to strive with them, until it brings them to a knowledge of the truth and the possession of the greater light and testimony of the Holy Ghost. If, however, he receive that greater light, and then sin against it, the Spirit of God will cease to strive with him, and the Holy Ghost will wholly depart from him. Then will he persecute the truth; then will he seek the blood of the innocent; then will he not scruple at the commission of any crime, except so far as he may fear the penalties of the law, in consequence of the crime, upon himself.

Jesus, the Father of this World.

I will read a little further:

> And that I am in the Father, and the Father in me, and the Father and I are one.

I do not apprehend that any intelligent person will construe these words to mean that Jesus and his Father are one person, but merely that they are one in knowledge, in truth, in wisdom, in understanding, and in purpose; just as the Lord Jesus himself admonished his disciples to be one with him, and to be in him, that he might be in them. It is in this sense that I understand this language, and not as it is construed by some people, that Christ and his Father are one person. I declare to you that they are not one person, but that they are two persons, two bodies, separate and apart, and as distinct as are any father and son within the sound of my voice. Yet, Jesus is the Father of this world, because it was by him that the world was made. He says:

> And the Father and I are one:
>
> The Father because he gave me of his fulness, and the Son because I was in the world and made flesh my tabernacle, and dwelt among the sons of men.
>
> I was in the world and received of my Father, and the works of him were plainly manifest;
>
> And John saw and bore record of the fulness of my glory: and the fulness of John's record is hereafter to be revealed:
>
> And he bore record, saying, I saw his glory that he was in the beginning before the world was;
>
> Therefore in the beginning the Word was, for he was the Word, even the messenger of salvation.
>
> The light and redeemer of the world; the Spirit of truth, who came into the world, because the world was made by him, and in him was the life of men and the light of men.
>
> The worlds were made by him: men were made by him: all things were made by him, and through him, and of him.
>
> And I, John, bear record that I beheld his glory, as the glory of the Only Begotten of the Father, full of grace and truth, even the Spirit of truth, which came and dwelt in the flesh, and dwelt among us.
>
> And I, John, saw that he received not the fulness at first, but received grace for grace;
>
> And he received not of the fulness at first, but continued from grace to grace, until he received a fulness:
>
> And thus he was called the Son of God, because He received not of the fulness at the first.

Glorious Possibilities of Man.

What a glorious thought is inspired in the heart when we read sentiments like this, that even Christ himself was not perfect at first; he received not a fulness at first, but he received grace for grace, and he continued to receive more and more until he received a fulness. Is not this to be so with the children of men? Is any man perfect? Has any man received a fulness at once? Have we reached a point wherein we may receive the fulness of God, of his glory and his intelligence? No; and yet if Jesus, the Son of God, and the Father of the heavens and the earth in which we dwell, received not a fulness at the first, but increased in faith, knowledge, understanding and grace until he received a fulness, is it not possible for all men that are born of women to receive little by little, line upon line, precept upon precept, until they shall receive a fulness, as he has received a fulness, and be exalted with him in the presence of the Father?

The revelation continues:

> And I, John, bear record, and lo, the heavens were opened, and the Holy Ghost descended upon him in the form of a dove, and sat upon him, and there came a voice out of heaven saying, This is my beloved son.
>
> This voice out of heaven came from God, the Father of our Lord and Savior Jesus Christ.
>
> And I, John, bear record that he received a fulness of the glory of the Father;
>
> And he received all power both in heaven and on earth, and the glory of the Father was with him, for he dwelt in him.
>
> And it shall come to pass, that if you are faithful you shall receive the fulness of the record of John.
>
> I give unto you these sayings that ye may understand and know how to worship, and know what you worship, that you may come unto the Father in my name, and in due time receive of his fulness.
>
> For if you keep my commandments you shall receive of his fulness, and be glorified in me as I am in the Father; therefore, I say unto you, you shall receive grace for grace.
>
> And now, verily I say unto you, I was in the beginning with the Father: and am the first-born.
>
> And all those who are begotten through me are partakers of the glory of the same, and are the church of the first-born.

Ye were also in the beginning with the Father, that which is Spirit, even the Spirit of truth,

And truth is knowledge of things as they are, and as they were, and as they are to come;

And whatsoever is more or less than this, is the spirit of that wicked one who was a liar from the beginning.

The spirit of truth is of God. I am the spirit of truth, and John bore record of me, saying—He receiveth a fulness of truth, yea, even of all truth.

And no man receiveth a fulness unless he keepeth his commandments.

He that keepeth his commandments receiveth truth and light, until he is glorified in truth and knoweth all things.

Man was also in the beginning with God. Intelligence, or the light of truth, was not created or made, neither indeed can it be.

All truth is independent in that sphere in which God has placed it, to act for itself, as all intelligence also, otherwise there is no existence.

Behold, here is the agency of man, and here is the condemnation of man; because that which was from the beginning is plainly manifest unto them and they receive not the light.

And every man whose spirit receiveth not the light is under condemnation.

For man is spirit. The elements are eternal, and spirit and element, inseparably connected, receive a fulness of joy:

And when separated, man cannot receive a fulness of joy.

Man to Become Like Christ.

In other words, the spirit without the body is not perfect, and the body without the spirit is dead. Man was ordained in the beginning to become like Jesus Christ, to become conformed unto his image. As Jesus was born of woman, lived and grew to manhood, was put to death and raised from the dead to immortality and eternal life, so it was decreed in the beginning that man should be, and will be, through the atonement of Jesus, in spite of himself, resurrected from the dead. Death came upon us without the exercise of our agency; we had no hand in bringing it originally upon ourselves; it came because of the transgression of our first parents. Therefore, man, who had no hand in bringing death upon himself, shall have no hand in bringing again life unto himself; for as he dies in consequence of the sin of Adam, so shall he live again, whether he will or not, by the righteousness of Jesus Christ, and the power of his resurrection. Every man that dies shall live again, and shall stand before the bar of God, to be judged according to his works, whether they be good or evil. It is then that all will have to give an account for their stewardship in this mortal life. The word of God is spoken to the children of men. It has been revealed from the heavens. It is extant in the world. It is in force upon the people. Those that reject it will have to answer for it before God, the judge of the quick and the dead; while those that receive and obey the word of the Lord and keep his commandments, as I have read, shall not only come to a knowledge of the truth, but shall look upon the face of the Redeemer and shall see and know him as he is. Furthermore, they will acknowledge that it is through the atonement and power of the Savior that they are brought again unto life immortal, to enjoy eternal felicity in the celestial kingdom of God, provided they have been obedient to his commandments. The Lord continues:

> The elements are the tabernacle of God; yea, man is the tabernacle of God, even temples; and whatsoever temple is defiled, God shall destroy that temple.
>
> The glory of God is intelligence, or, in other words, light and truth.
>
> Light and truth forsake that evil one.
>
> Every spirit of man was innocent in the beginning, and God having redeemed man from the fall, men became again in their infant state, innocent before God.
>
> And that wicked one cometh and taketh away light and truth, through disobedience, from the children of men, and because of the tradition of their fathers.

The word of the Lord is truth. You ask, What is truth? It is the truth that God lives. What more is truth? It is the truth that Jesus Christ is the Son of God, the Redeemer of the world; that he atoned for the sin of Adam, and that through our repentance and obedience to him we shall receive a forgiveness of our own sins, and shall be cleansed therefrom, and exalted again in the presence of God, from whence we came. It is truth that God has revealed to the world that except a man be born again he cannot see the kingdom of heaven. It is eternal truth that except a man be born of the water and of the Spirit he cannot enter into the kingdom of heaven. These are the Almighty's truths that he has revealed to the children of men, and upon these we will stand. We propose to bear our testimony to these truths, and to declare these principles to the children of men, as long as God will give us his Spirit, and we are entrusted with this mission to declare Jesus Christ and him crucified and risen from the dead, and Joseph Smith raised up by the power of God to restore the fulness of the everlasting Gospel and the authority of the Holy Priesthood to the earth in the dispensation of the fulness of times. We bear this testimony to the world, and we know that our testimony is true; for we have received of that Spirit of truth which is of God, and of which Jesus speaks here through the Prophet Joseph Smith. Therefore, our testimony is in force upon the world. Especially is it in force upon those who have yielded obedience to the message of salvation as it has been restored to the earth and declared unto you.

Personal Testimony.

Now, my brethren and sisters, I know that my Redeemer lives. I feel it in every fiber of my being. I am just as satisfied of it as I am of my own existence. I cannot feel more sure of my own being than I do that my Redeemer lives, and that my God lives, the Father of my Savior. I feel it in my soul; I am converted to it in my whole being. I bear testimony to you that this is the doctrine of Christ, the Gospel of Jesus, which is the power of God unto salvation. It is "Mormonism." But there is much more that could be said in relation to these matters. "Mormonism" has been interpreted by one who was inspired to mean "more good." We have accepted the term "Mormon." It having been applied to us by our enemies simply because we believed in the Book of Mormon, and we are not ashamed of it—we are not ashamed of "more good." We believe in every principle and precept of the Gospel, and in all the law of God. We believe that every principle is essential. We believe that we should do our duty to God and to our fellowmen. We should do unto others as we would have them do to us. We should observe the laws of chastity, honesty and uprightness, deal justly with our neighbors, and kindly and mercifully with the erring. We should seek to do good at all times and under all circumstances. The feeling should predominate in our hearts that we are here, not to do evil, but to do good; not to increase error, but to diminish it and to increase the knowledge of the truth; to make men happy, and to spread happiness abroad in the world by persuading men to do that which is right. There is no real happiness in wickedness. There is no real enjoyment in sin and transgression. The only source of real enjoyment and perfect happiness is in the observance of the laws of truth and righteousness.

The Lord bless you and help us all to live our religion and to keep the commandments of God, that we may look upon his face, and that we may see the Redeemer when he shall come to the earth again; for he will come, and when he does come again he will not come as the meek and lowly Nazarene, without "where to lay his head," and without respect and honor, but he will come as God out of heaven, clothed with power, glory, justice, judgment and truth. He will come with the hosts of heaven, and he will receive those who have kept his commandments in the earth as the church prepared for the Bridegroom, while he will take vengeance upon the ungodly.

This is not my doctrine; it is the declaration of the Bible, of the ancient prophets, and also of the modern prophets, who have spoken by inspiration. I am but repeating their words, and I tell you nothing new. God bless you and keep you in the path of duty, and deliver us all from evil, and help us to be steadfast and faithful to the covenants that we have made, and to the cause of Zion and of redemption for the living and the dead, is my prayer in the name of Jesus. Amen.